MW01077950

Quant Job Interview Questions and Answers

Second edition

Mark S. Joshi
Nicholas Denson
Andrew Downes

University of Melbourne

PILOT WHALE PRESS

PILOT WHALE PRESS
Melbourne

www.markjoshi.com

©Mark Suresh Joshi, Nicholas Denson, Andrew Downes 2008, 2013

National Library of Australia Cataloguing-in-Publication entry:

Author:	Joshi, Mark, S.
Title:	Quant job interview questions and answers / Mark Joshi; Andrew Downes; Nicholas Denson;
Edition:	Second edition;
ISBN:	9780987122827 (paperback)
Notes:	Includes bibliographical references and index.
Subjects:	Finance–Vocational guidance–Australia
Other Authors/Contributors:	Downes, Andrew, author. Denson, Nicholas, author.
Dewey Number:	657.02394

Contents

Preface to first edition   vii

    What this book is and is not   vii

    How to use this book   vii

    Website   viii

    Structure   viii

    The publication of this book   ix

Preface to second edition   xi

Chapter 1.   The interview process   1

   1.1.   Introduction   1

   1.2.   Getting an interview   1

   1.3.   The standard interview   3

   1.4.   The phone interview   5

   1.5.   The take-home exam   6

   1.6.   The exam   6

   1.7.   Follow-up   7

   1.8.   Dos and don'ts   7

   1.9.   When to apply?   9

   1.10.   The different roles   10

   1.11.   Sorts of employers   12

   1.12.   Where people go wrong   13

Chapter 2.   Option pricing   15

   2.1.   Introduction   15

   2.2.   Questions   16

   2.2.1.   Black–Scholes   16

   2.2.2.   Option price properties   17

   2.2.3.   Hedging and replication   19

2.2.4.   The Greeks   21
2.2.5.   General   21
2.2.6.   Trees and Monte Carlo   21
2.2.7.   Incomplete markets   22
2.3.   Solutions   22
2.3.1.   Black–Scholes   22
2.3.2.   Option price properties   35
2.3.3.   Hedging and replication   57
2.3.4.   The Greeks   66
2.3.5.   General   70
2.3.6.   Trees and Monte Carlo   72
2.3.7.   Incomplete markets   79

Chapter 3.   Probability   87
3.1.   Introduction   87
3.2.   Questions   88
3.2.1.   General   88
3.2.2.   Stochastic processes   93
3.3.   Solutions   95
3.3.1.   General   95
3.3.2.   Stochastic processes   144

Chapter 4.   Interest rates   171
4.1.   Introduction   171
4.2.   Questions   172
4.3.   Solutions   172

Chapter 5.   Numerical techniques and algorithms   181
5.1.   Introduction   181
5.2.   Questions   181
5.3.   Solutions   184

Chapter 6.   Mathematics   217
6.1.   Introduction   217
6.2.   Questions   217
6.2.1.   General   217
6.2.2.   Integration and differentiation   220

6.3.   Solutions   221

6.3.1.   General   221

6.3.2.   Integration and differentiation   250

Chapter 7.   Coding in C++   263

7.1.   Introduction   263

7.2.   Questions   266

7.3.   Solutions   274

Chapter 8.   Logic/Brainteasers   329

8.1.   Introduction   329

8.2.   Questions   330

8.3.   Solutions   333

Chapter 9.   The soft interview   355

9.1.   Introduction   355

9.2.   Soft questions and answers   355

9.3.   Finance data questions   361

Chapter 10.   Top ten questions   363

10.1.   Introduction   363

10.2.   Questions   363

Bibliography   365

Index   367

Preface to first edition

What this book is and is not

The purpose of this book is to get you through your first interviews for quant jobs. We have gathered a large number of questions that have actually been asked and provided solutions for them all. Our target reader will have already studied and learnt a book on introductory financial mathematics such as "The Concepts and Practice of Mathematical Finance." He will also have learnt how to code in C++ and coded up a few derivatives pricing models, and read a book such as "C++ Design Patterns and Derivatives Pricing."

This book is not intended to teach the basic concepts from scratch, instead it shows how these are tested in an interview situation. However, actually tackling and knowing the answers to all the problems will undoubtedly teach the reader a great deal and improve their performance at interviews.

Many readers may find many of the questions silly and/or annoying, so did the authors! Unfortunately, you have to answer what you are asked and thinking the question is silly does not help. Arguing with the interviewer about why they asked you it will only make things worse. For that reason, we have included many questions which we would never ask and think that no one should ask. That said, if the questions are too silly then you may want to consider whether you want to work for the interviewer.

How to use this book

We strongly advise you to attempt the questions seriously before looking at the answers. You will learn a lot more that way. You may also come up with different solutions. We have included a number of follow-up questions without solutions in the answers, which may or may not have been asked in a live interview. Tackling these will help you refine your skills. Some questions come up time and time again, so if you have actually learnt all the answers then there is no doubt you will eventually get some duplicates, but that is not really the point; it is more important to be able to tackle all the types of questions that arise and to identify your weaknesses so you can address them.

Eventually, of course, the interviewers will buy copies of this book to make sure that the questions they use are not in it. However, in the meantime, you can make the most of your comparative advantage...

Many candidates at their initial interviews seem to have a poor idea of what is required. If you find the questions in this book unreasonably hard, you are not yet ready. If you think that you will never be able to do them, then now is a good time to think of an alternative career. If you are on top of these sorts of questions, you should have no problem getting an entry level job. So use this book to judge when you are ready. If possible, get a friend, who is experienced, to give you a practice interview when you think you have reached that point.

Website

Inevitably, readers will have plenty of questions regarding this book's contents. For that reason, there is a forum on `www.markjoshi.com` to discuss its content. In particular, if you think a solution is wrong, or want a solution to a follow-up question, then this is the place to ask. There are also a lot of additional resources such as recommended book lists, discussion of problems, job adverts and career advice on that site.

Structure

This book is structured as follows: we start with a discussion of the interview process in Chapter 1 including how to get one as well as how to conduct yourself during one. We then move on to actual interview questions; each chapter contains some general discussion, a set of questions from real-life interviews, and then solutions with follow-up questions. We divide these into topics by chapter: option pricing, probability, interest rates, numerical techniques, mathematics, coding in

C++, and brainteasers. We then discuss how to handle a "soft interview", that is a non-technical interview, and list possible questions. We finish with a list of ten of the most popular questions from quant interviews.

The publication of this book

The reader may be curious to know how this book has been published. We decided not to go with conventional publishers for a number of reasons. The first is simply that the authors lose all control; once you have signed on the dotted line all the understanding and reassurances from your editor become worthless. A second is timing, a conventional publisher can easily take two years to get a book from draft to release. We have therefore gone with print-on-demand direct sales.

With this approach to publishing, the book is printed and bound after the order is made. There is therefore no overhead but the final product is of equally high quality. We hope that you will support this publishing revolution with your purchases and the books you write.

Preface to second edition

The release of the first edition curiously coincided with the global financial crisis. We hope that there was not a causal relationship. In 2013, we are now five years in to the "Great Recession" with no obvious end in sight. Quant jobs are thinner on the ground but hiring still takes place. The biggest change in the market is that you must make every interview count. Once upon a time, it was possible to simply prepare by going to enough interviews that you eventually learnt enough of the questions asked to do well. That is no longer a viable strategy, you now may only get a few interviews before hitting a long dry spell. In such circumstances, good interview preparation is essential. This book provides effective preparation without requiring you to fluff a few interviews.

Whilst the market has changed, the sort of questions asked has not changed greatly. The biggest change in the second edition is that we have included many more basic probability questions. These simply reflect the fact that our question gatherers were probed greatly in that area. The second greatest expansion has been in the C++ section reflecting the fact that a working knowledge of C++ is still expected for many jobs. CVA did not really exist in 2008; it is now an important part of the quant landscape, however. We therefore include it and also some discussion of the computation of VAR.

One curious aspect of the book is that despite the first edition's popularity, many candidates still get asked questions straight from it. So if you truly know all the contents, you will certainly get some easy wins. However, that is not really the point, the objective is to gain a working knowledge of the topics surveyed so that questions at this level become easy.

We wish you good luck in your job hunting.

Mark Joshi
Nick Denson
Andrew Downes
Melbourne 2013

CHAPTER 1

The interview process

1.1. Introduction

In this chapter, we look at how to get a job interview and then what happens once you have one. We also discuss the types of interview, the general process and what happens afterward. It is important to realise that how you behave in and approach the interview can have a marked effect on your chances. We round off with a discussion of the different roles, areas and types of employers.

There are, of course, many sorts of interviews and many ways for the interviewer to conduct it, but ultimately the interviewer wants to find out two things:

- Do you have the technical ability to do the job?
- Will you behave reasonably? That is, will you do what you are asked and get on with others.

The first will be assessed via a barrage of technical questions, and the second by observing your behaviour and on how you respond to general questions.

Most interviews focus largely on technical ability, since most candidates fail at this point. However, on the rare occasion there are multiple candidates who are good enough technically, other factors do become important.

1.2. Getting an interview

For many candidates, the biggest problem is getting the interview in the first place. There are many ways to get that far. The first thing to remember is that in hiring "like attracts like."

Do you know anyone with a similar background who's now working in the City? If so, ask if you can come down for a chat. This may translate rather quickly into a job offer. If a PhD student the year above you is applying for jobs in finance, make sure to make friends with him before he leaves. Keep in touch and when the time comes make use of the contact. Once you have exhausted all the people you know with similar backgrounds, try the ones with different backgrounds and then friends of friends.

Some places, for example BarCap, have quantitative associates programmes and you apply via the bank's web-site, otherwise interviews tend to come via recruitment consultants also known as "headhunters." Some recruitment firms now even map out the PhD classes in mathematics and physics departments at top universities: if you are looking for someone to sponsor your social events, they are a good place to start!

Headhunters generally call you down for a meeting to make sure that you are presentable. They then send you to a couple of interviews to see how you do. If you do well they will get very enthusiastic and then send you to lots of places. If you do badly they will quickly lose interest and it is time to find a new headhunter.

A much-discussed and difficult to answer question is how many firms to use at once. My inclination is to start with one or two and see how it goes. As long as they are getting you plenty of interviews, there is no point in registering somewhere else. But if they aren't, then it is time to try another firm.

An important fact to realise is that headhunters are paid by commission (e.g. 20% of your first-year package) on a placement basis. The motivations and incentives are therefore a lot like real estate agents:

- they really want to place you (good);
- they want you to get a high salary: commission is a percentage (good);
- they would much rather place you quickly in any job than slowly in a better one (not so good);
- they will be unhappy if you accept a job through someone else (no commission == no fee == very unhappy);
- they may or may not be interested in a long term relationship; you will be worth five times as much in five years to them.

A headhunter's business is relationships and information. They are therefore keen not to damage their reputation and also to get as much information as possible about who you know and who is doing what. Always bear this is mind when talking to them. Once you actually get a job, you will regularly get calls from them fishing for information and seeing if you are interested in roles they won't be keen to tell you much about until you are firmly their client. It is OK to talk to them but do NOT under ANY circumstances discuss any of your colleagues; this could get you fired. (For similar reasons, never ever talk to journalists but refer them to corporate communications or your boss.)

One headhunter firm that has its own guide to becoming a quant and has a good reputation is Paul and Dominic. The "Paul" is Paul Wilmott the financial mathematician. They have the advantage of actually understanding the job they are trying to place you in.

1.3. The standard interview

The most common interview consists of arriving at the bank's offices, you ask for some person whose name you have been given, you sit in the lobby and wait. Eventually someone comes and gets you, you are then shown into a meeting room. There may be one or several interviewers present. You have already had several chances to mess up. Make sure that:

- you arrive dead on time: being early really irritates, and being late displays disorganisation;
- you wear a suit and are looking well groomed;
- you know and remember the name of the person you are meeting;
- you have a copy of your CV with you, and do not expect them to have seen nor read it;
- you have had plenty to eat and are not suffering a sugar low since that will destroy thinking power;
- you switch off your mobile phone.

Arriving dead on time is an art: the only way to do it is to arrive with half an hour to spare, and then go and find a cafe where you can have something to eat or drink. Having a lemonade is a good idea to keep sugar levels up. Don't drink too much, however, or you will be rushing to the loo in the middle of the interview. Also try to assess how long the queue at reception is. If it is looking long you may need to join it ten minutes before your scheduled arrival time.

The interviewer may or may not be the person who fetched you from reception. When the interviewer arrives he (or she) will typically give you the chance to ask a few questions. Whilst it is good to ask a little, e.g. what the team does, where it sits, how many people are in it, what sort of role you are being considered for, it is best not to drag this part out since if you do badly in the technical interview it is all rather irrelevant. In addition, the interviewer may find too many questions at this stage annoying. There are often two or more interviewers rather than one, one will typically take the lead, however.

You will then be asked very technical questions and typically be given either a whiteboard or a sheet of paper to work through them. If you get stuck, the interviewer will generally help you out, the more help you need the worse you have done. Some interviewers always ask the same level of questions, others will make the questions harder if you get them right, and easier if you get them wrong. Sometimes the interviewer will vary the questions to try and find what you are good at, if anything.

Important points to remember are:

- Do not argue with them about why they asked something. If they asked, they want the answer. Disputing will make you look difficult and weak technically.
- The thinking process counts as well as the solution, so talk about how you are tackling it.
- They do not expect you to be able to do everything without help.
- If you are unsure of what they want, ask for clarification. For example, for a numerical or coding problem, do they just want a short solution, or do they want an optimal one?

Their expectations of you will be affected by your c.v. For example, if you say that have read the interviewer's book then you had better know it well. (Authors are very vain about their books so do not say anything critical about it either.) If you say you are an expert in a coding language, e.g. C++, then be sure you can back the statement up.

At the end, if you have done poorly, accept this graciously and ask for advice on what to read and how to improve. Do not get into an argument with the interviewer about what happened; just notch it up to experience and resolve to do better next time.

Banks in the UK tend not to bother with paying expenses and particularly not for first interviews. In the US, they will sometimes pay depending upon the length of the trip.

If you know that you will be there all day, it is worth taking some refreshments in your bag. Sugar lows and dehydration will badly affect your ability to think. Don't assume that it will have occurred to them that you need to eat and drink, just because you are there from nine to five. Goldman Sachs is most notorious for grilling you across long days by several people. They really do want you to meet everyone and if you cannot take the pace of the interviews, you won't be able to cope with working there.

1.4. The phone interview

Phone interviews are generally used when it is not convenient to see the candidate in person. They are often a pre-screen to check whether a proper interview is worth the effort when travel is involved. When a team is international then they are used by the overseas part of the team. You will never get a job without a face-to-face interview so this can only ever be one stage of the process.

The process is not hugely different from an in-person interview. Generally, there is only one interviewer and they ask you a series of questions and chat with you a little. The nature of the questions tends to be a little different since they need to work over the phone. For that reason, the fraction of brainteasers is higher than normal.

The important points to remember are:

- use the best phone line you can, (which is generally not a mobile;)
- speak loudly and clearly;
- do not give the impression that you are looking things up in a book or on the web;
- have pen and paper handy.

1.5. The take-home exam

This again is used to decide whether it is worthwhile to bother with a proper interview. The questions will largely reflect the interests of the hiring manager so they may focus on one tiny aspect of applied mathematics or probability theory or even physics.

Generally, they will e-mail it to you and expect a response within some set time period, e.g., 24 hours. Do not try to negotiate the time available to do it, since this gives the impression that you are weak mathematically and generally difficult. It is acceptable to ask that the start time be moved, e.g., to a Saturday so that you can devote yourself to it.

If you decide to copy out solutions from a book, try not to be too blatant and make sure you copy out the right material. One candidate copied out the code for a vanilla call option from the interviewer's book when asked to code up an Asian option pricer. His application was not taken further.

The presentation of the answers matters as well as correctness. So make sure your handwriting is clear and your steps are clearly explained.

1.6. The exam

The written exam which is not take-home is becoming more popular. Some banks are even setting a general exam for a large number of candidates at once and then taking the highest performers. This has the virtue of clarity and fairness. It also favours people who are good at exams rather than interviews, for better or worse.

The main problem is that the questions tend to reflect the background of the setter rather than relevance to the job. However, this is no different from interviews.

If you know you will be doing a written exam, then find out what the rules are. For example, is it open book? How long will it last? Are you allowed to use a calculator? Make sure to bring your own calculator – sitting in a room on your own with a defective calculator (or none at all) can be very stressful.

1.7. Follow-up

Most places will not give you feedback on the spot, but some occasionally will. If you got the interview via a recruitment agent, (i.e., headhunter) it will generally come that way. Otherwise, expect an e-mail a few days afterward. If you do not hear anything for a week or two, then it is perfectly reasonable to politely ask what is happening. If you have done well, they may move very quickly since very few really good candidates come along.

Bear in mind, that if they do not want you for the job, it does not mean that they think poorly of you. The first author of this book is in touch with quite a few people he met when turning them down for a job – often it just means that the preparation was not quite right or there was a better candidate. These candidates showed some potential and are now leading successful city careers after taking the feedback that they were given seriously. Related to this, remember that the quant circle is not very big so you will come across the same people repeatedly – don't destroy any relationships unnecessarily. Indeed, it is not unusual to find that after a takeover, you are working for the person who rejected you a year before.

It is very rare to get the job after the first interview. Instead, if you do well they will invite you back to meet more people. If they are organised and keen you may have several interviews in one day, or they may get you back again and again, until you have met everyone. After two or three rounds of this they will make a decision.

Generally the more times you are invited back, the keener they are. However, it can just reflect an inability to pool information. Going to ten interviews and then being told you are not getting the job because the second interview went badly is not unknown.

1.8. Dos and don'ts

Here's a checklist of things to do and not do:

- don't be late;
- don't be early;
- don't argue with the interviewer about why they've asked you something;
- do appear enthusiastic;
- do wear a suit;

- do be eager to please (they want someone who will do what they want, you must give the appearance of being obliging rather than difficult);
- don't be too relaxed (they may well conclude that you aren't hungry enough for success to work hard);
- don't tell them they shouldn't use C++ because *my niche language* is better;
- do demonstrate an interest in financial news;
- do be able to talk about everything on your CV (also known as resumé) –have a prepared 2 minute response on every phrase in it;
- do bring copies of your CV;
- don't expect the interviewer to be familiar with your CV;
- don't say you've read a book unless you can discuss its contents; particularly if they've written it;
- do be polite;
- do ask for feedback and don't argue about it (even if it is wrong try to understand what made the interviewer think that);
- don't say you want to work in banking for the money (of course you do, but it's bad form to say so);
- do say you want to work closely with other people rather than solo;
- don't say that you think that bankers are reasonable people – they aren't;
- do take a break from interviewing and do more prep if more than a couple of interviews go badly;
- don't use a mobile for a phone interview;
- do be able to explain your thesis – work out explanations for different sorts of people in advance;
- don't expect banks in the UK to pay for interview expenses;
- don't spend more on expenses than has been agreed;
- do ask about the group you'll be working in:
    - how much turnover is there? (This one is slightly risky in that some employers get upset if you ask this. If they do, it is probably a sign that people leave a lot which says a great deal in itself.)
    - where people go when they leave?
    - how many people are in the team?

– when can you meet the rest of the group? (only ask this if an offer appears imminent; if you can't meet the others, this is a big red flag: what's wrong with them?)
– how old the group is?
– what's the team's raison d'etre?
– is it expanding or contracting?
– what would a typical working day be?

- don't get on to the topic of money early in the process;
- don't be cynical about what bankers do;
- don't accept an offer made under pressure.

1.9. When to apply?

Most entry-level quants are hired because a specific team has a need for someone. This means that they want someone to start now and they want someone who will be productive quickly.

This means that you should not start applying unless you can start within the next two months. You should also wait until you are well-prepared. This is doubly the case in smaller places. In London or New York, it used to be that you could learn the hard way that you were not ready, but in today's market there may be only two or three possible employers so you had better be sure you perform at your best from the start.

How can you tell if you are ready? Here are some indicators:

- Could you get "A" in an exam on the contents of "The Concepts and Practice of Mathematical Finance" [6] ?
- Have you coded up some models in C++? (e.g. the computer projects at the end of that book.)
- Are you on top of the contents of "C++ Design Patterns and Derivatives Pricing" [7] ?
- Can you do the interview questions in this book without too much difficulty?
- Can you tackle the supplementary questions in this book?
- Have you successfully completed a practice interview?

The rules that apply to quantitative associates programs are different, since they will generally only be open at one point in the year. In these cases, find out what they want and what flexibility they have. Also, find out if failing one year will count against you the next year and take that into account too.

1.10. The different roles

It is important to realise that there are many different types of quants who do different sorts of things. There are pros and cons of each and it is worth considering what sort of role you want, and communicating that to potential employers. A brief list is:

(1) front office/desk quant;
(2) model validating quant;
(3) research quant;
(4) quant developer;
(5) statistical arbitrage quant;
(6) capital quant;
(7) portfolio theorist.

A *desk quant* implements pricing models directly used by traders. This can mean either very short term projects or longer term ones depending on the way the outfit is setup. The main advantage is that you are close to the real action both in terms of things happening and in terms of money. This is also a possible route into trading. The downside is that it can be stressful and depending on the outfit may not involve much research.

A *model validation quant* independently implements pricing models in order to check that front office models are correct. It tends to be more relaxed, and less stressful. The downsides are that model validation teams can be uninspired and far from the money. Also in some places, the quants spend their time running other peoples' models rather than coding their own which can be quite frustrating.

A *research quant* tries to invent new pricing approaches and sometimes carries out blue-sky research. These are the most interesting quant jobs for those who love mathematics, and you learn a lot more. The main downside is that it is sometimes hard to justify your existence.

Quantitative developers are programmers who generally implement other people's models. It is less exciting but generally well-paid and easier to find a job. This sort of job can vary a lot. It could be coding scripts quickly all the time, or working on a large system debugging someone else's code.

The *statistical arbitrage quant* works on finding patterns in data to suggest automated trades. The techniques are quite different from those in derivatives pricing. This sort of job is most commonly found in hedge funds. The return on this type of position is highly volatile!

A *capital quant* works on modelling the bank's credit exposures and capital requirements. This is less sexy than derivatives pricing but is becoming more and more important with the advent of the Basel III banking accord. You can expect decent (but not great) pay, less stress and more sensible hours. There is currently a drive to mathematically model the chance of operational losses through fraud etc, with mixed degrees of success. The biggest downside of going into this area is that it will be hard to switch to derivatives pricing later on.

Portfolio theorists use financial mathematics in the sense of Markowitz's portfolio theory rather than derivatives pricing and Black–Scholes. It is less technically demanding but there is certainly plenty of money in the area. There is a certain commonality between this area and capital modeling. Again it is hard to switch from this to derivatives pricing.

People do banking for the money, and you tend to get paid more the closer you are to where the money is being made. This translates into a sort of snobbery where those close to the money look down on those who aren't. As a general rule, moving away from the money is easy, moving toward it is hard.

1.11. Sorts of employers

There is quite a lot of variety in terms of sorts of employers. We give a rough catalogue:

- commercial banks, e.g., RBS, HSBC;
- investment banks, e.g., Goldman Sachs, Lehman Brothers was a classic example;
- hedge funds, e.g., the Citadel Group;
- accountancy firms;
- software companies.

Each of these has its pros and cons.

Large commercial banks tend to have large trading operations, but are influenced by the culture of the rest of the bank. The effect of this is that they tend to be less tough but also less exciting in terms of products and projects compared to investment banks or hedge funds. The advantages are shorter hours and better job security. The main disadvantage tends to be less money!

Investment banks, particularly American ones, tend to expect longer hours and have a generally tougher culture. They are much readier to hire and fire.

Hedge funds tend to demand a lot of work. They are very volatile and have been a big growth industry in recent years. They were, however, badly hit by the credit crisis; the industry is smaller than it was but it still exists. The packages tend to reflect very large risk premia.

In general, American banks and firms pay better but demand longer hours than European ones.

The big accountancy firms have quant teams for consulting. The main disadvantage is that you are far from the action, and high quality individuals tend to work in banks so it may be hard to find someone to learn from. Some firms are very good on external employee training, however, and will send employees on Masters courses or regular training courses.

There is an increasing move towards outsourcing quant modeling by purchasing off the shelf software models. One option is therefore to work for the software company instead. The issues are similar to those with working for accountancy firms. The growth in availability of open-source financial software such as QuantLib may hit these companies in the medium term.

1.12. Where people go wrong

A certain number of people try and fail to get quant jobs; it therefore has a reputation as a tough area to get into. The biggest reasons for failure are:

- mistaken ideas about the knowledge required;
- inability to code;
- personality defects;
- non-possession of appropriate degrees;
- lack of ability at mathematics;
- misperception of own ability.

If none of these apply, and you have done your preparation then you should be able to get a job.

What if some do apply? This book should make it clear what is required and how to acquire the necessary knowledge. If you don't know how to code, then you simply have to learn by picking up the books and coding some models. If you can't do this, try a different career.

If you have personality defects then well done for recognising the fact. Quant jobs are not an area where personality counts for a lot at entry level. Try reading a few books in the "self-help" section of the book-shop and work on your people skills. You only have to appear normal for a couple of hours to get the job.

The simple truth is that if you apply for quant jobs without something that says you are really good at maths in your c.v. then you won't get interviews. You therefore have to get a degree that demonstrates the ability and knowledge you claim, or do something that shows the requisite skills in other ways.

If you simply aren't that great at mathematics then this is not the career for you. Even if you manage to get that first job, you will be working day in, day out with people who love mathematics and can't imagine doing anything else. You will not thrive in that environment, better to find something you have natural talent in.

Inability to assess one's own ability quickly shows up when you think you are on top of everything and you start bombing the interviews. If you keep failing the interviews, it is a strong lesson that you need to reassess yourself. Getting a friend who is already in the quant area to do a practice interview is a good way to assess your ability. Working through the problems in this book and seeing how many you can do without help is another way.

Ultimately, there aren't really that many people who are very strong at mathematics. If you are one of those people, the quant career is attractive; if you aren't then it is very hard to get into.

CHAPTER 2

Option pricing

2.1. Introduction

The majority of work for quants in a bank is focused on the pricing of options. It is not surprising then that a large section of this book is dedicated to option pricing questions. Before even looking at financial models however, one needs to understand some of the more fundamental properties of option prices, such as no arbitrage bounds. For example, how does the price of a call option vary with time? What happens as volatility tends to infinity?

The classical model of Black and Scholes is almost certain to come up in any interview, so make sure you understand this model. You should be able to derive the pricing formula for at least a European call option and be able to extend it to different payoffs. It is also worth understanding the Greeks: what they mean and what they are in the Black–Scholes model.

Another key aspect of financial modeling is hedging and replication. Having a good understanding of what replication is and how you can replicate an unusual payoff with vanilla options is a valuable skill. Some banks manage to make large sums of money by replicating an exotic option with vanilla options, and you will be expected to have a good understanding of replication: both static and dynamic.

We briefly mention a few introductory books on option pricing. We also refer the reader to a much longer list on www.markjoshi.com.

This book of interview questions can be viewed as a companion book to the first author's book on derivatives pricing: "The Concepts and Practice of Mathematical Finance." The sequel, "More Mathematical Finance," is also relevant for readers wishing to get their knowledge up a level. For those who wish to have some alternatives, here are some standard choices:

- J. Hull, "Options, Futures and Other Derivatives," – sometimes called the "bible book." Gives a good run-down of how the markets work but is aimed at MBAs rather than mathematicians so the mathematics is quite weak.
- T. Björk, "Arbitrage Theory in Continuous Time." This book is on the theoretical side with the author having a background in probability theory, but he also has a good understanding of the underlying finance and he is good at translating intuition into theory and back.
- S. Shreve, "Stochastic Calculus for Finance Vols I and II." A careful and popular exposition of the theory.
- P. Wilmott, various books. Good expositions of the PDE approach to finance, but not so good on the martingale approach.
- M. Baxter and A. Rennie, "Financial Calculus." A good introductory book on the martingale approach which requires a reasonable level of mathematical sophistication but also has good intuition.

2.2. Questions

2.2.1. Black–Scholes.

QUESTION 2.1. Derive the Black–Scholes equation for a stock, S. What boundary conditions are satisfied at $S = 0$ and $S = \infty$?

QUESTION 2.2. Derive the Black–Scholes equation so that an undergrad can understand it.

QUESTION 2.3. Explain the Black–Scholes equation.

QUESTION 2.4. Suppose two assets in a Black–Scholes world have the same volatility but different drifts. How will the price of call options on them compare? Now suppose one of the assets undergoes downward jumps at random times. How will this affect option prices?

QUESTION 2.5. Suppose an asset has a deterministic time dependent volatility. How would I price an option on it using the Black–Scholes theory? How would I hedge it?

QUESTION 2.6. In the Black–Scholes world, price a European option with a payoff of

$$\max(S_T^2 - K, 0)$$

at time T.

QUESTION 2.7. Develop a formula for the price of a derivative paying

$$\max(S_T(S_T - K), 0)$$

in the Black–Scholes model.

QUESTION 2.8. Give me the price of a derivative which pays $\log(S_T)S_T$, you can assume that the Black–Scholes model is valid. How can we get the price more efficiently?

QUESTION 2.9. Prove that the implied vol of a put and the implied vol of a call (with the same strike) are the same.

2.2.2. Option price properties.

QUESTION 2.10. Sketch the value of a vanilla call option as a function of spot. How will it evolve with time?

QUESTION 2.11. Is it ever optimal to early exercise an American call option? What about a put option?

QUESTION 2.12. In FX markets an option can be expressed as either a call or a put, explain. Relate your answer to Question 2.11.

QUESTION 2.13. Approximately how much would a one-month call option at-the-money with a million dollar notional and spot 1 be worth?

QUESTION 2.14. Suppose a call option only pays off if spot never passes below a barrier B. Sketch the value as a function of spot. Now suppose the option only pays off if spot passes below B instead. Sketch the value of the option again. Relate the two graphs.

QUESTION 2.15. What is meant by put-call parity?

QUESTION 2.16. What happens to the price of a vanilla call option as volatility tends to infinity?

QUESTION 2.17. Suppose there are no interest rates. The spot price of a non-dividend paying stock is 20. Option A pays 1 dollar if the stock price is above 30 at any time in the next year. Option B pays 1 if the stock price is above 30 at the end of the year. How are the values of A and B related?

QUESTION 2.18. How does the value of a call option vary with time? Prove your result.

QUESTION 2.19. A put and call on a stock struck at the forward price have the same value by put-call parity. Yet the value of a put is bounded and the value of a call is unbounded. Explain how they can have the same value.

QUESTION 2.20. Suppose we price a digital call in both normal and log-normal models in such a way that the price of call option with the same strike is invariant. How will the prices differ?

QUESTION 2.21. What is riskier: a call option or the underlying? (Consider a one-day time horizon and compute which has bigger Delta as a fraction of value.)

QUESTION 2.22. If the stock price at time T is distributed as $N(S_0, \sigma^2)$ what is the expected value of an at-the-money European call expiring at time T?

QUESTION 2.23. Assume that the price of a stock at time T is $N(S_0, \sigma^2)$ where S_0 is the price now and that we know the price of an at-the-money European call expiring at T. How could we estimate σ?

QUESTION 2.24. A stock S is worth \$100 now at $t = 0$. At $t = 1$, S goes either to \$110 with probability = 2/3 or to \$80 with prob 1/3. If interest rates are zero, value an at-the-money European call on S expiring at $t = 1$.

QUESTION 2.25. Sketch the value of a vanilla call and a digital call as a function of spot. Relate the two.

QUESTION 2.26. Price a 1 year forward, risk free rate = 5%, spot = \$1 and a dividend of \$0.10 after 6 months.

QUESTION 2.27. What is the fair price for FX Euro/dollar in one year? Risk free rates and spot exchange rate given.

QUESTION 2.28. An option pays

$$\begin{cases} 1, & \text{if } S_1 > S_2, \\ 0, & \text{otherwise}, \end{cases}$$

at time T. If the volatility of S_1 increases, what happens to the value of the option?

QUESTION 2.29. In the pricing of options, why doesn't it matter if the stock price exhibits mean reversion?

QUESTION 2.30. What are the limits/boundaries for the price of a call option on a non-dividend paying stock?

QUESTION 2.31. What happens to the value of a call option after a 98th percentile fall in the stock price?

QUESTION 2.32. What is the price of a call option where the underlying is the forward price of a stock?

QUESTION 2.33. Prove that the price of a call option is a convex function of the strike price.

QUESTION 2.34. For an American option, when the risk-free interest rate increases, will it increase the possibility of early exercise?

QUESTION 2.35. What is a butterfly?

QUESTION 2.36. What is VAR and how do you compute it?

QUESTION 2.37. Assume you have markets quotes for an ITM put option and an OTM call option, both struck at K. Further, suppose that K is much larger than the current spot price. Which option should you use for calibration?

QUESTION 2.38. What is CVA and how do you compute it?

2.2.3. Hedging and replication.

QUESTION 2.39. What uses could an option be put to?

QUESTION 2.40. Suppose spot today is 90. A call option is struck at 100 and expires in one year. There are no interest rates. Spot moves log-normally in a perfect Black–Scholes world. I claim that I can hedge the option for free. Whenever spot crosses 100 in an upwards direction I borrow 100 and buy the stock. Whenever spot crosses 100 in a downwards direction I sell the stock and repay my loan. At expiry either the option is out-of-the-money in which case I have no position or it is in-the-money and I use the 100 dollar strike to payoff my loan. Thus the option has been hedged for free. Where is the error in this argument?

QUESTION 2.41. Team A plays team B, in a series of 7 games, whoever wins 4 games first wins. You want to bet 100 that your team wins the series, in which case you receive 200, or 0 if they lose. However the broker only allows bets on individual games. You can bet X on any individual game the day before it occurs to receive $2X$ if it wins and 0 if it loses. How do you achieve the desired pay-out? In particular, what do you bet on the first match?

QUESTION 2.42. Suppose two teams play five matches. I go to the bookmakers and ask to place a bet on the entire series. The bookie refuses saying I can only bet on individual matches. For each match I either win X dollars or lose X dollars. How would I construct a series of bets in such a way as to have the same payoff as a bet on the series?

QUESTION 2.43. You want to bet $64 at even odds on the CWS winning the World Series. Your bookmaker will only let you bet at even odds on each game. What do you do?

QUESTION 2.44. Suppose an option pays 1 if the spot is between 100 and 110 at expiry and zero otherwise. Synthesise the option from vanilla call options.

QUESTION 2.45. Suppose an option pays zero if spot is less than 100, or pays spot minus 100 for spot between 100 and 120 and 20 otherwise. Synthesise the option from vanilla options.

QUESTION 2.46. What is pricing by replication?

QUESTION 2.47. Replicate a digital option with vanilla options.

QUESTION 2.48. The statistics department from our bank tell you that the stock price has followed a mean reversion process for the last 10 years, with annual volatility 10% and daily volatility 20%. You want to sell a European option and hedge it, which volatility do you use?

QUESTION 2.49. A derivative pays

$$\frac{1}{\min(\max(S_T, K_1), K_2)},$$

with $K_1 < K_2$. Derive a model independent hedge in terms of a portfolio of vanilla options.

QUESTION 2.50. Given an Asian forward contract, price it using replication.

QUESTION 2.51. How would you hedge a butterfly with vanilla options?

QUESTION 2.52. How do you hedge a barrier option?

2.2.4. The Greeks.

QUESTION 2.53. What methods can be used for computing Greeks given a method for computing the price? What are their advantages and disadvantages?

QUESTION 2.54. How does the Gamma of a call option vary with time?

QUESTION 2.55. Suppose an option pays one if spot stays in a range $K1$ to $K2$ and zero otherwise. What can we say about the Vega?

QUESTION 2.56. All being equal, which option has higher Vega? An at-the-money European call option with spot 100 or an at-the-money European call option with spot 200? (A structurer asked this question and didn't want formulas.)

QUESTION 2.57. How do you construct a Vega neutral portfolio with vanilla call and put options?

2.2.5. General.

QUESTION 2.58. How accurate do you think a pricing function should be?

QUESTION 2.59. Assume you have a good trading model that you think will make money. What information would you present to your manager to support your claim?

2.2.6. Trees and Monte Carlo.

QUESTION 2.60. A stock is worth 100 today. There are zero interest rates. The stock can be worth 90 or 110 tomorrow. It moves to 110 with probability p. Price a call option struck at 100.

QUESTION 2.61. At the end of the day, a stock will be 100 with probability $p = 0.6$ and 50 with probability $1 - p = 0.4$. What is it trading for right now? Value an at-the-money European call option expiring at the end of the day. What if the actual stock price is 75 right now?

QUESTION 2.62. A stock is worth 100 today. There are zero interest rates. The stock can be worth 90, 100, or 110 tomorrow. It moves to 110 with probability p and 100 with probability q. What can we say about the price of a call option struck at 100.

QUESTION 2.63. Follow-up: given that we have seen that trinomial trees do not lead to unique prices, why do banks use them to compute prices?

QUESTION 2.64. Consider the following binomial tree. There are two identical underlying assets A and B with the same prices and volatility. If all were the same except that research suggests company A will do better than company B, how would the option prices compare?

QUESTION 2.65. Monte Carlo versus binomial tree – when shall you use one or the other?

QUESTION 2.66. Current stock price 100, may go up to 150 or go down to 75. What is the price of a call option based on it? What is the Delta?

QUESTION 2.67. Explain the Longstaff-Schwartz algorithm for pricing an early exercisable option with Monte Carlo.

2.2.7. Incomplete markets.

QUESTION 2.68. What is implied volatility and a volatility skew/smile?

QUESTION 2.69. What differing models can be used to price exotic foreign exchange options consistently with market smiles? What are the pros and cons of each?

QUESTION 2.70. Explain why a stochastic volatility model gives a smile.

2.3. Solutions

2.3.1. Black–Scholes.

Solution to Question 2.1. In the Black–Scholes world the evolution of the stock price S_t is given by

$$dS_t = \mu S_t dt + \sigma S_t dW_t,$$

for μ, $\sigma > 0$. We also assume the stock does not pay any dividends, there are no transaction costs and the continuously compounding interest rate is $r > 0$

(constant). The latter assumption implies the evolution of the risk-free asset B_t is given by

$$dB_t = rB_t dt.$$

We are interested in pricing an option which is a function of the stock price at time $T > 0$, S_T. One possible example is a call option with strike $K > 0$, that is a derivative which at time T pays

$$\max(S_T - K, 0).$$

While the form of the payoff is not particularly important, that it is a function of the stock price at time T, and only time T, is important. Under this condition we can show that the call option price is a function of current time t and current stock price S_t only (see e.g. [18] p.267, Theorem 6.3.1 or [6]). Thus we denote by $C(t, S_t)$ the call option price.

To price a derivative in the Black–Scholes world, we must do so under a measure which does not allow arbitrage (clearly the existence of arbitrage in any model is cause for concern). Such a measure is called a risk-neutral measure. One can prove that under this measure, the drift term of the stock price changes so that

$$dS_t = rS_t dt + \sigma S_t dW_t.$$

We are now ready to proceed with our derivation. In the risk-neutral world, $C(t, S_t)/B_t$ is a martingale and hence if we calculate its differential we know it must have zero drift. Applying Itô's lemma to $C(t, S_t)$ gives

$$dC(t, S_t) = \frac{\partial C}{\partial t} dt + \frac{\partial C}{\partial S_t} dS_t + \frac{1}{2} \frac{\partial^2 C}{\partial S_t^2} (dS_t)^2,$$

where the arguments of C and its partial derivatives are understood to be (t, S_t). Using the risk-neutral dynamics of S_t (and recalling that $(dW_t)^2 = dt$, $dW_t dt = (dt)^2 = 0$) gives

$$dC(t, S_t) = \left(\frac{\partial C}{\partial t} + \frac{\partial C}{\partial S_t} rS_t + \frac{1}{2} \frac{\partial^2 C}{\partial S_t^2} \sigma^2 S_t^2 \right) dt + \sigma S_t \frac{\partial C}{\partial S_t} dW_t.$$

Finally using the Itô product rule we can compute

$$d\left(\frac{C(t, S_t)}{B_t} \right) = \frac{1}{B_t} \left(\frac{\partial C}{\partial t} + \frac{\partial C}{\partial S_t} rS_t + \frac{1}{2} \frac{\partial^2 C}{\partial S_t^2} \sigma^2 S_t^2 - rC \right) dt + \sigma \frac{S_t}{B_t} \frac{\partial C}{\partial S_t} dW_t.$$

Since we know this is a martingale (the drift term is zero), we see that

$$(2.1) \qquad \frac{\partial C}{\partial t} + \frac{\partial C}{\partial S_t} r S_t + \frac{1}{2} \frac{\partial^2 C}{\partial S_t^2} \sigma^2 S_t^2 - r C = 0.$$

This is the Black–Scholes equation.

When considering the boundary conditions, we do need the form of the payoff function of the derivative. Here we take our example of the call option with strike K. We can approach the question regarding the boundary conditions in two ways. The first is simple, logical, but not entirely concrete: just think about it. Consider first the boundary condition for $S_t = 0$. If the stock price at time t is zero, it will be zero forever. To see this, either note that the stochastic differential equation for S_t becomes $dS_t = 0$ at time t, and hence the stock price never changes, remaining at zero. Alternatively, recall the solution to the stock price stochastic differential equation is given by

$$S_T = S_t \exp \left\{ \left(r - \frac{1}{2} \sigma^2 \right) (T - t) + \sigma (W_T - W_t) \right\},$$

so if S_t is zero then so is S_T. Thus the call option will be worthless, and we have the boundary condition $C(t, 0) = 0$, $t \in [0, T]$. As a more concrete approach, if we substitute $S_t = 0$ into the Black–Scholes equation, we end up with

$$\frac{\partial C}{\partial t}(t, 0) = r C(t, 0).$$

This is an ordinary differential equation which we can solve to give

$$C(t, 0) = e^{rt} C(0, 0).$$

We know $C(T, 0) = \max\{0 - K, 0\} = 0$. This gives $C(0, 0) = 0$, and in turn this implies $C(t, 0) = 0$ for all t.

The boundary condition at $S_t = \infty$ is a little harder to specify. For very large values of S_t, the option is almost certain to finish in-the-money. Thus for every dollar the stock price rises, we can be almost certain to receive a dollar at payoff, time T. This is sometimes written as

$$\lim_{S \to \infty} \frac{\partial C}{\partial S_t}(t, S_t) = 1.$$

Alternatively, one can observe that as the option gets deeper and deeper into the money, the optionality gets worth less and less so the boundary condition is that

$$C = S_t - K$$

for S_t large.

Note this is only one way to derive the Black–Scholes equation and it is wise to know many ways. For further details on the Black–Scholes equation and related background, see [6].

Here are some possible related questions:

- If the payoff function is instead $F(S_T)$ for some deterministic function F, what are the boundary conditions at $S_t = 0$ and $S_t = \infty$?
- Prove that the equation $S_t = S_0 \exp\left\{\left(r - \frac{1}{2}\sigma^2\right)t + \sigma W_t\right\}$ satisfies the stochastic differential equation given for S_t.
- Prove that the Black–Scholes formula for a European call option satisfies the Black–Scholes equation.
- Derive the equation if the stock pays continuous dividends at a rate d.
- Transform equation (2.1) into the heat equation using a change of variables.

□

Solution to Question 2.2. What sort of undergrad are we dealing with here? Obviously there is a large difference between a student directly out of high school and one nearing the end of their studies in probability theory or financial mathematics. The best interpretation of this question is to give an explanation which is as simple as possible.

One unavoidable, and somewhat technical, statement is that in the Black–Scholes world the arbitrage-free stock price evolves according to the stochastic differential equation

$$dS_t = rS_t dt + \sigma S_t dW_t,$$

where r is the risk-free rate of return (whether the undergrad understands much stochastic calculus is questionable, but short of giving a brief explanation of what the above equation represents there is little we can do to avoid using this). Here you should mention that 'arbitrage-free' essentially implies that there does not exist opportunities to make money for nothing without any risk in the market. One could also give an elementary explanation of what this equation represents; see the extension questions below. We require one other asset to use in the derivation, the risk-free bank account. This grows at the continuously compounding rate r and hence its value at time t, B_t, is given by

$$B_t = e^{rt} \Rightarrow dB_t = rB_t dt,$$

which is a result from ordinary calculus.

The final necessary piece of technical mathematics we require is Itô's formula: the stochastic differential equation of a function $f(t, S_t)$ is given by

$$df(t, S_t) = \frac{\partial f}{\partial t}(t, S_t)dt + \frac{\partial f}{\partial S}(t, S_t)dS_t + \frac{1}{2}\frac{\partial^2 f}{\partial S^2}(t, S_t)(dS_t)^2.$$

Evaluating this requires the relations $(dt)^2 = (dW_t)(dt) = 0$, $(dW_t)^2 = dt$. Here we can compare this result to those from ordinary calculus, noting the extra term as a consequence of differentiation using stochastic processes.

Next we state that the price of a derivative is a function of the current time t and the current stock price S_t (this can be proved, but is beyond the scope of the question). We therefore denote such a price by $C(t, S_t)$.

Finally we need that $C(t, S_t)B_t^{-1}$ is a martingale. How do we justify this, and what does it mean? A simple explanation of its meaning is that we expect it to have zero growth: our option price is expected to grow at the same rate as the bank account and hence the growth of each cancels out in the given process. This is what it means to be a martingale, we do not expect change over time so we have zero expected growth. We perhaps overused the word 'expected' here, but it should be emphasised that there will be changes in the discounted price, we just expect it to be zero on average. This translates to the discounted price having a zero drift term. We apply Itô's formula to calculate the drift (see Question 2.1), equate to zero and get

$$\frac{\partial C}{\partial t} + \frac{\partial C}{\partial S_t}rS_t + \frac{1}{2}\frac{\partial^2 C}{\partial S_t^2}\sigma^2 S_t^2 - rC = 0,$$

the Black–Scholes equation.

Here are some possible related questions:

- Give a non-technical explanation of the stochastic differential equation describing the evolution of the stock price.
- What is the mathematical definition of 'arbitrage free'? Explain this in everyday language.

□

Solution to Question 2.3. Exactly what is meant by 'explain' this equation is not entirely clear. We begin in the most obvious place, by stating the equation with an explanation of its terms. For a derivative paying a function of the stock price at some future time, the Black–Scholes equation is given by

$$\frac{\partial C}{\partial t} + \frac{\partial C}{\partial S_t} r S_t + \frac{1}{2} \frac{\partial^2 C}{\partial S_t^2} \sigma^2 S_t^2 - rC = 0,$$

where

$$t \text{ is the current time,}$$

$$S_t \text{ is the current stock price,}$$

$$C(t, S_t) \text{ is the price of the derivative,}$$

$$r \text{ is the risk-free interest rate,}$$

$$\text{and } \sigma \text{ is the volatility parameter of the stock price,}$$

(for a derivation see Question 2.1).

This is a partial differential equation describing the evolution of the option price as a function of the current stock price and the current time. The equation does not change if we vary the payoff function of the derivative, however the associated boundary conditions, which are required to solve the equation either in closed form or by simulation, do vary.

An important part of this equation are the assumptions underlying its derivation. Perhaps most importantly, we assume that under the risk-neutral measure the evolution of the stock price is given by

$$dS_t = r S_t dt + \sigma S_t dW_t.$$

As mentioned, we also assume the existence of a risk-free asset which grows at the continuously compounding rate r.

Here are some possible related questions:

- What are the boundary conditions needed to solve the equation associated with a payoff function $f(S_T)$?
- Explain the Itô formula.

□

Solution to Question 2.4. The first part of this question asks us to compare the value of call options struck on two different stocks which have the same volatility but different drifts, that is the evolution of the stocks S_t^1 and S_t^2 is given by

$$dS_t^1 = \mu^1 S_t^1 dt + \sigma S_t^1 dW_t,$$
$$dS_t^2 = \mu^2 S_t^2 dt + \sigma S_t^2 dW_t,$$

where $\mu^1 \neq \mu^2$. The answer is that despite their differing drifts, the prices of the options on the two stocks do not differ at all. The more interesting question is why they do not differ. Mathematically, we can consider the derivation of the Black–Scholes equation in Question 2.1. Here we see that the pricing of any derivative must be done in the risk-neutral measure in order to avoid arbitrage, and under the risk-neutral measure the drift of a stock is changed so that

$$dS_t^i = r S_t^i dt + \sigma S_t^i dW_t,$$

for $i = 1, 2$, where r is the risk-free rate of return. Financially (from [6], Section 5.7), 'this reflects the fact that the hedging strategy ensures that the underlying drift of the stock is balanced against the drift of the option. The drifts are balanced since drift reflects the risk premium demanded by investors to account for uncertainty and that uncertainty has been hedged away'. That is we can perfectly hedge the claim in the Black–Scholes world.

We now consider a call option on a stock with downward jumps at random times compared to a model without jumps. In fact, we treat the more general case of an option with a convex payoff (a call option is such an example). We assume the usual Black–Scholes diffusion model for the stocks, with one having an additional jump term.

To see how the prices compare, we carry out the Black–Scholes hedging strategy. This consists of an initial portfolio cost of $C_{BS}(0, S_0)$, where C_{BS} denotes the Black–Scholes (no-jumps) option price, and holding $\frac{\partial C_{BS}}{\partial S}$ units of the stock while the rest is in bonds. While a jump does not occur, the hedge works perfectly, and hence if no jumps occur the option's payoff is perfectly replicated.

The convex payoff of the call option leads to a convex Black–Scholes price. This implies that if we graph the price as a function of spot for any time t, any tangent of the graph will lie below it. The above Black–Scholes hedge we set up is constructed to be exactly the tangent through the point $(S_t, C_{BS}(t, S_t))$. When a jump occurs, we will move instantly along this tangent line, and hence finish at a point which is below the Black–Scholes price. We continue to hedge as before, and further jumps will add to this difference in the hedging portfolio and the Black–Scholes price. Hence if a jump occurs the portfolio value will be less than the Black–Scholes price.

Overall, we constructed a portfolio with initial cost $C_{BS}(0, S_0)$ which sometimes finishes with the same value as the option (if no jumps occur) and sometimes finishes with a lower value (if a jump occurs). Thus by no arbitrage considerations the value of the option on the stock with jumps must be greater than $C_{BS}(0, S_0)$.

For further information on pricing using a model with jumps, see [6] Ch.15.

Here are some possible related questions:

- Say instead of two constant, but different, drifts, we had one constant drift and one drift that was a deterministic function of time. How would the two option prices then compare?
- Is the jump model we considered a model which leads to a complete market? What is the limiting price of an option on this stock as the jump intensity, which determines the frequency of jumps, approaches zero?
- Can we apply the same considerations in a jump model to other options, for example a digital call option?

□

Solution to Question 2.5. Details of the following can be found in Section 6.11 of [6].

In a Black–Scholes world where the volatility follows a time-dependent (but still deterministic) function we can follow through the derivation of the Black–Scholes equation as per usual (see Question 2.1), however now the volatility σ is a function. This gives the modified version of the Black–Scholes equation,

$$\frac{\partial C}{\partial t} + \frac{\partial C}{\partial S_t} r S_t + \frac{1}{2} \frac{\partial^2 C}{\partial S_t^2} \sigma(t)^2 S_t^2 - rC = 0,$$

and the previous boundary conditions hold. From here it is not so clear how to proceed.

We instead consider pricing by using the martingale approach. Under the risk-neutral pricing measure, the evolution of the stock price is given by

$$dS_t = r S_t dt + \sigma(t) S_t dW_t,$$

or equivalently,

$$d(\log S_t) = \left(r - \frac{1}{2} \sigma(t)^2 \right) dt + \sigma(t) dW_t.$$

Our goal is to evaluate $\mathbb{E}(B_T^{-1} C(T, S_T))$, where the expectation is taken in the risk-neutral measure, B_t is the value of the risk-free asset and $C(t, S_t)$ is the value of the option at time t when the stock price is S_t. For this we need the distribution of S_T, or equivalently $\log(S_T)$. The above equation is just shorthand for

$$\log S_T - \log S_0 = rT - \frac{1}{2} \int_0^T \sigma(t)^2 dt + \int_0^T \sigma(t) dW_t.$$

If we recall some basic facts from stochastic calculus, we notice that for a deterministic function f, $\int_x^y f(t) dW_t$ is a normally distributed random variable with zero mean and variance $\int_x^y f(t)^2 dt$. If we define $\bar{\sigma}$ as the root-mean-square value of $\sigma(t)$, i.e.

$$\bar{\sigma} = \sqrt{\frac{1}{T} \int_0^T \sigma(s)^2 ds},$$

then we have

$$\log S_T - \log S_0 = \left(r - \frac{1}{2} \bar{\sigma}^2 \right) T + \bar{\sigma} \sqrt{T} Z,$$

where Z is a standard normal random variable. Here we notice that this is just the distribution at time T for the log of a geometric Brownian motion with constant volatility $\bar{\sigma}$, and we can price using this. For example, we have that the value of a European call option is just given by the Black–Scholes formula with σ replaced by $\bar{\sigma}$.

To hedge, we hold $\frac{\partial C}{\partial S}$ units of stock at a time. The only difference is, what value of volatility do we use? At time t, $C(t, S_t)$ is the value of the option with root-mean-square volatility taken over the time period $[t, T]$, and this is the value we use to find the hedge.

Here are some possible related questions:

- What changes if we use time-dependent drift?
- What changes if we use time-dependent interest rates?
- Where does the above argument break down if we introduce stochastic volatility?

$\square$

Solution to Question 2.6. The term 'in the Black–Scholes world' refers to the situation where the stock price S_t follows the stochastic differential equation

$$dS_t = \mu S_t dt + \sigma S_t dW_t,$$

for $\mu, \sigma > 0$ and where W_t is a Brownian motion. The question then asks us to compute, in the risk-neutral measure, the expectation

$$\mathbb{E}[\max(S_T^2 - K, 0)],$$

with appropriate discounting factors (a constant continuously compounding interest rate of r is assumed), where T is the maturity date and K is the strike price. The Black–Scholes PDE is still satisfied, with different boundary conditions, or you can use the more probabilistic approach of integrating the expectation against the appropriate density.

However all of this is a lot of work, and a large short-cut exists if we stop and think about it for a second. In the risk-neutral measure, the stock price follows the stochastic differential equation

$$dS_t = r S_t dt + \sigma S_t dW_t.$$

The solution to this is well-known and given by

$$S_t = S_0 \exp \left\{ \left(r - \frac{1}{2}\sigma^2 \right) t + \sigma W_t \right\}.$$

We are trying to price an option on S_t^2, so what process does S_t^2 follow? One option is to apply Itô's formula, alternatively we can look at the above expression and see immediately that

$$S_t^2 = S_0^2 \exp \left\{ \left(2r - \sigma^2 \right) t + 2\sigma W_t \right\}.$$

Comparing this with the original geometric Brownian motion, we have that in the risk-neutral pricing measure S_t^2 is again a geometric Brownian motion with diffusion 2σ and drift $2r - \sigma^2$.

We can therefore use the Black formula. We simply have to write the S_T^2 as

$$F_T(0)e^{-\nu^2 T/2 + \nu W_T},$$

compute the values of $F_T(0)$ and ν and plug them in.

Here are some possible related questions:

- Write down the boundary conditions satisfied by the new PDE.
- What are the Greeks of the option on S_t^2?

$\square$

Solution to Question 2.7. The trick to answering this question is to take the stock as numeraire. The price of an option is given by its pricing measure expectation

$$\frac{C_0}{N_0} = \mathbb{E}\left[\frac{S_T \max(S_T - K, 0)}{N_T} \right],$$

where C_0 is the option price and N_0 is a numeraire asset. By taking the stock as numeraire, $N_T = S_T$, we can simplify the expectation. We now just need to evaluate $S_0\mathbb{E}[\max(S_T - K, 0)]$ where the expectation is taken with the stock as numeraire. We can split this expectation into two parts

(2.2) $\mathbb{E}[\max(S_T - K, 0)] = \mathbb{E}[S_T \mathbb{1}_{S_T > K}] - \mathbb{E}[K \mathbb{1}_{S_T > K}],$

where $\mathbb{1}$ is the indicator function. Focusing on the last term, we need to know how the final stock price is distributed in the stock measure. It is (try to derive this yourself)

$$S_T = S_0 \exp\left\{\left(r + \frac{\sigma^2}{2}\right)T + \sigma\sqrt{T}N(0,1)\right\},$$

where $N(0,1)$ is a standard normal random variable. Since

$$\mathbb{E}[K\mathbb{1}_{S_T>K}] = K\mathbb{P}(S_T > K),$$

we can calculate this to be $KN(d_1)$ where d_1 is the same as in the Black–Scholes formula (see Section 6.13 of [6]).

Concentrating on the middle term in equation (2.2), we can rewrite the expectation as an integral

$$\mathbb{E}[S_T\mathbb{1}_{S_T>K}] = \frac{S_0}{\sqrt{2\pi}} \int_l^\infty \exp\left\{\frac{-x^2}{2}\right\} \exp\left\{(r + \frac{\sigma^2}{2})T + \sigma\sqrt{T}x\right\} dx,$$

with

$$l = \frac{\ln(\frac{K}{S_0}) - (r + \frac{\sigma^2}{2})T}{\sigma\sqrt{T}}.$$

To calculate the expectation we perform the usual trick of putting all the x terms inside the exponential and completing the square. It turns out to equal (again, try it yourself)

$$\mathbb{E}[S_T\mathbb{1}_{S_T>K}] = S_0 \exp\{(r + \sigma^2)T\}N(d_3),$$

where

$$d_3 = \frac{\ln(\frac{S_0}{K}) + (r + \frac{3\sigma^2}{2})T}{\sigma\sqrt{T}}.$$

So combining the expectations the price of an option paying $\max(S_T(S_T - K), 0)$ in the Black–Scholes world is given by

$$S_0\left(S_0 \exp\{(r + \sigma^2)T\}N(d_3) - KN(d_1)\right),$$

with

$$d_i = \frac{\ln(\frac{S_0}{K}) + (r + \frac{i\sigma^2}{2})T}{\sigma\sqrt{T}}.$$

Here are some possible related questions:

- How will the price of this option compare to that of a European call?
- Why would a bank be reluctant to sell an option such as this?

☐

Solution to 2.8. The inefficient way is to compute the expectation of the pay-off in the risk-neutral measure and discount. An efficient way is to use the stock measure, that is we take the stock price as numeraire. We then have

$$D(0) = S_0 \mathbb{E}_S \left(\log S_T \right)$$

with the expectation taken in the stock measure. In that measure,

$$dS_t = (r + \sigma^2)S_t dt + \sigma S_t dW_t,$$

and, it follows from Itô's lemma that

$$d \log S_t = (r + 0.5\sigma^2)dt + \sigma dW_t.$$

This implies

$$\log S_T = \log S_0 + (r + 0.5\sigma^2)T + \sigma\sqrt{T}Z,$$

with Z a standard normal. The expectation is now trivial and we get

$$D(0) = S_0(\log S_0 + (r + 0.5\sigma^2)T).$$

For more discussion of the use of the stock measure, see [6].

Here are some possible related questions:

- What if there are dividends?
- Price a contract paying $S_T(\log S_T)^2$.
- Price a contract paying $S_T^2 \log S_T$.

☐

Solution to Question 2.9. The key to this one is put-call parity.

$$C = F + P.$$

Observe that this must hold both in the market and in the Black–Scholes model, since both must not allow any arbitrages. Also the value of F is model independent and so must be the same in both. So if $\hat{\sigma}$ is such that

$$P_{\text{market}} = P_{\text{BS}}(\hat{\sigma}),$$

then it immediately follows that

$$C_{\text{market}} = C_{\text{BS}}(\hat{\sigma}).$$

Here are some possible related questions:

- Prove that the strike of the call is the same as that of the put in a delta neutral straddle.
- If we were to calculate a Black–Scholes implied vol for an American call and put, would these vols have to be the same?

$\square$

2.3.2. Option price properties.

Solution to Question 2.10. Figure 2.1 shows the value of vanilla call options

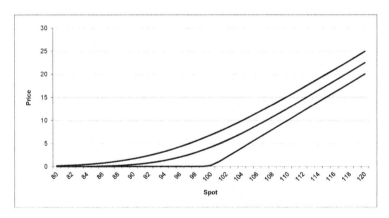

FIGURE 2.1. Vanilla Call options of varying time to expiry with strike 100, volatility of 10% and a risk-free rate of 5%. The highest graph has 1 year to expiry, the lowest has 1 day.

with 1 year, 6 months and 1 day to expiry. It is unlikely you will sketch these graphs perfectly in an interview, however there are a few important features that should be preserved:

- The vanilla call option value is monotone increasing in spot.
- The value is a convex function of spot, that is the price lies above all of the possible tangent lines.
- A vanilla call option (on a non-dividend paying stock) with longer time to expiry than an equivalent option is always worth at least as much.

As the last bullet point suggests, the option value decreases as time to expiry decreases and the value approaches its payoff.

Here are some possible related questions:

- Sketch the value of a vanilla put option as a function of spot.
- Sketch the value of a digital call/put option as a function of spot.
- Sketch the value of a vanilla call/put option as a function of volatility.

□

Solution to Question 2.11. The short answer is that it is never optimal to early exercise an American call option (assuming the underlying stock does not pay dividends), but it can be optimal to early exercise an American put option.

For the American call option, consider a portfolio consisting of one option C and K zero coupon bonds B, which expire at time T. At time T if the non-dividend paying stock price S is above K then the portfolio will be worth

$$(S_T - K) + K = S_T.$$

If the stock price is below K the portfolio will be worth K. Therefore our portfolio is worth $\max\{S_T, K\}$, which is never less than the stock price and sometimes more. The principle of no arbitrage implies that the portfolio must be worth more than the stock at all previous times, giving

$$C_t + KB_t > S_t, \ \forall t < T.$$

Rearranging, this yields

$$C_t > S_t - KB_t.$$

Assuming interest rates are non-negative i.e. $B_t < 1$ we have

$$C_t > S_t - K,$$

which says that an option will always be worth more than its value if exercised immediately. Unfortunately there isn't an equivalent argument for put options, and there are times when the optionality value is worth less than receiving the payoff today and hence it is optimal to early exercise. For more details on optimal exercise times of American put options see [14].

Here are some related possible questions:

- What about when the stock pays dividends, is it ever optimal to early exercise an American option?
- What if there are negative interest rates?
- What can be said about the relationship between the price of European and American call options? Put options?

□

Solution to Question 2.12. The answer to this question is not initially obvious if one is thinking about the quoted exchange rate, rather than what actually happens when the option is exercised. Consider an option on the AUDUSD exchange rate where AUD\$1,000,000 is sold to buy USD\$800,000 on the option's exercise date. This option could be considered both a call on USD and a put on AUD.

If we take the current exchange rate to be AUD\$1 = USD\$0.75, the call option will have a strike of 0.80 and a notional of AUD\$1,000,000. The put will have spot equal to 1.00, strike of $0.75/0.80 = 0.9375$ and a notional of AUD\$800,000.

After answering this and the previous question the interviewer may ask, why is it never optimal to early exercise the call when it is equivalent to a put, which can be optimally early exercised? The answer is that the notional amount in the foreign currency will grow at its risk free rate, which is equivalent to paying dividends and hence the optimal early exercise arguments do not apply.

□

Solution to Question 2.13. This question is designed to test one's basic feel for the price of an option. An easy way to answer is by using the approximation formula for at-the-money options. It states that an option's price is approximately

$$0.4 S_0 \sigma \sqrt{T}.$$

(The derivation of this formula can be found in [6].) To answer the question we need to know the volatility, which for simplicity we could assume to be 10%. The price of a one month at-the-money call option with million dollar notional and spot 1 is worth approximately $11,500.

Here are some possible related questions:

- What is the approximate price of a put option with the same characteristics as above? (Note that the approximation formula is the same for puts and calls as we are at-the-money, by put-call parity).
- How accurate is the approximation above?

☐

Solution to Question 2.14. After recognising the first option as a down-and-out

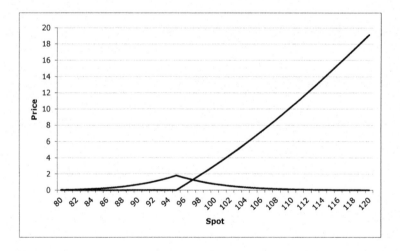

FIGURE 2.2. A down-and-out barrier option (increasing line) and a down-and-in barrier option (humped line), with strike 100 and barrier 95.

call, the value should look something similar to the increasing line in Figure 2.2, which is a sketch of a 1 year call with barrier at 95. The key features are zero value for spot below the barrier, increasing value with spot, and similarity to a vanilla call option when far from the barrier.

The second option in Figure 2.2 is a down-and-in call with the same parameters. The key to this question is relating the two values, which simply follows from the rule

$$\boxed{\text{out + in = vanilla.}}$$

The two option values when added together should look the same as a vanilla call option. (See Figure 2.1). To see why this relationship holds, see Section 8.1 of [6].

Here are some possible related questions:

- Why should out + in = vanilla?
- Sketch the value of a call option with a barrier above the strike. Approximately what will the sensitivities (Delta and Gamma) look like when the spot is close to the barrier?

□

Solution to Question 2.15. Put-call parity states that a European call option minus a European put option, with the same underlying asset, strike price and time to maturity, is equal to the forward contract. Using C for call, P for put and F for the forward contract we have

$$\boxed{C - P = F.}$$

Put-call parity is a very useful concept in options pricing and it is model independent, so it must hold no matter which model one is working with. Put-call parity could be used, for example, to price a put option instead of the required call option, due to the fact a put option is sometimes easier to price as its payoff is bounded. The parity gives the call option from the calculated put and forward contract. It can also be used to prove that the drift of the underlying asset does not affect the price of an option.

Here are some possible related questions:

- Does put-call parity hold for options with early exercise features, e.g. American options?
- Prove put-call parity.

□

Solution to Question 2.16. The price of a vanilla call option is monotone increasing in volatility, so as volatility tends to infinity the option price will tend to its maximum value. We know that the upper bound for the price of a call option is the stock price, so as volatility tends to infinity the price of a call option tends to a value less than or equal to the stock price. Of course, we still need to show that the limit is the stock price. Now assume that we are in a Black–Scholes world, with the option price given by the Black–Scholes formula. We can then argue that as volatility tends to infinity

$$d_1 = \frac{\log(\frac{S}{K}) + (r + \frac{\sigma^2}{2})T}{\sigma\sqrt{T}} \to \infty \ \text{ as } \ \sigma \to \infty.$$

Similarly,

$$d_2 = \frac{\log(\frac{S}{K}) + (r - \frac{\sigma^2}{2})T}{\sigma\sqrt{T}} \to -\infty \ \text{ as } \ \sigma \to \infty.$$

The corresponding normal cdf of d_1 and d_2 will then be 1 and 0 respectively. So as volatility tends to infinity the option's price will tend to the spot price.

Here are some possible related questions:

- What happens to the price of a vanilla call option as volatility tends to zero?
- What happens to the price of a vanilla call option as time to expiry tends to infinity?

□

Solution to Question 2.17. The key to this question is relating the American optionality of option A to the European optionality of option B in terms of probabilities. Clearly if option B pays a dollar then option A must also, but the converse is not true. Thus A must be worth more than B. For example, assume that the stock follows Brownian motion. As there are no interest rates this Brownian motion will have zero drift in the risk-neutral measure. If the stock reaches 30 before expiry, then in the risk-neutral measure there is a 50% chance it will be above 30 at expiry. In terms of the two options, if A pays off there is a 50% chance B will pay off, therefore B will be worth half the value of A.

If we were to assume that the stock follows Geometric Brownian motion it will have a negative drift in the case of zero interest rates (due to the $-\sigma^2 T/2$ term). We no longer have that option B is worth half the value of option A, it will be worth less than half the value of A.

Here is a related question:

- In general, what can we say about the value of American digital options compared to European digital options?

$\square$

Solution to Question 2.18. We will take the underlying asset to be non-dividend paying and consider two arbitrary expiry times T_1 and T_2 with

$$T_1 < T_2.$$

Take an American option C_1 which expires at time T_1 and an American option C_2 expiring at time T_2. C_2 carries all the rights of C_1, because it can be exercised at any time before T_1 and it also carries extra rights, because it can be exercised after T_1 whereas C_1 cannot. Therefore C_2 must be worth at least as much as C_1 as the extra rights will have a non-negative value.

We have shown that as time to expiry increases the option value increases, which makes intuitive sense as extra time gives us more optionality, which our bank/broker will no doubt charge us extra for.

Note this argument applies equally well to European call options since they will have the same value as American call options (see Question 2.11).

Here are some possible related questions:

- Prove this result for European options without using American options.
- Will this relationship always hold for European options on dividend-paying assets?

□

Solution to Question 2.19. This is a strange question, but interviewers tend to like asking curly questions. Put-call parity holds even though the value of a call is unbounded. One could argue that it doesn't matter that the call value is unbounded, the put and call must have the same value by put-call parity.

Another approach is to discuss how options are priced. The price of a derivative is given by the integral of the payoff multiplied by the risk-neutral density, then discounted. The payoff for a call option is unbounded, however when this is multiplied by the risk-neutral density it will be bounded. This is because the risk-neutral density will rapidly decay to zero for any reasonable model.

Here are some possible related questions:

- What is the rate of decay of the Black–Scholes density?
- What does it mean for a model to have fat tails?
- Suppose we worked in the Bachelier model, what would happen?

□

Solution to Question 2.20. The question can be divided into:

- What effect does skew have on the price of a digital option?
- What skew arises in a normal model?

All volatility smile questions about European options with single time payoffs, i.e. options that pay $f(S_T)$ at time T, are best resolved by using replication arguments.

We can replicate a digital call option using a limit of call spreads. Thus we take for some small ϵ, $0.5/\epsilon$ call options struck at $K - \epsilon$ and $-0.5/\epsilon$ call options struck at $K + \epsilon$. The value of this portfolio is equal

$$\frac{C(K - \epsilon) - C(K + \epsilon)}{2\epsilon}.$$

Letting ϵ tend to zero, we get

$$-\frac{\partial C}{\partial K}.$$

This is the value of the call option as a function, if we have a smile and we are using Black–Scholes values with implied volatility, $\hat{\sigma}$, we must consider

$$-\frac{\partial}{\partial K}\left(\text{BS}(K, \hat{\sigma})\right) = -\frac{\partial \text{BS}}{\partial K} - \frac{\partial \text{BS}}{\partial \hat{\sigma}}\frac{\partial \hat{\sigma}}{\partial K}.$$

The first term is the price in a model with no smile, that is a log-normal model. Since Vega is always positive for a vanilla call option, the correction is positive for downwards sloping smiles and negative for upwards sloping ones.

A normal model can be crudely written as a log-normal model with volatility σ/S. The volatility therefore goes up when spot goes down and we have a negative skew.

In conclusion, the price of a digital call option will increase when we switch from a log-normal model to a normal one. See [6], Chapter 7 for further discussion of the issues raised in this example.

Here are some possible related questions:

- What happens with a digital put? (This is trivial!)
- Can you think of a case where the correction would be negative?
- What about a double digital?

□

Solution to Question 2.21. The Delta of a call option is always between zero and one. The Delta of a stock is always one. The risk of the stock is therefore always bigger; this is, however, misleading in that the value of the stock is generally much, much higher than that of the option. If we put all our money into stocks or call options, it is the call option portfolio that would be riskier.

Recall that the Delta of a call option is $N(d_1)$. After we divide by the Black–Scholes value, we have to compare

$$\frac{N(d_1)}{S_t N(d_1) - Ke^{-r(T-t)} N(d_2)} \quad \text{and} \quad \frac{1}{S_t}.$$

Since $N(d_2)$ is always positive, the first of these is bigger than the second, and so the Delta as a fraction of the value is bigger.

Why is the Delta the correct quantity to observe? If we are not Delta-hedged then the main component of our profit and loss when spot moves by ΔS will be

$$\Delta S \times \frac{\partial \text{Value}}{\partial S}.$$

Here are some possible related questions:

- What about put options?
- What about a portfolio of calls and puts?
- Can you derive the Delta of a call option?

$\square$

Solution to Question 2.22. One of the most important results in mathematical finance is that option prices are given as their pay off integrated against a risk-neutral probability density and then discounted. For the price of a European call option we have

$$e^{-rT} \int_{-\infty}^{\infty} \max(S_T - K, 0) p(S_T) dS_T,$$

where p is the risk-neutral density. We will assume the interviewer has given us the risk-neutral distribution for the stock price and that interest rates are zero. Note that we can write

$$S_T = S_0 + \sigma N(0, 1),$$

where $N(0, 1)$ is a standard normal random variable. Also, we have that the option is at-the-money, so $K = S_0$. The call option price is equal to

$$\frac{1}{\sqrt{2\pi}} \int_{-\infty}^{\infty} \max(S_0 + \sigma x - S_0, 0) e^{-\frac{x^2}{2}} dx.$$

The integrand will be non-zero if and only if $x > 0$, so we can rewrite this as

$$\frac{1}{\sqrt{2\pi}} \int_0^\infty \sigma x e^{-\frac{x^2}{2}} dx.$$

All we need to do now is note that

$$\frac{d}{dx} e^{-\frac{x^2}{2}} = -x e^{-\frac{x^2}{2}},$$

and we obtain

$$\frac{-\sigma}{\sqrt{2\pi}} \left[e^{-\frac{x^2}{2}} \right]_0^\infty = \frac{\sigma}{\sqrt{2\pi}}.$$

Compare this to the approximation for an at-the-money European call option in Question 2.13, which assumed a log-normal distribution for the underlying stock price. As $1/\sqrt{2\pi} \approx 0.4$, we now see how the rough relationship between log-normal and normal models came about in Question 2.20.

Here are some possible related questions:

- What are some of the practical flaws with pricing call options in this model?
- Suppose the two models give the same price at the money, how will the prices below the money compare?
- Why is the relationship between normal and log-normal models above only approximate?
- How good will the approximation between normal and log-normal models be? Consider at-the-money and out-of-the money options.

□

Solution to Question 2.23. We will use the result of the previous question, where the at-the-money call option price, C was given by

$$C = \frac{\sigma}{\sqrt{2\pi}}.$$

It now straightforward to see that volatility is found by multiplying the price by $\sqrt{2\pi}$.

Here are some possible related questions:

- Assuming a Black–Scholes world, if we know the stock price and the price of a 1 year at-the-money European call, how can we estimate σ?
- How would you estimate σ if you had no option price information?

☐

Solution to Question 2.24. Assuming zero interest rates the option will be worth $20/3$ (for working see Question 2.61).

Here are some possible related questions:

- Why should the probabilities be $2/3$ and $1/3$?
- Price the same European call but with a strike of 90 and 110.
- What if the probabilities were $1/4$ and $3/4$?

☐

Solution to Question 2.25. For a sketch of a vanilla call see Figure 2.1 and for

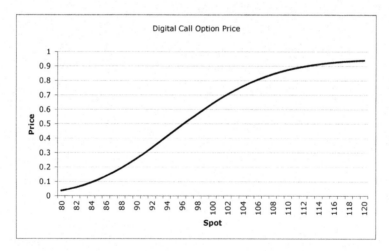

FIGURE 2.3. Digital call option with strike 100, volatility 10%, risk free rate 5% and 1 year to expiry.

a digital call see Figure 2.3. When relating the two graphs the key features are:

- As spot increases the slope of the call option price increases, until it approaches a constant slope of 1. However, the digital call option price flattens out as the option approaches deep in-the-money. This is caused by the digital payoff being capped at 1.
- A vanilla call option's price is convex, a digital call is not. The digital call looks like a cumulative distribution function.

Here is a related question:

- Plot a digital put on the same graph as a digital call. For what value of spot will the two lines intersect?

□

Solution to Question 2.26. To value this forward, we need to remember the simple formula for the forward price at time T of a non-dividend paying stock,

$$F_T = S_0 e^{rT}.$$

When the stock pays its dividend in 6 months time the price will drop by the dividend amount, so we need to take this into account in the forward price. We simply just subtract the suitably accumulated dividend amount, giving

$$F_T = S_0 e^{rT} - d e^{r(T-T_d)},$$
$$= 1 e^{0.05} - 0.1 e^{0.05(0.5)},$$

giving a forward price of 0.95.

Here are some possible related questions:

- Why is the forward price of a stock equal to the formula above? (Think in terms of a forward contract.)
- Why do some banks price options using the forward price instead of the spot price? (Hint: interest rates.)
- Adjust the forward price for a continuous dividend rate.

□

Solution to Question 2.27. This question is simply asking what the forward foreign exchange rate is between the Euro and US dollar. We can work out what the forward rate should be by thinking in terms of investing the current spot exchange rate for one year.

We assume that the current exchange rate between the two currencies is S. How could we lock in the exchange rate in one years time? Consider buying 1 US dollar today, which has been bought by borrowing S Euros. This portfolio will have zero value. In one years time the US dollar amount will have grown by the US interest rate, d, and the loan will have grown by the Euro interest rate, r. As the portfolio had zero initial value, it must have zero future value (otherwise an arbitrage opportunity exists).

Putting the value in one year's time into equation form

$$0 = (1 + d) - S(1 + r), \text{ and thus}$$
$$1 = S\frac{1 + r}{1 + d}.$$

So the original 1 US dollar has turned into $S(1 + r)/(1 + d)$ and this is the fair forward foreign exchange rate.

Here are some possible related questions:

- If the forward price was trading above this amount, set up an arbitrage portfolio.
- If the forward price was below, set up an arbitrage portfolio.
- Do you think that forward prices are good predictors of future exchange rates?

□

Solution to Question 2.28. This option is similar to a Margrabe option, but with a digital payment. A Margrabe option pays $\max(S_1(t) - S_2(t), 0)$, for more details see Section 11.6 of [6].

To answer this question we will make a few simplifying assumptions: the volatility of S_2 does not change and the correlation between S_1 and S_2 is zero. We have two situations to consider, $S_1(t) > S_2(t)$ and $S_1(t) \leq S_2(t)$, that is we are currently either in or out-of-the-money.

If we are in-the-money then an increase in the volatility of S_1 will create a higher probability in the risk-neutral world of finishing below S_2, so the option price will decrease. If we are out-of-the-money, then the extra volatility is good for those long the option as it means S_1 is more likely to finish above S_2 so the option value will increase.

Here are some possible related questions:

- We now take the correlation between S_1 and S_2 to be non-zero. What affect will correlation have on the price of the option, assuming everything else remains constant?
- How sensitive will the value of this option be to interest rates?

□

Solution to Question 2.29. A possible mean reversion process for a stock is

$$dS_t = \alpha(\mu - S_t)dt + \sigma S_t dW_t,$$

where α is the mean reversion rate and μ is the long term mean. These are the real world dynamics of the stock process, but to price an option we are only interested in the risk-neutral dynamics. When we move to the risk-neutral dynamics the drift of the stock becomes rdt as we saw in Question 2.1. Therefore the real world drift, be it mean reverting or not, does not change the price of the option.

Here are some possible related questions:

- What is the financial interpretation if the drift of a stock is equal to r?
- When changing between probability measures, in what way does the volatility change?

□

Solution to Question 2.30. We have already seen that the price of a European call option on a non-dividend paying stock is always more than its intrinsic value, see Question 2.11. What about the upper bound? A call option gives the holder the right, but not the obligation to purchase a stock at a future point in time. So at expiry the most we can hold is one stock. Therefore the option cannot be worth more than the stock price as our maximum payoff is the stock price.

The price bounds for a European call C_t on a non-dividend paying stock S_t with strike K are

$$S_t - KB_t < C_t < S_t,$$

where B_t is the price of a zero-coupon bond expiring at the same time as the option.

Here are some possible related questions:

- If we denote a call option by $C(K, T)$, where K is the strike and T is the expiry, what can we say about the function C in terms of K?
- What can we say about $C(K, T)$ in terms of T? (Assume non-dividend paying stock.)

$\square$

Solution to Question 2.31. This question relates to the concept of Value at Risk (VAR), which is the key measurement for the risk in a bank's trading book. If applying for a job in Risk Management it is very important that you know what VAR is and that you also know some of the common calculation methods, see [**9**] or [**4**].

To answer the question we will need to assume a distribution for the stock price. We will work in the Black–Scholes world where the stock is distributed as

$$S_T = S_0 \exp \left\{ \left(r - \frac{\sigma^2}{2} \right) T + \sigma \sqrt{T} N(0, 1) \right\},$$

where $N(0, 1)$ is a standard normal random variable. Finding the 98th percentile move in the stock requires looking up the value where 98 percent of the standard normal's probability lies above this value. Using the inverse normal the value is -2.05. We will assume some initial market values $S_0 = 100$, $r = 0$, $T = 1$, and $\sigma = 0.1$. Using these parameters the price of call option with strike 100 is 3.99, using the Black–Scholes formula.

We now calculate the 98th percentile fall in the stock price over the coming year. If the stock price fell this much it would be worth

$$100 \exp(0.5(0.1^2) + 0.1(-2.05)) = 81.03.$$

This translates to the call option being worth a measly 0.06.

Here are some possible related questions:

- How would the 98th percentile move in the stock price vary with time?
- What if the stock had a distribution with 'fatter tails' than a log-normal distribution. Would the value of the call be more or less?

□

Solution to Question 2.32. The option's price is given by the Black formula, which is derived in a similar way to the Black–Scholes formula, but instead we assume the forward price follows a geometric Brownian motion (try the derivation for yourself). If we denote the forward price of the stock as F, the call price, C, is given by

$$C = e^{-rT} \left[FN(d_1) - KN(d_2) \right],$$

where

$$d_i = \frac{\log\left(\frac{F}{K}\right) + (-1)^{i-1}\frac{1}{2}\sigma^2 T}{\sigma\sqrt{T}},$$

and $N()$ denotes the standard Normal cumulative distribution function. The Black formula is commonly used in interest rate markets to price swaptions and caps.

Here is a related question:

- What is the benefit of pricing an option on the forward instead of the spot? (Hint: interest rates.)

□

Solution to Question 2.33. The following is based on the proof in Section 2.8 of [6].

To prove the call option is a convex function of the strike price we consider the price as a function of strike, and prove that a line joining any two points on the graph of this function lies on or above the graph. This is a necessary and sufficient property of convex functions.

Let $C(K)$ denote the call option price as a function of strike K. Then this is equivalent to saying, for $K_1 < K_2$,

$$(2.3) \qquad \theta C(K_1) + (1 - \theta)C(K_2) \geq C\left(\theta K_1 + (1 - \theta)K_2\right),$$

for all $0 \leq \theta \leq 1$.

The important thing to note here is that the final payoff is convex in strike for a fixed value in the underlying, that is the function

$$(S_T - K)^+$$

is convex in K. With this in mind, consider a portfolio long θ call options struck at K_1, long $(1-\theta)$ options struck at K_2 and short one option struck at $\theta K_1 + (1-\theta)K_2$ (all options with the same maturity). Since the final payoff is convex in strike, (2.3) holds at the expiry of the options and we therefore have that our portfolio has non-negative value at expiry. This implies, by no-arbitrage considerations, that the portfolio must be of non-negative value at all times before expiry, and hence (2.3) holds at these times and we have proved convexity of the call option price.

Here are some possible related questions:

- Sketch the shape of the value of a call option as a function of strike.
- Prove that a portfolio with non-negative value at expiry must have non-negative value at all times before expiry.
- What other property (besides the one used in the proof above) does a convex function have?
- In the Black–Scholes model, prove the call option price is a convex function of spot.

$\square$

Solution to Question 2.34. We recall from Question 2.11 that it is never optimal to early exercise an American call option on a non-dividend paying stock. We will therefore consider American put options, where there are optimal early exercise times. Consider a deep ITM put option, if we were to exercise it today then we would earn interest on our profits between now and the option's expiry. As interest rates increase, our potential interest earnt will also increase, making it more likely to early exercise the option.

Here is a possible related question:

- Which other market parameters will increase the possibility of early exercise for an American put option?

□

Solution to Question 2.35. A butterfly is a common trading strategy that is made up of four vanilla options with the same expiry but different strikes. It consists of being short a call and put option with strike K (known as a straddle,) long a put option with strike K_1 and long a call option with strike K_2 (known as a strangle), where $K_1 < K < K_2$.

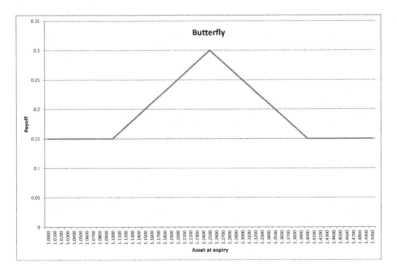

FIGURE 2.4. Butterfly payoff

Butterflies are typically used by investors who believe that the underlying asset will not deviate too far from its current value, since no movement results in the largest payoff, see the example in Figure 2.4.

Butterflies are one of the three main products quoted in a vanilla FX option market, the other two being ATM straddles and risk reversals. Brokers will quote butterflies as the vol difference between the strangle and straddle vol and quants will use this vol when constructing the vol surface.

Here are some possible related questions:

- Name another common trading strategy and give an example of why a company would use this to hedge an underlying exposure.
- What is the relationship between a butterfly and the second order Greek, volga?
- What is a risk reversal?

□

Solution to Question 2.36. VAR or Value At Risk is one of the key measurements used by market risk to monitor a bank's trading book. It is usually defined as the percentile of the loss distribution from a portfolio over a fixed period of time. For example, a trading book is said to have a VAR of $1 million when there is a 99% chance it will not lose more than that in the next trading day. There are many ways to calculate VAR, but one of the most common is via historical simulation. This simple method typically involves taking the previous 500 days market moves and applying them to the current market conditions and then revaluing the trading portfolio for each of them. This produces 500 profit and loss numbers which are sorted from biggest loss to biggest gain, giving the loss distribution. The VAR number for a given confidence interval, e.g. 99%, will be the number of the largest loss inside this range, e.g. the 5th largest loss.

Here are some possible related questions:

- Given the VAR for two individual portfolios, what is the VAR for the combined portfolio? Discuss.
- Describe at least one shortcoming of historical simulation and how it could be improved.
- Suggest an alternative method of computing VAR and give its benefits/drawbacks compared to historical simulation.

□

Solution to Question 2.37. When calibrating a model to the market we usually know the underlying asset price and we are interested in calibrating our model to the vols from the vanilla option market to be able to price exotic options. Market-quoted vanilla options are almost always OTM and it is likely that any ITM options have had their value inferred from OTM options. The reason for this is that an OTM option's value is driven more by its optionality, rather than its intrinsic value. We would therefore use the OTM option for calibration.

Here are some possible related questions:

- Given a set of options to calibrate to, but a model that can only calibrate to a subset of these, what criteria would you use to chose the calibration instruments?
- Which model would you prefer, one that can perfectly calibrate to the market or one that has more realistic dynamics?

$\square$

Solution to Question 2.38. CVA or credit valuation adjustment is the price adjustment made to a portfolio based on the risk of the trading counterparties defaulting on their obligations. This only applies to over-the-counter (OTC) transactions, because exchange-traded contracts are protected from default by the exchange. In the past a derivative portfolio was marked to market and all cash flows were assumed to have risk-free values. However, since the 2008 global financial crisis banks have realised that it is important to take the counterparty's credit quality into account. The Basel III framework is one of the main drivers of CVA, which requires banks to report it on their balance sheet.

To demonstrate how CVA is calculated we initially consider a single contract between a bank and a counterparty. If the counterparty defaults during the life of the contract then there are two outcomes for the bank. If the contract is in-the-money for the counterparty then the bank closes out the position by paying out the market value of the contract, resulting in a zero net loss. If the contract is in-the-money for the bank, then the bank needs to replace the contract by going into the market and entering into a similar contract, resulting in a net loss equal to the contract's market value. The exposure to the bank at time t for a contract valued at V is therefore

$$\max[V(t), 0].$$

A bank will often have many contracts against a counterparty so it needs to accumulate the contracts to compute an overall counterparty exposure. It is often possible to net off contracts which have a negative and positive value between the bank and a counterparty, so assuming netting is possible over all n individual contracts V_i, the counterparty exposure is

$$f(t) = \max \left[\sum_{i=1}^{n} V_i(t), 0 \right].$$

The CVA for this counterparty is calculated as the expected future exposure at the time of default, τ. If we denote the expiry of the longest contract as T and the recovery amount at default R, the future loss is

$$L = \mathbb{E}(f(\tau)(1 - R)).$$

The CVA is given as the expected value of this future loss. How do we calculate this expectation? We know today what the overall counterparty exposure is, but how do we calculate its future value? One approach is to simulate the underlying asset for each contract V_i and value them at a discrete set of possible future default dates. For a good overview on how this is done, see [15]. The probability that a counterparty defaults at a future date can be inferred from market-traded credit default swaps, and we can compute the expectation as a sum.

This gives an overview of the CVA for an individual counterparty, however banks often have many counterparties. It is not necessarily the case of summing up individual CVAs, we need to take into account the codependence of counterparties' defaults.

Here are some possible related questions:

- What factors should a good CVA model capture?
- How often should CVA risk be managed, at deal time only, daily or monthly?
- What is right way/wrong way risk?
- Calculate the CVA on a vanilla option.

- Calculate the CVA on an interest rate swap. Plot the exposure profile over the life of the contract.

□

2.3.3. Hedging and replication.

Solution to Question 2.39. The short answer to any question about participation in the financial markets is that there are three sorts of behaviours:

- hedging,
- speculation,
- arbitrage.

A hedger uses financial products to reduce risk. For example, an exporter who is paid in foreign currency may use an option to guard against the possibility that the exchange rate moves against him.

A speculator takes on risk with the belief either that the compensation for the additional risk makes it worthwhile or because he has specific views on how an asset will behave, and the product allows him to make a profit from these views if they are correct.

An arbitrageur exploits mis-pricing in the market, and makes money by buying risk in one place and selling it in another.

Here are some possible related questions:

- Which category do you think most participants in the market fall into?
- Which category do you think this bank falls into?
- Which category do you think personal investors fall into?

□

Solution to Question 2.40. This is a tricky one in that you often find that the questioner does not really understand the problem either.

The fundamental problem is that the hedging strategy is not well defined. For example, when you first touch 100, how do you know whether the stock will go up or down? It is not clear at that time whether 100 will be crossed so you cannot know what to hold. Thus you really need to buy at $100 + \epsilon$ and sell at $100 - \epsilon$. You then lose 2ϵ for each crossing, and the strategy is no longer riskless.

The properties of Brownian motion actually make the problem worse. If it hits a level then it will hit it again infinitely often in an arbitrarily small amount of time. So even in retrospect, it's hard to know when the crossing occurred.

Here are some possible related questions:

- Do you think this would be an effective approach in practice?
- Does the fact that you do not know which way the stock would go when it hits 100 make sense financially?

$\square$

Solution to Question 2.41. The key to this sort of the problem is to identify which sort of option pricing problem it is equivalent to. Here we have a digital option that pays $+100$ if A win 4 or more matches and -100 otherwise.

The underlying is simply a random walk that goes up or down one at each step. So in option pricing terms, the question is how do you replicate a digital option on a 4-step symmetric binomial tree? Once you have identified this fact it should be easy.

We can compute the hedge at the first step by computing the value in the up and down states. In the up state, the value will be 100 times the probability of 3 or more up moves out of six less 100 times the probability of 2 or fewer. The probability of 3 or more up moves is equal to one minus the probability of 2 or less up moves: using binomial coefficients, this is equal to

$$1 - \left(\frac{1}{2}\right)^6 (1 + 6 + 15) = \frac{42}{64} = \frac{21}{32}.$$

The value in the up state is therefore

$$100 \times \frac{21}{32} - 100 \left(1 - \frac{21}{32}\right).$$

The value in the down state is the negative of this by symmetry.

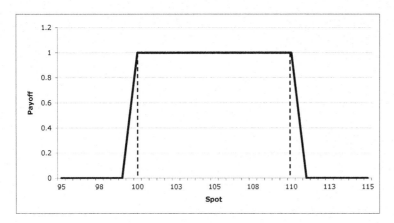

FIGURE 2.5. Option payoff profile

The bet we place on the first match is therefore

$$100 \times \frac{42}{32} - 100 = 31.25,$$

and we are done.

Here are some possible related questions:

- Work out the entire betting strategy.
- What if there were only 5 matches?
- Could you do this if the sizes of all bets had to be decided in advance of the series?

$\square$

Solution to Question 2.42. See Question 2.41. $\square$

Solution to Question 2.43. See Question 2.41. $\square$

Solution to Question 2.44. One can clearly not do this precisely since call options are continuous and the double digital option which we are being asked to replicate is not.

However, there is a standard approach to replicating jumps which is to use a call spread. Let $C(K)$ denote a call option struck at K. We pick a small $\epsilon > 0$, and take

$$1/\epsilon \text{ of } C(K - \epsilon) \text{ and } -1/\epsilon \text{ of } C(K).$$

Outside the interval $K - \epsilon$ to K this matches a digital call option struck at K.

So for this problem we take $1/\epsilon$ of the following portfolio:

- A call option struck at $100 - \epsilon$.
- Minus 1 call option struck at 100.
- Minus 1 call option struck at 110.
- A call option struck at $110 + \epsilon$.

Figure 2.5 shows the replicating portfolio with the solid lines and the double digital option with the dotted lines.

Here are some possible related questions:

- Would the price for your portfolio be higher or lower than the true price?
- How would you get a portfolio that was a close approximation on the opposite side?
- Must the price of the portfolio converge to the true price as $\epsilon \to 0$? (See Chapter 6 of [**6**].)

$\square$

Solution to Question 2.45. The key to this sort of problem is to identify that the payoff is a straight line which changes gradient at various points. Every time you need to change gradient by x you add x call options. If there are jumps, then you use call spreads as in Question 2.44. If there is value when spot equals zero, then you can use put options or zero-coupon bonds.

For this example, we have:

- $+1$ gradient at 100,
- -1 gradient at 120,
- no jumps,
- no value when spot equals zero.

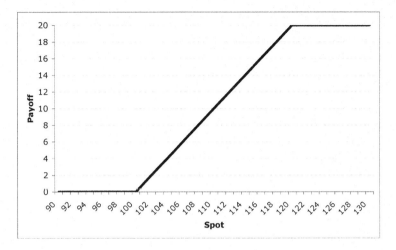

FIGURE 2.6. Payoff profile for Question 2.45.

So our portfolio is one call option struck at 100 and minus one struck at 120. Figure 2.6 plots the payoff profile.

Here are some possible related questions:

- Synthesise a payoff of $S - 100$.
- Synthesise a payoff of zero for $S < 90$, linearly increasing to 20 at 100 then back to zero at 110 and zero above 110.

□

Solution to Question 2.46. Pricing by replication involves trading in financial instruments in such a way as to match the payoff of another instrument that is most likely exotic. For example, a barrier option can be priced using a portfolio of vanilla options whose payoff matches that of the barrier option. See Section 10.2 of [6] for details. One of the main benefits of pricing exotic options by (static) replication with vanilla options is that the exotic will be priced in a way that is consistent with the current volatility smile.

There are two main types of replication methods that one should be aware of: static and dynamic. Static replication involves setting up a portfolio today and then not having to do any further trading (or at most trading on a finite number of future dates). Dynamic replication involves continuously trading in the underlying and is the method required to hedge an option using the stock and bond in the Black–Scholes model.

Here are some possible related questions:

- What are some of the practical problems of dynamic replication?
- Given the choice between two different static replicating portfolios that match an option's payoff, what criteria would you use to decide between the two?

□

Solution to Question 2.47. See Question 2.44.   □

Solution to Question 2.48. As we know from Question 2.16, European call and put options are monotone increasing in volatility, so if we use the lower volatility we will underprice the option. Which volatility do we use? The choice becomes clear when we think about how we would actually hedge the short position in this option.

We will assume we are in the Black–Scholes world and therefore will dynamically (or at least daily) hedge our option position. Due to the frequent hedging we are exposed to daily volatility and we must use the 20% volatility to price the option.

Here are some possible related questions:

- What would happen if we bought an option off a bank using the 10% volatility?
- What if we could statically hedge the option today, does this change which volatility we use?

□

Solution to Question 2.49. When trying to replicate a derivative the best way

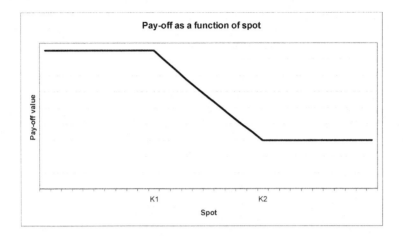

FIGURE 2.7. The derivative's payoff in Question 2.49.

to start is by sketching its payoff. For this derivative it is easier to think of the denominator on its own then consider the actual payoff. The denominator will pay K_1 for $S_T < K_1$ then increase linearly until $S_T > K_2$ where its payoff will be K_2. The actual payoff will be the inverse of this, which will look something like Figure 2.7.

The payoff is not linear between K_1 and K_2, therefore we will not be able to exactly replicate it with vanilla options, but we can get close. If we make the approximation that the payoff is linear between K_1 and K_2 and use the techniques discussed in Question 2.45 our replicating portfolio will contain

- $1/K_1$ zero coupon bonds expiring at time T;
- a call option struck at K_1 with notional $a = \frac{(1/K_2)-(1/K_1)}{K_2-K_1}$; and
- and a call option struck at K_2 with notional $-a$.

This approximation will be good for K_1 close to K_2, but will deteriorate as the two values of K are further apart.

There are two ways to improve our replication. We can either select a finite number of points in the interior and then do piecewise straight lines between them, or we can write the payoff as a continuous super-position of options. In the second case, we have an uncountably infinite number of options but can replicate precisely. The key is that the second derivative of a call option with respect to strike is a delta function.

Here are some possible related questions:

- What is the final stock value that will result in the maximum error from our replicating portfolio? What is the error?
- Improve the approximation of the replicating portfolio between K_1 and K_2.
- Say you can no longer trade zero coupon bonds. Change the replicating portfolio below K_1 using only vanilla options.

$\square$

Solution to 2.50. First, we have to establish the pay-off. An Asian option pays a function of the average of the stock price. So a forward contract will pay

$$A_T - K$$

(or its negative) where A_T is the average up to time T. We therefore have averaging dates $t_j, j = 1, 2, \ldots, n$ and we receive

$$\frac{1}{n} \sum_{j=1}^{n} S_{t_j} - K,$$

at time T. We assume that there is a riskless bond worth e^{rt} at time t. We also assume that S_t is the price process of a non-dividend-paying stock.

To replicate $-K$ is easy, we just take $-Ke^{-rT}$ bonds at time 0. To replicate

$$\frac{1}{n} S_{t_j}$$

at time t_j is also easy. We take $1/n$ stocks at time 0 and then sell them at t_j. However, we want the pay-off at time T. So we actually need

$$\frac{1}{n} e^{-r(T-t_j)} S_{t_j}$$

at time t_j. We can achieve this via by holding

$$\frac{1}{n} e^{-r(T-t_j)}$$

stocks from zero 0 to t_j. We then use the value to buy riskless bonds.

In conclusion, the cost of our replicating portfolio is

$$\frac{1}{n} S_0 \sum_{j=1}^{n} e^{-r(T-t_j)} - e^{-rT} K.$$

We are done.

Here are some possible related questions:

- How can we find the price of an Asian put, given the price of an Asian call with the same strike?
- The argument above is for arithmetic Asian options. What about geometric Asians?
- What if interest rates are not assumed to be constant?

□

Solution to Question 2.51. We have seen in the answer to Question 2.35, that a butterfly consists of four vanilla options. So as a hedge we would take the opposite position in these four options.

Here are some possible related questions:

- How are butterflies used to hedge exotic options?
- Which of these two options is more likely sensitive to changes in a butterfly volatility, a single no touch or a double no touch?

□

Solution to Question 2.52. There are many possible ways to hedge a barrier option and even within the same bank two traders will often put on different hedges. The approach discussed in the solution to Question 2.46 is one reasonable method and some banks have used this for their front office pricing. To keep things simple, however, we will present an alternative approach to illustrate some of the key ideas.

As an example, consider a knock-out call option with strike, K, and an out-of-the-money barrier, B. The first item in our hedging portfolio will be a vanilla call option with the same strike and expiry as the barrier option. To reduce the cost of the hedge we need to account for the knock-out barrier. One approach is to short a put option with the same maturity but strike B/K. This is the strike of the original option geometrically reflected in the barrier and so the call and the put have similar values at the time of knock out.

Here are some possible related questions:

- What dynamics (if any) have we hedged with the above example.
- What are some of the issues with the example hedge given above and how would you improve them?
- Give an example of how you would hedge a double no-touch option. What market dynamics would you try to capture that differ from the hedge above?

□

2.3.4. The Greeks.

Solution to Question 2.53. There are many different ways to compute the Greeks, but we will focus our answer on three popular methods:

- finite-difference approximations,
- pathwise method,
- likelihood ratio method.

Finite-difference approximations involve calculating the price for a given value of a parameter, say spot, then changing the parameter value slightly, by ϵ, and recalculating the price. If we let f be the payoff and θ the parameter we are interested in, an estimate of the sensitivity will be

$$\Delta = \frac{f(\theta + \epsilon) - f(\theta)}{\epsilon}.$$

This method has the advantage that it is easy to implement and does not require too much thought, apart from choosing an appropriate ϵ. It is however, a biased estimate of the sensitivity. This bias can be reduced by using a central-difference estimator

$$\Delta = \frac{f(\theta + \epsilon) - f(\theta - \epsilon)}{2\epsilon},$$

although we will now have to calculate three prices (as we usually have to calculate $f(\theta)$), which could become slow. There is also an issue with discontinuous payoffs. For example, if we want to estimate the Delta for a digital call we will get Δ being zero except for the small number of times when it will be 1. For these paths our estimate of Δ will then be very big, approximately of the order ϵ^{-1}.

The pathwise method gets around the problem of simulating for different values of θ by first differentiating the option's payoff and then taking the expectation under the risk-neutral measure

$$\Delta = e^{-rT} \int \frac{\theta_T}{\theta_0} f'(\theta_T) \Phi(\theta_T, \theta_0) d\theta_T,$$

where Φ is the density of θ in the risk-neutral measure. The pathwise method has a few advantages: it is an unbiased estimate, only requires simulation for one value of θ and is usually more accurate than a finite-difference approximation. It does become more complicated when the payoff is discontinuous (e.g. digital or barrier options), but to get around this we can write $f = g + h$, with g continuous and h piecewise constant.

The likelihood ratio method is similar to the pathwise method, but instead of differentiating the payoff we differentiate the density Φ

$$\Delta = e^{-rT} \int f(\theta_T) \frac{\Psi}{\Phi}(\theta_T) \Phi(\theta_T) d\theta_T,$$

where Ψ is the derivative of Φ by θ. One advantage with the likelihood ratio method is that only one value of θ needs to be simulated to calculate both the price and the sensitivity. We also do not need to worry about discontinuities in the payoff function as we are are differentiating the density. The main disadvantage with this method is needing to explicitly know the density. For more details regarding these three methods, see Chapter 7 of [4].

Here are some possible related questions:

- What is the likelihood ratio in the Black–Scholes model?
- What is Malliavin calculus?
- Why might importance sampling help?

□

Solution to Question 2.54. The Gamma of an option is the second derivative

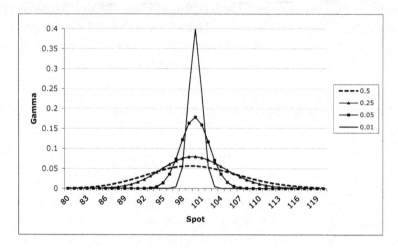

FIGURE 2.8. The Gamma of a vanilla call option struck at 100 as
a function of spot for varying expiries (in years).

of the price with respect to spot, or the derivative of the option's Delta. We cannot
expect to draw the Gamma perfectly in an interview, however it should look similar
to Figure 2.8. The key features are:

- the Gamma for a long position in a vanilla call or put option is always positive;
- as the option's maturity approaches, the Gamma will become more spiked at the strike price.

The positivity of Gamma is due to call and put options being convex functions of
spot as the second derivative for any convex function is positive. Why does the
Gamma become more spiked as maturity approaches? If we think about the option's
Delta for short maturities, it will behave almost like a step function, jumping from
zero below the strike to one above it. The derivative of Delta will reflect this jump
and therefore produce a spiked Gamma.

Here are some possible related questions:

- What does the Gamma express in terms of hedging costs?
- Is it possible to have an option with zero Gamma?
- Why do call and put options have the same Gamma?

☐

Solution to Question 2.55. This option, known as a double no-touch, will have a negative Vega. Vega measures the change in option price for a 1% change in volatility. If volatility increases then the probability in the risk-neutral measure of hitting either barrier $K1$ or $K2$ increases and so the option price will decrease, giving a negative Vega.

Here are some possible related questions:

- What about the Vega for a double one-touch?
- Sketch the Vega for a digital call option and explain its features.

☐

Solution to Question 2.56. One way to answer this question is to firstly think about how the values of the two options differ. Both of these options are at-the-money, so doubling the value of spot will double the strike and hence the value of the option, the factor of two multiplies through. Therefore the option with spot 200 (option B) will be worth twice as much as the option with spot 100 (option A).

The Vega of option B will be twice the Vega of option A, as the two will multiply through the Vega as well.

Here are some possible related questions:

- What happens when the spot of each option moves by say 10%, will the relationship between the Vegas change?
- Consider the same two options, what can we say about the difference between the Gammas?

☐

Solution to Question 2.57. Firstly we need to know what the current Vega of the portfolio is. The Vega for the portfolio will be the sum of all the individual instrument's Vegas, so we find these and add them up. If this value is non-zero we will have to use an option to make it zero. We can use either a call or put as the Vega of a vanilla call is the same as a put, due to put-call parity and the forward contract having zero Vega.

We take an option which expires at a similar time to the portfolio and find its Vega. We then buy/sell enough of these options to make the Vega of our portfolio zero.

It is possible that the interviewer may want to know how to construct a non-trival portfolio from nothing using calls and puts. In that case, we could go make a call spread centred at the current strike. So we go long a call with strike below the current spot price and short with one with strike than it.

Here are some possible related questions:

- Assuming Black–Scholes and given our portfolio is now Vega neutral, will it be Gamma neutral?
- If we don't believe in Black–Scholes will our portfolio be Gamma neutral if it is Vega neutral?

□

2.3.5. General.

Solution to Question 2.58. There are many ways to answer this question. The answer the interviewer was looking for was $1E - 4$, that is one basis point. Another approach is to consider the uncertainty in the inputs. For example, volatility is estimated rather than observed so an error that is small compared to one Vega is sufficient.

One could also mention that it is error as a fraction of the uncertain part of the price that is important, not as a fraction of the total price. For example, a deeply-in-the-money option is almost all intrinsic, it is the estimate of the value of the optionality that matters.

Here are some possible related questions

- How much is the Vega on a one-year at-the-money call option if the stock price is 100?
- If your model were inaccurate, how would you spot the fact?

□

Solution to Question 2.59. We will answer this question assuming two different models. Firstly we consider a *statistical arbitrage* model and then secondly assuming we have a model for pricing exotic derivatives.

Statistical arbitrage involves exploiting small mispricings in the market, usually by buying and selling stocks to create a portfolio which has minimal risk, but potential for profit. This portfolio of stocks will often be very large, and thus requiring a large amount of computational power. Therefore one aspect of a good model is that it returns trade information in a useful time frame.

What other information would you use to prove your model is a good one? A good check is to back-test the model, seeing how the trades it suggested actually worked on historic data. One could then argue if it made money in the past it should make money in the future. An important test is that it should work "out of sample" that is if we train on a set of data then it should work on real data that it has not been trained on.

Typically, statistical arbitrage (also known as "stat arb" or "stab art") works well in normal times but fails when turbulence occurs. You therefore might want to demonstrate that it still works in a period of turbulence. If you could prove that your model not only makes money in benign markets, but it also does well during a market crash, then your manager will no doubt be interested to hear more.

Another point to consider is whether the trading strategy takes into account bid-offer spreads and other transaction costs. It is easy to find strategies that work when these are ignored, and this will be one of the first things your boss seizes upon.

A related issue is liquidity. Many funds and most spectacularly, LTCM, have failed because of a sudden liquidity drought. How much money will your strategy lose in such a case?

Now considering exotic derivatives; the first piece of evidence to present would be that your model reproduces the prices of basic instruments. If the model cannot accurately price vanilla options and discount bonds, then traders will need a lot of convincing that it will price exotic instruments correctly.

The second piece of evidence to present comes down to what a model should actually do. Apart from giving prices, a model's main purpose is to suggest a hedging strategy. Therefore a new model that provides more accurate hedging ratios, will be popular automatically. How could you provide proof that the hedging is more accurate? Once again we could run back-testing on market data. If the variance of the profit and loss to a trading book is less under your new model than the current model, the hedging is more accurate and hence you have a better model.

In addition, you will have to discuss the advantages of the model over the old. These could include

- speed;
- realism;
- ease of calibration;
- ability to easily specify new products.

Here are some possible related questions:

- Discuss some of the main reasons why hedge funds have found themselves in trouble using statistical arbitrage models.
- If you had a perfect model for a stock process, what features would the model most likely have?

$\square$

2.3.6. Trees and Monte Carlo.

Solution to Question 2.60. This is a standard trick question to see if you make the mistake of using p in the answer. This precise example is discussed in detail in [6] so if you claim to have read it, make you sure that you can do this question.

The easiest solution is simply to use risk-neutral evaluation. The risk-neutral probability of an up-move is 0.5 by symmetry. The value of a call option is 10 in the up-state and 0 in the down-state so the answer is

$$10 \times 0.5 = 5,$$

since there are no interest rates.

One could also use a hedging argument. We could hold δ stocks and minus one option. We choose δ so that the portfolio has the same value in both states. The two values are

$$110\delta - 10 \text{ and } 90\delta.$$

These are equal if and only if $\delta = 0.5$. The value is then 45.

By no arbitrage, this portfolio is also worth 45 today. So

$$50 - \text{Option} = 45,$$

and the option price is 5.

A third method of doing this problem is to use the stock and bond to replicate the option payoff, which obviously leads to the same value.

Here are some possible related questions:

- Price using the stock and bond to replicate the option payoff.
- What about a put struck at 100? (There's a very easy solution!)
- How will introducing interest rates affect the price?
- Without computations, how will the price with the branches at 80 and 120 compare?

□

Solution to Question 2.61. A simple answer is that it could be worth anything between those values. However, given it is a short time horizon we can proceed as if these probabilities are both real world and risk-neutral. For the given probabilities to be risk neutral we need (neglecting interest rates as the time scale is very small)

$$\mathbb{E}(S_T) = S_0.$$

We then have that the stock is currently trading at

$$S_0 = 100 \times 0.6 + 50 \times 0.4 = 80.$$

An at-the-money European call option will have a strike of 80. There is a 60% chance in the risk-neutral measure that it will pay off 20 and a 40% chance it will pay off nothing. Its value must therefore be $20 \times 0.6 = 12$.

If the actual stock price is 75, then we can compute the risk-neutral probabilities and these will be different from the real-world ones.

Here are some possible related questions:

- Explain why an at-the-money put option expiring at the end of the day is worth 12 also. Do not use probabilities in the explanation.
- What if tomorrow's stock prices could go up from today's prices by 20 with probability 0.6 and down 10 with probability 0.4? Price a call option expiring tomorrow.

$\square$

Solution to Question 2.62. This example is analysed in detail in [**6**], Chapter 3. The essential point is that the model is incomplete so we can only bound the option price.

The easiest approach is risk-neutral evaluation. As usual, the real-world probabilities are irrelevant provided they are non-zero. The condition that the expected stock price is today's price is that the probability of an up-move and a down-move are the same. Our three probabilities are therefore

$$p, 1 - 2p, p.$$

These must all be positive for the risk-neutral measure to be equivalent to the real-world measure. This means that p lies in the open range $(0, 0.5)$. The price of the call option can therefore vary between zero and 5.

We also look at how to do this via hedging as the interviewer may insist on that approach. The price will be less than that of any super-replicating portfolio, and more than that of any sub-replicating portfolio.

Clearly, zero sub-replicates so the price is positive. The portfolios in this problem are just multiples of the stock and the bond; their value is a straight line as a function of the stock price. The three points we have to consider

$$(90, 0), (100, 0), \text{ and } (110, 10).$$

We can fit a straight line through any two. For the first two, we just have the zero line and get a lower bound of zero.

For the first and last, we get 0.5 stocks and -45 bonds. This will dominate the price at 100 since it has value 5 rather than zero there. The value of this super-replicating portfolio is 5 so the price is less than 5.

For the final two points, the line has slope 1, so we hold 1 stock and -100 bonds. This has value zero today so we get the same lower bound of zero. In fact, we could consider any portfolio with a holding of θ stocks and -100θ bonds, for $0 \leq \theta \leq 1$ and get a lower bound of zero, which passes through the middle point.

Making a formal argument that there are no sub-replicating portfolios of higher value is a little tedious, but it is clear geometrically.

Here are some possible related questions:

- Why do the risk-neutral and replication arguments give the same answer?
- How would you make a price when the market is incomplete?
- Suppose the price of the call option struck at 100 is 2.5, what is the price of a call option struck at 95?

□

Solution to Question 2.63. The crucial point here is that when using a model as a computational device, we are not doing no arbitrage arguments. Instead, we are approximating a given risk-neutral measure. In this case, the risk-neutral measure we are approximating is geometric Brownian motion with a growth rate of r.

We can think of four operations:

- Passing to the risk-neutral measure.
- Discretisation with a trinomial tree.
- Pricing.
- Passing to the limit.

The crucial point here is that the first two of these do not commute.

One reason why a trinomial tree is a useful computational device is that it does not naturally oscillate in the same was as a binomial tree. That is if the number of time steps in the tree changes by one, the price will not change as much as in a binomial tree. Trinomial trees also have much flexibility in terms of node placement since one can play with 3 node locations and two probabilities, whereas with a binomial tree there are two node locations and one probability. We have to match two quantities (at least asymptotically): mean and variance. This means that one can adapt node placement to the product, so, for example, nodes lie on barriers.

Here are some possible related questions:

- What properties must a trinomial tree have to converge to the Black–Scholes price?
- Is it necessary for the discretised tree to be risk-neutral?
- Are trinomial trees better than binomial ones?

□

Solution to Question 2.64. If two assets have the same price and volatility then their option prices will be the same. This will be true whether we are looking at a binomial tree or we are in the Black–Scholes model. When pricing an option using a binomial tree we are using risk-neutral probabilities and these do not depend on research that says A will perform better than B.

This question is analogous to why the drift of the stock price does not affect the option price. See Questions 2.1 and 2.29.

Here is a related question:

- In what sort of market could the prices of the two options differ? Why?

□

Solution to Question 2.65. The great virtue of a binomial tree is that it is easy to do early exercise. Its rate of convergence for continuous payoffs including American options is $1/n$, where n is the number of steps. Since the number of computations increases as n^2, this means that the rate of convergence is $t^{-1/2}$ where t is computational time. (Your interviewer may not know this...) For higher dimensional trees, convergence will be slower. Path-dependence is not natural in trees but can be dealt with by using an auxiliary variable which increases the dimension by 1.

The great virtues of Monte Carlo are:

- Convergence is order $t^{-1/2}$ in all dimensions.
- Path-dependence is easy.

The great downside is that early exercise is hard (see Question 2.67). The other downside is slowness of convergence in low dimensions, although it is no slower than a binomial tree, there are other faster lattice methods in low dimensions.

The convergence speed and early exercise can be coped with, but it requires much work. As a rule of thumb, use binomial trees for low-dimensional problems involving early exercise, and Monte Carlo for high-dimensional problems involving path-dependence.

Here are some possible related questions:

- How would you price a path-dependent option with early exercise features on a tree? For example, an American Asian option.
- How would you price a path-dependent option with early exercise features by Monte Carlo? For example, an American Asian option.
- What's the fastest way to do one-dimensional numerical integrations?
- How would you speed up a Monte Carlo simulation?

□

Solution to Question 2.66. The problem does not state the strike so we will assume that it is 100. It also does not state the interest rate, so we will assume it is zero.

The risk-neutral probability of an up-move is $1/3$ by inspection, or by solving the equation

$$150p + 75(1 - p) = 100.$$

The value is therefore

$$\frac{50}{3} + \frac{2}{3} \times 0 = 16\frac{2}{3}.$$

To get the Delta, we need to find the hedge that eliminates all risk.

This will be the amount of stock, δ, such that

$$150\delta - 50 = 75\delta.$$

We solve this to get

$$\delta = \frac{50}{75} = \frac{2}{3}.$$

Here are some possible related questions:

- What if there is a 10% interest rate across the time period?
- Why is the probability of the up move not stated?
- What use is a binomial tree?
- Suppose we define Δ to mean sensitivity to the initial spot, and the move sizes are constant as we change spot, what is Δ then?

$\square$

Solution to Question 2.67. As we saw in Question 2.65 it is difficult to use Monte Carlo for products with early exercise features, such as American options. The Longstaff–Schwartz method is one way to handle early exercise using Monte Carlo.

When pricing an early exercisable product, we need to know at a given time whether it will be worth more by exercising now or by holding onto it. The value of holding onto the option, known as the continuation value, is what the Longstaff–Schwartz method estimates via regression. The Longstaff–Schwartz method is commonly used for such products as Bermudan swaptions.

Before we jump into the algorithm, a few details are necessary. A regression needs to be carried out against some basis functions, for example we might regress y against some explanatory variables x and x^2. Choosing good basis functions that will estimate the continuation value accurately is very much an art.

The Longstaff–Schwartz algorithm is:

(1) Run a certain number of Monte Carlo paths (e.g. 1000) and store the exercise value divided by the numeraire at each possible exercise date for each path. We also need to store the value of the basis functions at the same points.

(2) With all this data we now look at the second last exercise date. We perform a regression (usually least-squares) of the value at the last exercise date against the basis functions. This gives coefficients, α_i, for the basis functions.

(3) Using these coefficients we can calculate the continuation value at the second last exercise time for each path, using for example $y = \alpha_1 x + \alpha_2 x^2$.

(4) We now replace the deflated exercise value stored initially with the continuation value, if the continuation value is greater.

(5) Continue back through the exercise dates until reaching time 0. The (biased) value of the product will be the average of the time zero values multiplied by the initial numeraire value.

Here are some possible related questions:

• Why will the above algorithm produce a biased price? Will the bias be large? Suggest a way to remove the bias.

• How else could one fit early exercise into Monte Carlo?

• What are some useful basis functions when pricing a Bermudan swaption?

□

2.3.7. Incomplete markets.

Solution to Question 2.68. Implied volatility is simply the volatility implied from the market price of an option, using some model. It is usually calculated by taking the option's price and finding the volatility in the Black–Scholes formula that returns the same price. For example, consider an at-the-money European call option with 1 year to expiry, spot value 100 and a risk free rate of 5%. If the market price of this option is $6.80, then the implied volatility will be 15%.

If one calculates the implied volatility of options with the same expiry date but different strike prices and plots the volatilities, there is often a smile or skew shape. A volatility smile will look something like Figure 2.9.

There are many possible explanations for why some markets exhibit volatility smiles. One possible explanation is that the market is more likely to move up or

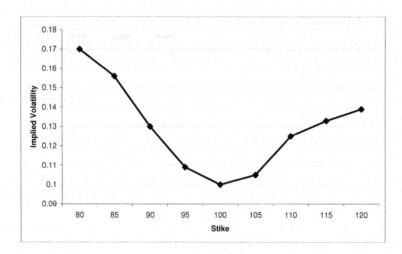

FIGURE 2.9. Volatility smile.

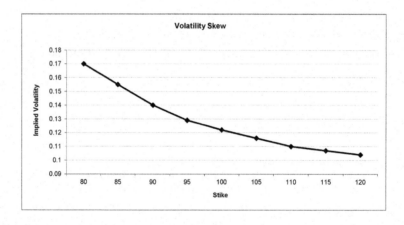

FIGURE 2.10. Volatility skew.

down by a large amount than is assumed within the Black–Scholes model. Hence the smile reflects the market's view of the imperfections in the Black–Scholes model.

A volatility skew is similar to a smile, but it is only downward sloping, compared to the more symmetric smile. A volatility skew could look something like Figure 2.10.

For a detailed discussion of volatility smiles and skews see Chapter 18 of [6].

Here are some possible related questions:

- Which shape will the implied volatility take for equity markets, skew or smile? Explain.
- When did the volatility smile first appear in the equity market and why?
- If the market was pricing options incorrectly and the smile was not a persistent feature, describe an arbitrage opportunity.

□

Solution to Question 2.69. There are many different option pricing models that capture some of the features of market smiles. The large number of models makes it too difficult to cover them all in detail, so we focus our answer on four popular models: jump diffusion, stochastic volatility, Variance Gamma and local volatility. For details of the first three models we refer the reader to [**6**]; see Chapter 22 of [**22**] for local volatility.

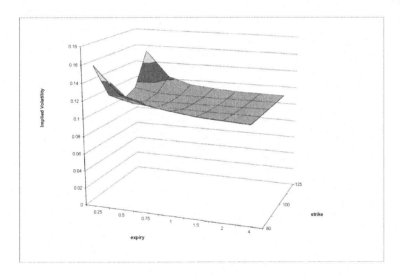

FIGURE 2.11. Jump diffusion implied volatility smile.

Jump diffusion models have the foreign exchange rate moving as geometric Brownian motion with an added random jump component. The jump component is usually a Poisson process. If S_t is the exchange rate, we could have

$$\frac{dS_t}{S_t} = \mu dt + \sigma dW_t + (J - 1)dN_t,$$

where J is a random jump size (J could be log-normally distributed, for example) and N_t is the Poisson process. Jump diffusion models produce what is known as a floating smile. This means that the smile moves when spot moves, so that the bottom of the smile will remain at-the-money. As floating smiles are a feature of foreign exchange markets this is an advantage of jump diffusion models.

One disadvantage of jump-diffusion model is that the smiles produced flatten with maturity quickly; this is not observed in most markets. See Figure 2.11 for an example in which the smile has largely disappeared after after 2 years.

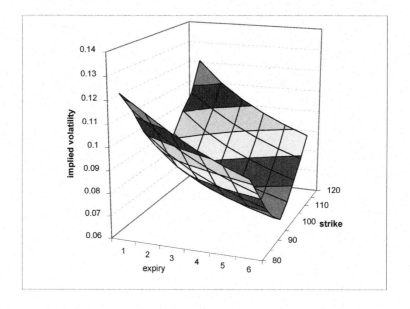

FIGURE 2.12. Heston model implied volatility smile.

Stochastic volatility models take both the foreign exchange rate and volatility process to be stochastic. There are many popular forms for the volatility process;

the Heston model, for example, uses

$$\frac{dS_t}{S_t} = \mu dt + \sqrt{V_t}dW_t^{(1)},$$

$$dV_t = \kappa(\theta - V_t)dt + \sigma_V \sqrt{V_t}dW_t^{(2)},$$

where θ is the long term average volatility, κ is the rate at which the process reverts to its mean, σ_V is the volatility of volatility, and $W_t^{(1)}$ and $W_t^{(2)}$ are Brownian motions with correlation ρ.

Stochastic volatility models also produce a floating smile and their smile shape can be easily changed by tweaking the parameters. For example, skew can be introduced by having ρ non-zero, the flattening out of the smile can be adjusted by the mean reversion parameter κ, etc. Figure 2.12 shows an example smile from the Heston model.

Having the flexibility of changing the smile shape has its disadvantages in that all these parameters need to be fitted in a stable and consistent way with the market, which is not a straightforward task.

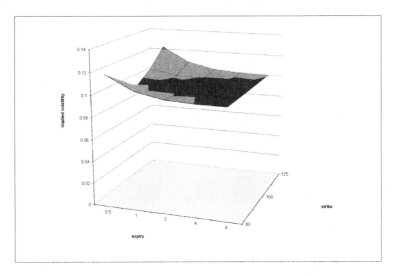

FIGURE 2.13. Variance Gamma implied volatility smile.

Variance Gamma models take the foreign exchange rate and time as a random process. The idea is that foreign exchange rates move when market information arrives and this information arrival is itself a random process. For example, if a large amount of information is arriving then we can expect high volatility, however on a day with minimal information arrival we can expect low volatility. To define a Variance Gamma model we let $b(t; \theta, \sigma)$ be a Brownian motion, i.e.

$$db_t = \theta dt + \sigma dW_t$$

and we let

$$X(t; \sigma, \nu, \theta) = b(T_t; \theta, \sigma),$$

where T_t is the time t value of a Gamma process with variance rate ν.

Variance Gamma smiles are similar to jump diffusion smiles, compare Figure 2.11 and 2.13. The smiles tend to flatten out over time as the model becomes more similar to a pure diffusive model.

Local volatility models derive the volatility surface from quoted market prices and then use this surface to price more exotic instruments. It turns out that under risk-neutrality there is a unique diffusion process consistent with market prices. The unique volatility function $\sigma(S_t, t)$ is known as the local volatility function.

Once this local volatility surface has been found, exotic instruments can be priced consistently with market prices. The problem however, is that the volatility surface is the market's current view of volatility and this will change in the future, meaning the exotic options will no longer be consistent with market prices.

Here are some possible related questions:

- Which of the above models are incomplete and why?
- Discuss the features of equity and interest rate smiles as compared to foreign exchange smiles.
- Given the four models above, you have to use one. What criteria would you use to pick a model?

□

Solution to Question 2.70. A stochastic volatility model takes volatility to be driven by a random process. It is then possible that the volatility will become large causing large movements in the underlying asset price. These large moves give the distribution of the underlying asset fatter tails than in the Black–Scholes model.

This means that options away from the money will be priced more expensively than in Black–Scholes leading to a volatility smile.

Another way to think about why the smile occurs is by looking at the second derivative of the option price with respect to the volatility. In the Black–Scholes world our Vega sensitivity (how good our volatility hedge is) will be zero. However, a stochastic volatility model will not necessarily have a non-zero derivative of Vega, therefore there is *Vega convexity* which is related to the volatility smile.

Here are some possible related questions:

- Explain why a jump-diffusion model and a Variance Gamma model produce smiles.
- Explain why a jump-diffusion model's smile flattens out with time, whereas a stochastic volatility model's smile may not.

□

CHAPTER 3

Probability

3.1. Introduction

This chapter focuses on questions from probability and stochastic processes. There is an inevitable overlap with Chapter 2, since random processes are at the core of modern pricing theory.

Problems range from the elementary, e.g., "what is the expectation of a single roll of a fair die?", to the rather hard. The interviewer is looking for two things: the ability to think probabilistically, and evidence of having studied stochastic processes. We have divided the questions between general problems many of which involve coin tosses, and questions about stochastic processes.

For the more challenging questions, we include references to allow the reader to study all the details. Before attempting quant job interviews, a study of probability theory is a must; here are several excellent books on the topic:

"Elementary Probability Theory" by Kai Lai Chung is a great place to start. The text is primarily aimed at people doing a first undergraduate course in probability. The book also includes a chapter on financial mathematics.

"Probability and Random Processes" by Geoffrey Grimmett and David Stirzaker is slightly more challenging than Chung. The book is clearly presented and well worth reading.

Another excellent book covering basic probability (and continuing to more advanced topics) is William Feller's two volume "An Introduction to Probability Theory and its Applications". Volume I covers discrete distributions and events, Volume II moves onto the continuous treatment. The explanations are presented in a clear and concise manner.

If you have some probability knowledge, "Probability with Martingales" by David Williams is a great place to start for discrete time martingales. The style is clear and informative while presenting solid mathematical ideas.

Following on from this, try the two volume set "Diffusions, Markov Processes and Martingales" by Chris Rogers and David Williams. Much of the material from Williams is repeated quickly in this book, before they proceed to discuss the basics of Brownian motion and continuous time martingales. The second volume discusses stochastic calculus.

"Introduction to Stochastic Integration" by Kai Lai Chung and Ruth Williams is a very readable account of stochastic integration theory. It assumes knowledge of continuous time martingales, however, so you must learn that elsewhere first.

If you want books with a more mathematical finance approach, "The Concepts and Practice of Mathematical Finance" by the first author of this book, Mark Joshi, is an excellent place to start.

"Stochastic Calculus for Finance" Volumes I and II by Steven Shreve are also a great introduction. Relative to "The Concepts and Practice of Mathematical Finance", this book tends to focus on the mathematics rather than the finance.

3.2. Questions

3.2.1. General.

QUESTION 3.1. Consider the following game. The player tosses a die once only. The payoff is 1 dollar for each dot on the upturned face. Assuming a fair die, at what level should you set the ticket price of this game?

QUESTION 3.2. Suppose we play a game. I roll a die up to three times. Each time I roll, you can either take the number showing as dollars, or roll again. What is your expected winnings?

QUESTION 3.3. Let's play a game. There are four sealed boxes. There is 100 pounds in one box and the others are empty. A player can open a box and take the contents as many times as they like, but each time they do so they must pay X. Assuming this is a fair game, what is the value of X?

QUESTION 3.4. We play a game: I pick a number n from 1 to 100. If you guess correctly, I pay you $\$n$ and zero otherwise. How much would you pay to play this game?

QUESTION 3.5. Suppose you have a fair coin. You start with a dollar, and if you toss a H, your position doubles, if you toss a T, your position halves. What is the expected value of the money you have if you toss the coin infinitely?

QUESTION 3.6. Suppose we toss a fair coin, and let N denote the number of tosses until we get a head (including the final toss). What is $\mathbb{E}(N)$ and $\text{Var}(N)$?

QUESTION 3.7. We play a game, with a fair coin. The game stops when either two heads (H) or tails (T) appear consecutively. What is the expected time until the game stops?

QUESTION 3.8. For a fair coin, what is the expected number of tosses to get three heads in a row?

QUESTION 3.9. You toss a biased coin. What is the expected length of time until a head is tossed? For two consecutive heads?

QUESTION 3.10. I have a bag containing nine ordinary coins and one double-headed one. I remove a coin and flip it three times. It comes up heads each time. What is the probability that it is the double-header?

QUESTION 3.11. I take an ordinary-looking coin out of my pocket and flip it three times. Each time it is a head. What do you think is the probability that the next flip is also a head? What if I had flipped the coin 100 times and each flip was a head?

QUESTION 3.12. You throw a fair coin one million times. What is the expected number of strings of 6 heads followed by 6 tails?

QUESTION 3.13. Suppose you are throwing a dart at a circular board. What is your expected distance from the center? Make any necessary assumptions. Suppose you win a dollar if you hit 10 times in a row inside a radius of $R/2$, where R is the radius of the board. You have to pay 10c for every try. If you try 100 times, how much money would you have lost/made in expectation? Does your answer change if you are a professional and your probability of hitting inside $R/2$ is double of hitting outside $R/2$?

QUESTION 3.14. A woman has two babies. One of them is a girl, what is the probability that the other is a boy?

QUESTION 3.15. A family has two children of whom you know at least one is a girl. What is the probability that both are girls? What if you know that the eldest is a girl? What if you know that they have a girl called Clarissa?

QUESTION 3.16. What is the probability that the fourth business day of the month is Thursday?

QUESTION 3.17. You are playing Russian Roulette. There are precisely two bullets in neighbouring chambers of the six shooter revolver. The barrel is spun. The trigger is pulled and the gun does not fire. You are next, do you spin again or pull the trigger?

QUESTION 3.18. Consider a deck of 52 cards, ordered such that $A > K > Q > \ldots > 2$. I pick one first, then you pick one, what is the probability that my card is larger than yours?

QUESTION 3.19. Suppose 2^n teams participate in a championship. Once a team loses, it is out. Suppose also that you know the ranking of teams in advance and you know that a team with a higher rank will always win the game with a team of lower rank. In the beginning, all teams are randomly assigned to play with each other. What would be the probability that in the final, the best team will play the second best?

QUESTION 3.20. A drawer contains 2 red socks and 2 black socks. If you pull out 2 socks at random, what's the probability that they match.

QUESTION 3.21. If I draw two cards from an ordinary deck with replacement, what is the probability that they are both aces? Without replacement?

QUESTION 3.22. Suppose we have an ant traveling on edges of a cube, going from one vertex to another. The ant never stops and it takes him one minute to go along one edge. At every vertex, the ant randomly picks one of the three available edges and starts going along that edge. We pick a vertex of the cube and put the ant there. What is the expected number of minutes that it will take the ant to return to that same vertex?

QUESTION 3.23. You have been captured and blindfolded by pirates, then placed somewhere on a five-meter-long wooden plank. Disorientated, each step you take is a meter long but in a random direction – either toward the sharks waiting at one end or eventual freedom at the other. If x (integer) is the distance in meters you start from the safe end, determine the probability of your survival as a function of x.

QUESTION 3.24. Romeo and Juliet have agreed to meet for a date sometime between 9pm and 10pm. Each of them randomly picks a time within this interval and shows up and waits for the other for fifteen minutes. What is the probability that they will actually meet?

QUESTION 3.25. A plane has one hundred seats and there are exactly one hundred people boarding. They line up at the gate In exactly the same order as the order of the seats on the plane, from 1 to 100. However, the first person is Grandma who doesn't see well, so instead of taking the first seat on the plane, she picks a random seat and sits down. Now, the rule is: when any other person enters the plane, he or she will try to sit at his own seat. If this is not possible, this person chooses one of the free seats randomly. Eventually, everyone boards the plane. What is the probability that the last person (number 100) will sit at his assigned seat number?

QUESTION 3.26. Suppose three assets A, B, C are such that the correlation coefficient of A and B is 0.9 and the correlation coefficient of B and C is 0.8. Is it possible for A and C to have correlation coefficient 0.1?

QUESTION 3.27. Let x, y be uniformly distributed on $[0, 1]$ and separate the unit interval $[0, 1]$ into 3 pieces, what is the probability that the 3 pieces of the line can be constructed into a triangle?

QUESTION 3.28. What is the distribution function of a standard uniform $U(a, b)$ random variable?

QUESTION 3.29. Suppose $x_1, x_2, \ldots, x_n$ are independent identically distributed from $[0, 1]$ and uniform on the interval. What is the expected value of the maximum? What is the expected value of the difference between the maximum and the minimum?

QUESTION 3.30. Give an example of a distribution with infinite variance.

QUESTION 3.31. Suppose the random variable X has a probability density function $f_X(x)$. What density function does $g(X)$ have?

QUESTION 3.32. What is the distribution function and density function of the kth order statistic?

QUESTION 3.33. Let X and Y be two independent uniform random variables on the unit interval $[0, 1]$. What is the probability density function of $X + Y$?

QUESTION 3.34. What does the Central Limit theorem say?

QUESTION 3.35. Prove that a covariance matrix is positive definite.

QUESTION 3.36. Explain change of measure. Give an example when a change of measure is useful in Monte Carlo.

QUESTION 3.37. If X is $N(\mu, \sigma)$ and $\lambda > 0$, calculate the values of $\mathbb{E}(X^2)$ and $\mathbb{E}(\exp(\lambda X))$.

QUESTION 3.38. If $M(x)$ is the cumulative Gaussian function and X is $N(0, 1)$ then what is $\mathbb{E}[M(X)]$?

QUESTION 3.39. Suppose you have a jar with 1000 coins, one with 2 heads and the rest normal. You choose a coin at random and get 10 heads from 10 tosses. What is the probability that you chose the coin with two heads?

QUESTION 3.40. Urn A contains 5 white balls and 2 red balls. Urn B contains 4 red balls and 4 black balls. You randomly pick an urn and draw a ball (without replacement). You then repeat the process of selecting an urn and drawing out a ball. What is the probability the first ball drawn was red, given that the second ball was black?

QUESTION 3.41. Given a coin, how do you use it to choose one out of three events? What's the average number of tosses you need to do this?

QUESTION 3.42. Suppose you have a biased coin with $\mathbb{P}(H) = 0.45$ and $\mathbb{P}(T) = 0.55$. We play a game where if the coin results in a head you get 1 point otherwise you get -1 point. If after 3 tosses you have at least 1 point then you win $100 otherwise you win nothing. What is the value of the game to you? Generalise to N tosses.

QUESTION 3.43. Draw 3 cards from a deck of 52 cards (no jokers). What is the expected value of the 3 cards? Assume the value of a jack is 11, a queen 12 and a king 13.

QUESTION 3.44. Draw 3 cards from a deck of 52 cards (no jokers). Observe the value of the 3 cards, then replace the card with the lowest value with another card in the deck. What is the expected value of the 3 cards? Assume the value of a jack is 11, a queen 12 and a king 13.

QUESTION 3.45. Draw 4 cards from a deck of 54 cards (with 2 jokers). What is the expected value of the 4 cards? Assume the value of a jack is 11, a queen 12, a king 13 and a joker 100.

QUESTION 3.46. Given a die, what's the expected number of throws till you see a six?

QUESTION 3.47. What is the probability of seeing the same number on a roulette wheel with two zeros plus the usual 36 numbers and on the sum of two dice?

QUESTION 3.48. Three ants on different corners of triangle. Each chooses a direction of travel randomly and they all travel at the same positive speed. What is the probability of no collision?

QUESTION 3.49. If I toss a coin N times, and you toss a coin $N + 1$ times, what is the probability that you will have more heads than me? Prove it.

QUESTION 3.50. There are 10 red, 20 blue, and 30 green balls in a bag. You keep taking one out at random. What is the probability that when you take the last red one out, there is at least one blue and one green ball still in the bag?

QUESTION 3.51. You toss a coin twice. If two heads come up then you get 0 dollars, if one head comes up then you get 1 dollar, if two tails come up you re-toss the two coins. What is the expected value of this game?

QUESTION 3.52. The probability of rain on Saturday is 60%, and rain on Sunday is 70%. What's the probability of some rain on the weekend if they are independent?

QUESTION 3.53. Toss a coin N times what is the probability that there are no HH sequences?

QUESTION 3.54. Let X and Y be two Gaussian random variables with distributions $N(0, a)$ and $N(0, b)$, respectively. Suppose that X and Y are correlated with correlation ρ. What is $\mathbb{E}[X - Y | 2X + Y]$?

3.2.2. Stochastic processes.

QUESTION 3.55. What is Brownian motion?

QUESTION 3.56. Suppose we are doing a random walk on the interval $[0, 1000]$, starting at 80. So, with probability $1/2$, this number increases or decreases by one at each step. We stop when one of the boundaries of the interval is reached. What is the probability that this boundary will be 0?

QUESTION 3.57. If S_t follows a log-normal Brownian motion, what process does the square of S_t follow?

QUESTION 3.58. Suppose you have a call option on the square of a log-normal asset. What equation does the price satisfy?

QUESTION 3.59. Assume the stock price process S_t follows the stochastic differential equation

$$dS_t = \alpha(\mu - S_t)dt + S_t\sigma dW_t,$$

with α, σ and $\mu > 0$. What sort of qualitative behaviour does the stock price exhibit? What is the impact of the parameters α and μ? What effects do they have on the price of a call option on this stock?

QUESTION 3.60. Given that $dS_t = \mu S_t dt + \sigma S_t dW_t$, give an SDE for $\log(S_t)$.

QUESTION 3.61. Show that the process

$$X_t = \cosh(\lambda W_t)\exp(-\lambda^2 t/2)$$

is a martingale.

QUESTION 3.62. If W_t is a standard Brownian motion, is W_t^3 a martingale?

QUESTION 3.63. Apply Itô's formula to 2^{W_t}, where W_t is a Brownian motion, is it a martingale?

QUESTION 3.64. Given two independent Brownian motions W_t and Z_t, what is the distribution of $\frac{W_t}{Z_t}$? What stochastic differential equation is satisfied by the ratio?

QUESTION 3.65. Solve the SDE of the Ornstein-Uhlenbeck process.

QUESTION 3.66. Calculate $\mathbb{E}(W_s W_t)$ where W_t is standard Brownian motion.

QUESTION 3.67. If we have a Brownian motion, X_t, $X_0 = 0$, $X_1 > 0$, what is the probability of $X_2 < 0$?

QUESTION 3.68. Let W_s be a Brownian bridge, that is a Brownian motion constrained such that $W_0 = 0$ and $W_t = x$. What is the distribution of W_s, for $0 \leq s < t$?

QUESTION 3.69. We often write $dt = (dW_t)^2$. What does this mean?

QUESTION 3.70. Why is Itô's lemma true?

QUESTION 3.71. If N_t is a Poisson process with parameter λ, what is

$$\mathbb{E}\left(N_{t_2}|N_{t_1} = k\right),$$

where $t_2 > t_1$?

QUESTION 3.72. Given two independent Poisson random variables X and Y with parameters λ and μ respectively, what is the probability that the sum of the two variables is equal to n?

QUESTION 3.73. What is the probability that a Brownian motion will cross the level 1 before time T?

QUESTION 3.74. For a Brownian motion W_t, what is the probability that it hits 1 before it hits -2? What is the expected value of the stopping time to hit either of these levels? Repeat both questions for the stochastic process X_t satisfying $dX_t = \mu dt + dW_t$.

QUESTION 3.75. Let W_s be a Brownian motion. What are the mean and variance of $I(T) = \int_0^T W_s ds$?

QUESTION 3.76. What is the correlation between 2 Brownian motions at time t_1 and t_2? Assume that they are jointly normal with correlation ρ.

3.3. Solutions

3.3.1. General.

Solution to Question 3.1. This is a simple question asking us to calculate the expected number of dots on the upturned face of a fair die. Evaluating this in the standard way gives

$$\mathbb{E}(\text{number of dots}) = 1 \times \frac{1}{6} + 2 \times \frac{1}{6} + \cdots + 6 \times \frac{1}{6} = 3.5.$$

The ticket level is slightly more interesting, after all we want to make a profit. To avoid going broke we need to charge at least $3.5, however perhaps we can play on people's enjoyment of gambling and charge slightly more than this fair price.

Here are some possible related questions:

- Evaluate the expectation for an $n-$sided die, with n a positive integer.
- What is the expectation of the sum of two rolls?
- What is the probability of getting seven with two rolls?

□

Solution to Question 3.2. This problem should be approached from the end. If instead I only offered you one roll of the dice, what are your expected winnings? Clearly the answer here is

$$\mathbb{E}(1 \text{ die}) = \sum_{i=1}^{6} i\frac{1}{6} = 3.5.$$

Now if I offer you two dice, you can either take the result of the first roll, or proceed onto the second die. The optimal strategy is to take the first roll if it is better than your expected winnings from the second roll, or continue otherwise. Thus we take the first roll if it is 4 or greater, otherwise we continue, giving

$$\mathbb{E}(2 \text{ dice}) = \mathbb{E}(\max\{\text{first roll, expected winnings from 1 die}\})$$

$$= \frac{1}{6} \times 6 + \frac{1}{6} \times 5 + \frac{1}{6} \times 4 + \frac{1}{2} \times 3.5 = 4.25.$$

Repeating the same idea for the third die gives

$$\mathbb{E}(3 \text{ dice}) = \mathbb{E}(\max\{\text{first roll, expected winnings from 2 dice}\})$$

$$= \frac{1}{6} \times 6 + \frac{1}{6} \times 5 + \frac{2}{3} \times 4.25 = 4\frac{2}{3}.$$

Note that this is essentially the problem of pricing an option on a multinomial tree, and this is why the problem is very popular with interviewers.

Here are some possible related questions:

- How many rolls would I need to offer you before you will only accept a 6 on the first roll?

- What sort of option does this problem relate to?
- How does your answer change if the payment is the square of the number showing?
- What effect will it have if I charge you $1 for each additional roll?

$\square$

Solution to Question 3.3. Since this is a fair game, we must have that by playing optimally the player has an expected cost equal to their expected winnings. What is the optimal strategy? Say we set a price Y to play the game. The price is 'fair' in the sense that the player will not, on average, incur a loss by playing at least once. If they do not win on their first pick, then clearly it is optimal to continue playing. If it was worth playing when the odds of picking the correct box were $1/4$, then if you can play for the same price with the increased odds of $1/3$ it is worthwhile.

So we have that the optimal strategy is to continue playing until you pick the correct box. This means every time we play this strategy, we will win the 100 pounds. Thus we need to find a price X such that the expected cost of playing until you win is 100. Note

$$\mathbb{E}(\text{cost}) = X\mathbb{P}(\text{win on first attempt}) + 2X\mathbb{P}(\text{win on second attempt})$$
$$+ 3X\mathbb{P}(\text{win on third attempt}) + 4X\mathbb{P}(\text{win on fourth attempt}).$$

We are dealing with conditional probabilities, that is the probability of winning on your second attempt is the probability of picking the correct box the second time after not picking it the first time. Thus, for example, $\mathbb{P}(\text{win on second attempt}) = \frac{3}{4} \times \frac{1}{3}$. This gives the equation for X

$$100 = 2.5X,$$

and solving we see $X = 40$.

As a quick 'sanity check', why must the price be at least 25 (think about it before you read on)? If the price was less than 25, playing just once would be a game favourable to the player. While this might seem trivial, such checks can be quite handy as a quick way to detect silly mistakes.

Here are some possible related questions:

- Instead of maintaining a constant price, if you choose to continue playing after two incorrect guesses the price changes to Z. What is the fair value of X and Z?
- Generalise the above problem to the case of n boxes.

$\square$

Solution to Question 3.4. When you are asked a question like this, they are asking for the expected value under an optimal strategy. They generally don't want you to get into a discussion of risk preferences.

Note that this is really a game theory question. Each player has to pick a strategy. In this case, an optimal strategy will be one in which the expected winnings is independent of the strategy the opponent picks.

Clearly, it is better for the payer to choose a small number so that he has to pay less. On the other hand, if he always goes for a small number then he is more likely to have to pay out since the receiver will then also go for a small number.

The solution is to pick k with probability proportional to $1/k$. We therefore pick k with probability

$$\frac{1}{k} \left(\sum_{j=1}^{100} \frac{1}{j} \right)^{-1} .$$

Our expected pay-out is then

$$\left(\sum_{j=1}^{100} \frac{1}{j} \right)^{-1} ,$$

whatever the other person does. Note that the expected value decreases as the size of the set of numbers increases, as one would expect.

Here are some possible related questions:

- What if you receive the number squared?
- Why should the value decrease as the number of numbers increases?
- Do you think many people would play this game well?

- If you charge an incorrect price, in what sense would you lose money?
- Do you think that this game would work well for fleecing people at a fairground?

□

Solution to Question 3.5. We work out what happens with one toss, then n tosses, and then let n tend to infinity.

Let X denote a toss, then

$$\mathbb{E}(X) = \frac{1}{2}2 + \frac{1}{2}\frac{1}{2} = \frac{5}{4}.$$

Provided the tosses are independent, the product of expectations is the expectation of the product. Let X_j be the effect of toss j. This means that

$$\mathbb{E}\left(\prod_{j=1}^{n} X_j\right) = \prod_{j=1}^{n} \mathbb{E}(X_j),$$

$$= \left(\frac{5}{4}\right)^n.$$

This clearly tends to infinity as n tends to infinity.

Here are some possible related questions:

- Suppose your position increases by a factor of x on a H instead of 2. Classify the long term behaviour as a function of x.
- Suppose your position increases by a factor of x on a H and is multiplied by y with $y < 1$ otherwise. Classify the long term behaviour as a function of x and y.

□

Solution to Question 3.6. The random variable N has a *geometric* distribution. Some care should be taken to avoid ambiguities arising from the inclusion of the final toss – some definitions include it, giving a state space $\{1, 2, 3, \ldots\}$, while others do not, giving a state space $\{0, 1, 2, \ldots\}$. Here we use the former, although this is not simply a question asking you to recite expectations and variances of common distributions so the definition is not important as long as we are clear. You may well already know the answer, but odds on if you're being asked this in an interview they want to see if you can derive it, so keep the answer to yourself and just use it to check what you arrive at from first principles.

Given our definition of N, it is clear that if $N = k$, then we had $k - 1$ consecutive tails followed by 1 head. From this we conclude

$$\mathbb{P}(N = k) = 0.5^{k-1}0.5 = 0.5^k,$$

for $k = 1, 2, \ldots$ Using the standard calculation for $\mathbb{E}(X)$ we have

$$\mathbb{E}(X) = \sum_{k=1}^{\infty} 0.5^k k.$$

If you remember the formula for this series then you are done. If you don't, or forget it under the pressure of the interview, here's a nice trick for quickly calculating it (which is easily extended to similar problems):

$$\mathbb{E}(X) = 0.5^1 + 2 \times 0.5^2 + 3 \times 0.5^3 + \cdots$$
$$\Rightarrow 0.5\mathbb{E}(X) = 0.5^2 + 2 \times 0.5^3 + 3 \times 0.5^4 + \cdots$$
$$\Rightarrow 0.5\mathbb{E}(X) = 0.5^1 + 0.5^2 + 0.5^3 + \cdots,$$

the final line being the difference of the first two. This is also just the sum of the probabilities $\mathbb{P}(N = k)$ and hence adds to 1, thus $\mathbb{E}(X) = 2$. Applying the same technique (twice) gives

$$\mathbb{E}(X^2) = \frac{2 - 0.5}{0.5^2} = 6,$$

and so $\text{Var}(X) = 2$.

Here are some possible related questions:

- I pay you \$1 at the end of this year, \$2 at the end of next year and so on. The effective annual interest rate is i. Derive, from first principles, the value of this payment stream.
- Derive the expectation and variance of a Poisson random variable.
- What is the mean and expectation if we redefine N to be the number of tails before we toss a head?

□

Solution to Question 3.7. We begin by deriving the distribution of the game length. Let N denote the number of throws until the game stops, $N \in \{2, 3, \ldots\}$. For the event $\{N = k\}$ to occur, we can start with any throw. However after this the remaining sequence of $k - 1$ throws are exactly determined. For example, for the game to end in four throws if we begin with a H we need the sequence THH while if we begin with a T we need the sequence HTT. A determined sequence of $k - 1$ throws occurs with probability 0.5^{k-1}, so

$$\mathbb{P}(N = k) = 0.5^{k-1}.$$

This gives the expectation as

$$\mathbb{E}(N) = \sum_{k=2}^{\infty} k 0.5^{k-1} = 2 \times 0.5 + 3 \times 0.5^2 + \cdots.$$

Thus

$$0.5\mathbb{E}(N) = 2 \times 0.5^2 + 3 \times 0.5^3 + \cdots,$$

and taking differences gives

$$0.5\mathbb{E}(N) = 2 \times 0.5 + 0.5^2 + 0.5^3 + \cdots.$$

Observing that this is a geometric series (plus an additional term), we have

$$\mathbb{E}(N) = 3.$$

Here are some possible related questions:

- What is the variance of N?
- How is the expectation changed if we alter the game so we need three consecutive occurrences of either heads or tails to end the game?

□

Solution to Question 3.8. There are many ways to do this. One particularly nice way using pricing ideas is via a gambling strategy. It is always good to answer questions in a quant job interview using methods that appear finance related.

We gamble in such a way that we make money on heads but such that if we get a T on toss n, our position is $-n$.

We therefore gamble one unit on the first toss and on each toss after a T. After one head, we gamble three. This guarantees that if we get a T next then we go to minus n. After two heads, we are therefore up four, and so we gamble seven to get us to $-n$ again if the next toss is tails. Our gambling winnings is a martingale, since we are making finite trades in a martingale. (Any bounded trading strategy in a martingale is a martingale.)

After three heads, our position is $11 - (n - 3) = 14 - n$. The time taken to get three heads is a stopping time with finite expectation, so if we stop at it, we still have a martingale (Optional Sampling theorem). Thus

$$\mathbb{E}(14 - n) = 0,$$

and we are done.

We really need to show that the stopping time has finite expectation. This is easy. The probability that coins $3k, 3k + 1, 3k + 2$ are all heads is $1/8$. So the probability that we have not obtained three heads in a row after $3k$ draws is less than

$$(1/8)^k.$$

The expected time to achieve three heads is therefore less than

$$\sum_k (3k)(1/8)^k,$$

which is clearly finite.

The book by Williams, [21], is a good reference for this material.

Here are some possible related questions:

- What's the answer for n heads?
- Show that the expected time is always an integer.
- A monkey types letters from the alphabet plus the space bar with equal probability at the rate of one a second. How long would it take him to type the string "option pricing"?
- A monkey type letters from the alphabet plus the space bar with equal probability at the rate of one a second. How long would it take him to type the string "Black-Scholes"? (trick question)

□

Solution to Question 3.9. Let the probability of a head be p. The probability of a head on throw j but not on the first $j - 1$ throws is

$$p(1 - p)^{j-1}.$$

The expected time is therefore

$$p \sum_{j=1}^{\infty} j(1 - p)^{j-1}.$$

We need to compute this infinite sum. We know

$$\frac{1}{1 - x} = \sum_{j=0}^{\infty} x^j.$$

Differentiating, we get

$$\frac{1}{(1 - x)^2} = \sum_{j=1}^{\infty} j x^{j-1}.$$

Let $x = 1 - p$. We get that the infinite sum is $1/p^2$. The answer is therefore $1/p$.

That's the brute force solution. We can also solve this using martingales, which gives an easier generalisation to the two Heads case. The solution is also more financial which is always good when doing a quant job interview.

Suppose we receive $1 - p$ dollars when we toss a head, and pay p dollars when we toss a tail. Our expected gain per toss is then zero. If X_k is our position after k tosses, then this is a martingale.

The time of the first head is a stopping time. Its expectation is finite because the probability of not getting a head in the first k tosses is $(1 - p)^k$ which goes to zero rapidly. This means that X_k stopped at the first head is a martingale, and its expected value is $X_0 = 0$, using the Optional Sampling theorem.

Our position if we terminate at k tosses is

$$(1 - p) - (k - 1)p.$$

The expected value of this is zero, so rearranging we get

$$\mathbb{E}(k) = \frac{1}{p}.$$

Now consider the second part of this problem. We construct a strategy so that if we get a T on toss k then our position is $-kp$. The main difference is that we now have to handle the case of getting a head then a tail.

If we threw a tail on toss $k-2$ but a head on toss $k-1$ then our position before toss k is

$$(1-p) - (k-2)p.$$

If we bet y dollars on toss k then our position after a tail on toss k is

$$(1-p) - (k-2)p - yp.$$

We choose y to make this equal to $-kp$. The solution is

$$y = \frac{1+p}{p}.$$

The value of our position after two successive heads is then

$$-(k-2)p + 1 - p + (1-p)\frac{1+p}{p}.$$

The expected value of this is again zero so we can solve for the expected value of k and get

$$\mathbb{E}(k) = 2 + \frac{1-p}{p}\left(1 + \frac{1+p}{p}\right).$$

Here are some possible related questions:

- Suppose the coin is fair, what is the expected number of tosses to get four heads in a row?
- Suppose the coin is fair, what is the expected number of tosses to get five heads in a row?
- Suppose the coin is fair, what is the expected number of tosses to get four heads in total?
- Suppose the coin is fair. I gain one on a head. I lose one on a tail. I quit when my position is $+1$. What's the probability that the game terminates? What's my expected winnings when the game ends? Explain.
- What are the hypotheses of the Optional Sampling theorem?

$\square$

Solution to Question 3.10. We can do this using Bayes' theorem: if the events A_j partition our sample space, Ω, that is

$$A_i \cap A_j = \emptyset, \text{ for } i \neq j,$$
$$\cup A_i = \Omega,$$

then for any event $B \subset \Omega$,

$$\mathbb{P}(A_i|B) = \frac{\mathbb{P}(B|A_i)\mathbb{P}(A_i)}{\sum\limits_{j=1}^{N} \mathbb{P}(B|A_j)\mathbb{P}(A_j)}.$$

Here we take A_1 to be the event that the double-headed coin is drawn, and A_2 to be that any other is drawn. We have

$$\mathbb{P}(A_1) = \frac{1}{10} \text{ and } \mathbb{P}(A_2) = \frac{9}{10}.$$

The probability of three heads with a fair coin is clearly $1/8$, so we get

$$\frac{1 \times \frac{1}{10}}{1 \times \frac{1}{10} + \frac{9}{10} \times \frac{1}{8}} = \frac{8}{17}.$$

Here are some possible related questions:

- What if there are two double-headed coins?
- How many tosses would you need to be 95% sure that the coin is double-headed?

$\square$

Solution to Question 3.11. *If the coin is fair* then the number of heads in a row before you flip has no effect on the probability of another head so the answer is $1/2$.

If the interviewer flips 100 heads in a row, then it is unlikely that the coin is fair since the probability of this happening is 2^{-100}. In fact, in that case the most likely cause is that the coin is double-headed.

To properly answer this question, we really need a *prior distribution*: what is our view that the coin is fair before we receive any information? Given we are in an interview and the interviewer may play tricks on us, let's say that we estimate that the coin is double-headed with $p = 1\%$ probability before we receive any information.

This is a Bayesian approach to the problem, and we can apply Bayes' theorem. In fact, we are back in the situation of Question 3.10, and we can proceed in the same fashion. The probability that the coin is double-headed after N heads and no tails is

$$\frac{p}{p + (1 - p)2^{-N}}.$$

After 100 throws this will be very close to 1 for any reasonable p.

You might mention that this problem comes up in the play "Rosencrantz and Guildenstern are dead" by Tom Stoppard. If you do not know this play, it is very funny and there is a great film version. It is based on two minor characters from "Hamlet."

Here are some possible related questions:

- Do you think that people are Bayesians?
- At what N would you get suspicious? (e.g. when would you be 99% sure that the coin is fixed?)
- Suppose the coin instead of always tossing heads, alternated in such a way to give the sequence $HTHTHTHTHTHT...$ what then?

$\square$

Solution to Question 3.12. This one looks hard but is not. There are $1,000,000 - 11$ possible slots for the sequence to occur. In each one of these slots, the probability is

$$2^{-12}.$$

The answer is therefore

$$\frac{1,000,000 - 11}{2^{12}}$$

which is 244.14. (How would you do this quickly and approximately in your head?)

Many readers are probably wondering why this simple multiplication was justified. The crucial point is the linearity of expectation; this does not require independence. Let I_j have value 1 if the sequence starting at toss j is correct and zero otherwise. We want to evaluate

$$\mathbb{E}\left(\sum I_j\right).$$

However, this is just equal to

$$\sum \mathbb{E}(I_j),$$

since finite sums commute with expectation.

Here are some possible related questions:

- What is the expected number of sequences of six tails, if we do not allow overlaps?
- What is the probability of getting at least one sequence of six heads followed by six tails? (very hard!)

$\square$

Solution to Question 3.13. We first assume that the probability of landing in a subset of the board is equal to its area divided by the area of the board. This means that we (almost) always hit the dartboard but beyond that all points are equally likely. The dart board has radius R so the probability of landing inside a circle of radius s is

$$\left(\frac{s}{R}\right)^2.$$

The density of the radius is therefore the derivative of this with respect to s which is

$$\frac{2s}{R^2}.$$

The expected distance from the centre is then

$$\int_0^R \frac{2s}{R^2} s\, ds = \frac{2}{3}\frac{R^3}{R^2} = \frac{2R}{3}.$$

The probability of landing in a circle of radius $R/2$ is $1/4$, to do this ten times in a row has probability

$$2^{-20}.$$

This is roughly a millionth. If we do this one hundred times, our expected winnings are

$$\frac{1}{10000}.$$

We would have pay

$$100 \times 0.1 = 10$$

dollars to play so this would be a very bad deal.

If we were better at darts and the winning probability was $2/3$ per throw, then the probability of getting ten in a row is

$$\frac{2^{10}}{3^{10}} = \frac{1024}{59049} \sim \frac{1}{50}.$$

After 100 attempts, we would win about 2 dollars so we would expect to be down 8 dollars. It is still a bad deal.

Here are some possible related questions:

- For the player hitting the board at random, if the game is modified to work with a different radius, what radius is the break-even point?
- What would a fair price for the original game be for the better darts player?
- Formulate and solve the three-dimensional analogue of this game.

$\square$

Solution to Question 3.14. See extended problem below. $\square$

Solution to Question 3.15. These problems are trickier than they first appear. The key is to identify the possible sample points and their probabilities.

Here we have two children. The possibilities are, with eldest first,

$$BB \text{ w.p. } 0.25,$$
$$BG \text{ w.p. } 0.25,$$
$$GB \text{ w.p. } 0.25,$$
$$GG \text{ w.p. } 0.25.$$

The probability of the event that at least one is a girl is 0.75. The probability of both being girls is 0.25.

We compute

$$\mathbb{P}(GG| \text{ at least one } G) = \frac{\mathbb{P}(GG)}{\mathbb{P}(\text{at least one } G)},$$

and get $1/3$. Note that the answer is not 0.5.

If the eldest is a girl, then we divide by 0.5 instead of 0.75 and get 0.5.

The last part is simply to throw you and is no different from the event that at least one is a girl.

Here are some possible related questions:

- A dictator decides that to increase the number of sons in his realm, a family that has had a girl is allowed no more children. Would this work?
- Suppose there are three children, what's the probability all three are girls if one is?
- Suppose there are three children, what's the probability all three are girls if the middle child is a boy?
- Suppose there are three children, what's the probability that two are girls if the middle child is a boy?

☐

Solution to Question 3.16. Note the crucial point that the question refers to *business* days. We will take business days to be Monday to Friday. However, in an interview one should mention that there are other non-business days such as bank holidays, Good Friday and Christmas. Note that Thanksgiving is always on a Thursday.

Given this, the important thing is that the fourth business day will be a Thursday if the first day of the month is a Saturday, Sunday or a Monday. The probability is therefore 3/7.

Here are some possible related questions:

- An event happens on business day k of the month. We want to minimise the number of times it happens on a Monday. What k do we choose? (We prefer smaller k if equal probability.)
- What is the probability that the third of January 2015 is a business day?

☐

Solution to Question 3.17. Assuming you haven't left the interview by now, here's the idea. If you spin again, you clearly have a $1/3$ probability of being shot, as two out of six chambers are loaded.

What is the probability if you don't spin again? The initial spin must have taken you to one of the four empty chambers. Only one of these precedes a loaded chamber. Thus if you don't spin again, you have a $1/4$ chance of being shot.

If you're still sitting there, don't spin again.

Here are some possible related questions:

- How do the odds change if we load three contiguous chambers?
- What if there are three rounds in alternating chambers?

□

Solution to Question 3.18. As usual, we can make this problem a lot simpler by using symmetry. We first divide into the two cases: they have the same rank or different ranks. The probability the second card has the same rank is $3/51$. So the probability of different ranks is $48/51$.

If they are of different ranks then the probability is $1/2$ by symmetry.

So the answer is
$$\frac{1}{2}\frac{48}{51} = \frac{24}{51}.$$
Here are some possible related questions:

- What is the probability that the second card has the same suit?
- Suppose one suit is a trump suit. What is the probability that the second card would beat the first card in a trick? (i.e. it is a trump and the first card is not, or it is higher than the first card and in the same suit.)

□

Solution to Question 3.19. The first point to observe here is that the probability is not one: simply by bad luck, the second best team could play the best in the first round, and be knocked out.

We can think of a tree with the winner at the top. It has two branches below it corresponding to each of the semi-finals. Each semi-final has two branches corresponding to quarter finals. The best two teams will meet before the final if and only if they are below the same semi-final.

Since the winning teams takes up one of the places in its half, the probability is $\frac{N}{2N-1}$ if there are $2N$ teams.

Here are some possible related questions:

- There are M teams in a knock-out tournament. How many matches must be played to determine who wins?
- There are M teams in a knock-out tournament. How many rounds must be played to determined who wins? (A round means any number of simultaneous matches with a team in a maximum of one match.)

$\square$

Solution to Question 3.20. After we have pulled out one sock, there are three socks left. Only one of these matches the original sock so the probability is $1/3$.

Here are some possible related questions:

- What if there were n different colours and you pull out two?
- What if there were n different colours and you pull out three?
- If there are 20 red socks and 20 black socks in a drawer, how many would you have to pull out to be sure of having a matching pair? (the answer is not 21.)

$\square$

Solution to Question 3.21. "With replacement" means that I put the card back and reshuffle the deck before drawing the second time. This means that both draws are the same (that is they have the same probability distribution) and are independent of each other.

There are 13 ranks of card and 4 of each card. The probability of getting an ace on a single draw is therefore

$$1/13,$$

and of two with replacement is

$$1/169.$$

Without replacement, we need the probability that the second is an ace given that the first one is. There are 3 aces and 51 cards left so the probability is

$$\frac{3}{51} = \frac{1}{17}.$$

The probability of two aces is therefore

$$\frac{1}{13} \times \frac{1}{17} = \frac{1}{221}.$$

Here are some possible related questions:

- What's the probability I am dealt two aces at Pontoon?
- What's the probability of getting 3 aces with and without replacement?
- What's the probability of getting an ace and a king without replacement?

$\square$

Solution to Question 3.22. Once we place the ant on a vertex, we will refer to this vertex as vertex 0, being zero distance from the starting position. Note that due to the symmetry of the cube, the expected number of minutes for the ant to return is a function of only the distance from this original position, which of the three vertices of distance one (for example) the ant is on is irrelevant. Let $f(n)$ denote the expected number of minutes for the ant to return from a vertex n units from the starting position, $n = 0, 1, 2, 3$. We want to find the value of $f(0)$.

When we place the ant, it will travel to another vertex (taking one minute), and then be a distance of one from the origin. Thus

$$f(0) = 1 + f(1).$$

From a distance of one, it has a $1/3$ chance of returning to the origin in one minute, or a $2/3$ chance of taking one minute to travel to a vertex which is a distance of 2 from the origin. This gives

$$f(1) = \frac{1}{3} + \frac{2}{3}(f(2) + 1).$$

Arguing similarly gives

$$f(2) = \frac{2}{3}(f(1) + 1) + \frac{1}{3}(f(3) + 1)$$
$$f(3) = 1 + f(2).$$

Solving this system of equations gives $f(0) = 8$.

Here are some possible related questions:

- Instead of constantly moving, the ant gets tired and rests for one minute with probability $1/4$. What is the new expected time?
- Repeat the question assuming the ant is walking on a regular tetrahedron.

$\square$

Solution to Question 3.23. Begin by making the obvious assumption that your steps have a uniform distribution on ± 1, so you move one meter toward or away from safety with probability 0.5. We then let $f(x)$ denote the probability of your survival from the starting position x, that is

$$f(x) = \mathbb{P}(\text{ You finish at the safe end } | \text{ you start } x \text{ meters from the safe end }).$$

There are (at least) two ways to approach this sort of question: recursion and a martingale approach. We focus on the recursive approach and leave the martingale as an extension.

As a recursive exercise, the reasoning goes as follows. If we start at $x = 1$, we head to safety with probability 0.5 or to a position two meters from safety with probability 0.5. From the second outcome, we survive with probability $f(2)$ – the process is Markov so it is just as if we had started from this position. We thus have

$$f(1) = 0.5f(0) + 0.5f(2) = 0.5 + 0.5f(2),$$

since clearly we have $f(0) = 1$ and $f(5) = 0$.

Arguing in the same manner gives the system of equations

$$f(2) = 0.5f(1) + 0.5f(3),$$
$$f(3) = 0.5f(2) + 0.5f(4),$$
$$f(4) = 0.5f(3) + 0.5f(5) = 0.5f(3).$$

Solving this system of equations (by hand, it is easiest to start with the final equation and substitute backwards) we obtain the solution

$$f(1) = \frac{4}{5}, \qquad f(2) = \frac{3}{5}, \qquad f(3) = \frac{2}{5}, \qquad f(4) = \frac{1}{5}.$$

As a quick sanity check, the probability of surviving from $x = 1$ should be the same as the probability of being eaten from $x = 4$ due to symmetry, which it is.

Here are some possible related questions:

- Solve the question using a martingale approach.
- Extend to an n meter long plank using both approaches.
- When would you prefer a shorter plank and when would you prefer a longer one?

□

Solution to Question 3.24. Clearly, one can do this by integration. Here's a simpler solution. The first thing to do is to phrase the problem in terms of a two-dimensional event. We pick two independent uniforms x, y from $[0, 1]$ and the question is what is the probability $|x - y| \leq 0.25$? In other words, what is the probability that a pair (x, y) picked from the uniform distribution on the square

$$[0, 1] \times [0, 1]$$

lies in the set

$$E = \{(x, y) \mid |x - y| \leq 0.25\}.$$

We need to identify the geometry of E. This set will be a strip inside $[0, 1] \times [0, 1]$, with sides $y = x + 0.25$ and $y = x - 0.25$. Clearly, the complement of this set is two congruent right-angled triangles. The two short sides of these are of length 0.75. The two triangles together therefore give a square of side $3/4$. Its area is therefore $9/16$. And the answer is

$$1 - \frac{9}{16} = \frac{7}{16}.$$

Note the use of symmetry and 2-dimensional geometry in this probability problem.

Here are some possible related questions:

- Romeo and Juliet both wait x minutes. What is the probability?
- Romeo is twice as keen as Juliet and so waits $2x$ minutes. What is the probability?

$\square$

Solution to Question 3.25. There are a number of ways to do this. Most of these are tricky and complicated algebraically. However, if we condition on the right event it becomes easy.

Every person who does not sit in their own seat can do three things. Sit in seat 1, sit in seat 100 or force someone else to sit in the wrong seat.

If they sit in seat 1, then every subsequent person sits in the correct seat, and therefore so does the last passenger.

If they sit in seat 100, then the last passenger sits in the wrong seat.

If they sit in any other seat, we are back in the same situation with fewer passengers and seats.

Consider the last passenger who has a choice. This is a passenger below 100 who has been displaced. Since he is the last one displaced he must either sit in seat 100 or seat 1.

The answer is therefore $1/2$, since the probability of sitting in either of these two seats is equal.

Here are some possible related questions:

- What happens with N seats?
- An officious steward tries to make displaced passengers sit in seat 1. He succeeds with probability 0.9. What's the probability of passenger 100 being in the right seat?

• What if grandpa comes as well? The first two passengers sit in two independent seats at random.

□

Solution to Question 3.26. The question is equivalent to asking is the matrix

$$M = \begin{pmatrix} 1 & 0.9 & 0.1 \\ 0.9 & 1 & 0.8 \\ 0.1 & 0.8 & 1 \end{pmatrix}$$

positive definite (see Question 3.35). This can be done by the methods outlined in Question 6.9. We choose the last method mentioned. Clearly the upper-left 1-by-1 corner of M has positive determinant. The upper-left 2-by-2 corner of M has determinant 0.19, also positive. Finally, M has determinant -0.316, which is negative and hence the matrix is not positive definite.

Thus it is not a covariance matrix, and hence it is not possible for A and C to have correlation coefficient 0.1.

Here are some possible related questions:

• Given the correlation coefficients for the pairs (A, B) and (B, C), what are the allowable range of values for the correlation of (A, C)?
• What if the correlation of A and B is x and of B and C is y?
• Suppose you were given a correlation that was not positive definite, how might you turn it into a valid correlation matrix?

□

Solution to Question 3.27. First, we need to transform the condition into something less opaque. The three pieces will form a triangle if the longest piece is smaller in size than the sum of the other two. This will happen if and only if the biggest piece is of size less than a half. Unfortunately, we do not know at the start which piece will be longest. However, this happens if precisely one of x and y is less than $\frac{1}{2}$, and $|x - y| < \frac{1}{2}$. (If both were in the same half interval, the longest piece would contain the other half interval.)

As usual when drawing two points, it is best to think of of (x, y) as a point in the unit square. We work out the geometry of the valid set in order to compute its area. The condition that precisely one is less than $\frac{1}{2}$, means that if we divide into four squares of size $\frac{1}{2}$, we are in the top left or the bottom right. Our remaining constraint says that we are below the diagonal from bottom left to top right in the top left square, and above the same diagonal in the bottom right square.

The set therefore consists of two half small squares, and is of area equal to one small square. The answer is therefore $\frac{1}{4}$.

Here are some possible related questions:

- What if the second point is chosen to break the longer segment left after the first point has been chosen?
- What's the probability that the triangle is right angled?
- Suppose we take n points with $n > 3$. What's the probability of forming an n-gon?

□

Solution to Question 3.28. This is a reasonably straightforward question, and there are two ways to approach it. Firstly, recall the density function of a $U(a, b)$ random variable is given by

$$f(x) = \frac{1}{b - a}, \qquad a \leq x \leq b,$$

and $f(x) = 0$ outside this interval. Then the distribution function, $F(x)$ is given by

$$F(x) = \int_a^x f(y)dy$$
$$= \frac{x - a}{b - a},$$

for $a \leq x \leq b$, $F(x) = 0$ for $x < a$ and $F(x) = 1$ for $x > b$.

The alternative is just to recall the 'idea' behind the uniform distribution: probability is spread uniformly over the interval. Thus the probability a random variable takes a value in a given interval is simply proportional to the length of that interval, $\mathbb{P}(x \leq U(a, b) \leq y) = k(y - x)$ for some constant k and $a \leq x \leq y \leq b$.

Since $\mathbb{P}(a \leq U(a,b) \leq b) = 1$ we see $k = \frac{1}{b-a}$ and hence

$$F(x) = \mathbb{P}(a \leq U(a,b) \leq x) = \frac{x-a}{b-a}.$$

Here are some possible related questions:

- What is the distribution function of an $\exp(\lambda)$ random variable?
- What is the distribution function of a standard Cauchy random variable?
- What is the probability density function of a $N(0,1)$ random variable?

$\square$

Solution to Question 3.29. We want the distribution of the maximum of n independent uniform random variables.

It is easy to find the cumulative distribution function of the maximum of n independent random variables: it is simply the product of the individual ones. To see this, observe

$$\mathbb{P}(\max(x_i) \leq x) = \mathbb{P}(x_i \leq x \ \forall i),$$

$$= \prod_{i=1}^{n} \mathbb{P}(x_i \leq x),$$

where the second equality uses the independence of the random variables.

We now have a program to attack this problem:

- compute the cumulative probability of a uniform;
- take the nth power;
- differentiate to get the probability density function;
- multiply by x and integrate to get the expectation.

The density of a uniform, U, is 1 between zero and one, and 0 otherwise. Integrating, we get

$$\mathbb{P}(U < x) = x,$$

for $x \in [0, 1]$. This means that the cumulative distribution function of $\max x_j$ is given by

$$\mathbb{P}(\max x_j \leq x) = \begin{cases} 0 \text{ for } x \leq 0, \\ x^n \text{ for } x \in (0, 1), \\ 1 \text{ for } x > 1. \end{cases}$$

Differentiating the probability density function, we get

$$nx^{n-1},$$

for $x \in [0, 1]$ and zero elsewhere. Multiplying by x and integrating from zero to one, we obtain

$$\mathbb{E}(\max x_j) = \frac{n}{n+1},$$

and we have completed the first part. For the second part, by symmetry the expectation of $\min x_j$ is

$$\frac{1}{n+1}.$$

Since taking expectations is linear, we have

$$\mathbb{E}(\max x_j - \min x_j) = \frac{n-1}{n+1}.$$

Here are some possible related questions:

- What is the expectation of $|x_1 - x_2|$?
- What is the density of $x_1 + x_2$?
- What is the expectation of $\min x_j + \max x_j$?

$\square$

Solution to Question 3.30. The Cauchy distribution has density function

$$\frac{1}{\pi} \frac{1}{1 + x^2}.$$

Clearly, the second moment does not exist as we would have to integrate

$$\frac{x^2}{1 + x^2}$$

which tends to one as x goes to plus or minus infinity.

It is worth noting that the expectation of this distribution does not really exist either, as the integral of

$$\frac{x}{1+x^2}$$

is

$$\frac{1}{2}\log(1+x^2),$$

which is divergent as $x \to \infty$. The integral from $-R$ to R is zero for any R, however, so the integral exists in a principal-value sense and is zero. Note that if your interviewer is a physicist, he may not get all these subtleties and may even regard your awareness of them as a negative.

Here are some possible related questions:

- Give an example where the expectation exists properly but the variance does not exist.
- Do you know of, or can you construct, other densities with infinite variance?
- If $\mathbb{E}[|X|^k]$ exists, does $\mathbb{E}[|X|^m]$ exist for $0 \leq m \leq k$? Prove it.

□

Solution to Question 3.31. This question tests your basic understanding of the definition of a probability density function. Recall

$$f_X(x) = \frac{d}{dx}F_X(x) = \frac{d}{dx}\mathbb{P}\left(X \leq x\right),$$

denoting by $F_X(x)$ the distribution function of X. Let $Y = g(X)$. Then the question is to evaluate

$$f_Y(x) = \frac{d}{dx}F_Y(x) = \frac{d}{dx}\mathbb{P}\left(Y \leq x\right),$$

where $f_Y(x)$ is the probability density function of Y and $F_Y(x)$ is its distribution function. Continuing, assuming $g(x)$ has an differentiable inverse $g^{-1}(x)$,

$$
\begin{aligned}
f_Y(x) &= \frac{d}{dx}\mathbb{P}\left(Y \leq x\right) \\
&= \frac{d}{dx}\mathbb{P}\left(g(X) \leq x\right) \\
&= \frac{d}{dx}\mathbb{P}\left(X \leq g^{-1}(x)\right) \\
&= \frac{d}{dx}F_X\left(g^{-1}(x)\right) \\
&= f_X\left(g^{-1}(x)\right)\frac{d}{dx}g^{-1}(x).
\end{aligned}
$$

Here are some possible related questions:

- What is the distribution function of $Y = g(X)$? (This should be obvious from the above working).
- Can you conclude $\mathbb{E}(Y) = g(\mathbb{E}(X))$? Give a counter-example. What approximation can we use instead?
- What is Jensen's inequality?

$\square$

Solution to Question 3.32. The kth order statistic is the kth smallest value in a sample of n from a random distribution. Let the random variables $X_1, X_2, \ldots, X_n$ be independent and identically distributed. Label the smallest value $X_{(1)}$, the next smallest $X_{(2)}$ and so on up to $X_{(n)}$. Then the value of the kth order statistic is $X_{(k)}$, for $1 \leq k \leq n$.

Let $F(z)$ denote the distribution function of the X_i's and $f(z)$ the density function. The question asks us first to determine the distribution of the kth order statistic, that is

$$\mathbb{P}(X_{(k)} \leq x).$$

To have $X_{(k)} \leq x$ we need to have at least k of the n X_i's less than or equal to x. Each of the n independent trials has probability $F(x)$ of being less than or equal to x, thus the number of trials less than or equal to x has a Binomial distribution with n trials and probability $F(x)$. That is

$$\mathbb{P}(X_{(k)} \leq x) = \mathbb{P}(\text{at least } k \text{ successes from a } Bi(n, F(x)) \text{ distribution})$$

$$= \sum_{j=k}^{n} \mathbb{P}(j \text{ successes})$$

$$= \sum_{j=k}^{n} \binom{n}{j} (F(x))^j (1 - F(x))^{n-j}.$$

To find the density function we take the derivative with respect to x:

$$\frac{d}{dx} \mathbb{P}(X_{(k)} \leq x)$$

$$= \frac{d}{dx} \left(\sum_{j=k}^{n} \binom{n}{j} (F(x))^j (1 - F(x))^{n-j} \right)$$

$$= \sum_{j=k}^{n-1} \binom{n}{j} \left(j(F(x))^{j-1} f(x)(1 - F(x))^{n-j} \right.$$

$$\left. - (n - j)(F(x))^j (1 - F(x))^{n-j-1} f(x) \right) + nf(x)F(x)^{n-1}$$

$$= nf(x) \sum_{j=k}^{n-1} \left(\binom{n-1}{j-1} (F(x))^{j-1} (1 - F(x))^{n-j} \right.$$

$$\left. - \binom{n-1}{j} (F(x))^j (1 - F(x))^{n-j-1} \right) + nf(x)F(x)^{n-1}$$

$$= nf(x) \left(\sum_{j=k-1}^{n-2} \binom{n-1}{j} (F(x))^j (1 - F(x))^{n-j-1} \right.$$

$$\left. - \sum_{j=k}^{n-1} \binom{n-1}{j} (F(x))^j (1 - F(x))^{n-j-1} \right) + nf(x)F(x)^{n-1}.$$

Written in this form, it is obvious that the majority of terms will cancel. This leaves

$$\frac{d}{dx} \mathbb{P}(X_{(k)} \leq x) = \frac{n!}{(n - k)!(k - 1)!} f(x)(F(x))^{k-1} (1 - F(x))^{n-k}.$$

Here are some possible related questions:

- Simplify this if the X_i's are exponentially distributed.
- Now consider the joint random variable $(X_{(k_1)}, X_{(k_2)})$. What is its distribution function?

$\square$

Solution to Question 3.33. We'll begin with the more general case of two independent random variables X and Y with densities $f(x)$ and $g(x)$ respectively. We start by considering the distribution function of $X + Y$, and condition on the value of Y:

$$\mathbb{P}(X + Y \le z) = \int \mathbb{P}(X + Y \le z | Y = y) g(y) dy$$

$$= \int \mathbb{P}(X \le z - y) g(y) dy,$$

due to the independence of the two random variables. To find the density, take a derivative with respect to z, giving the density as

$$h(z) = \int_{-\infty}^{\infty} f(z - y) g(y) dy.$$

This is called the *convolution* of the two densities.

In our case, we have

$$f(x) = g(x) = \begin{cases} 1, & 0 \le x \le 1, \\ 0, & \text{otherwise.} \end{cases}$$

The next step is the most important when considering such convolutions. How do the above restrictions to intervals for $f(x)$ and $g(x)$ translate to restrictions on $f(z - y)$ and $g(y)$? This is not very difficult, but requires attention to detail. We have

$$f(z - y) = \begin{cases} 1, & z - 1 \le y \le z, \\ 0, & \text{otherwise,} \end{cases}$$

and $g(y)$ is done in the obvious manner. This gives

$$h(z) = \int_{\max\{z-1,0\}}^{\min\{z,1\}} 1 dy.$$

We must therefore break the integral into separate cases, a situation which is quite common in these problems.

For $z \leq 0$, we therefore clearly have $h(z) = 0$. For $0 \leq z \leq 1$,

$$h(z) = \int_0^z 1 dy = z,$$

and for $1 \leq z \leq 2$

$$h(z) = \int_{z-1}^1 1 dy = 2 - z.$$

Finally, for $z \geq 2$, $h(z) = 0$.

Here are some possible related questions:

- Repeat the question if X and $-Y$ have exponential distributions.
- Derive the density of the product of the random variables X and Y.
- Derive the density of the ratio of the random variables X and Y, X/Y.

$\square$

Solution to Question 3.34. The following information, along with further details, can be found in [3], VIII.4.

There are actually several forms of the Central Limit theorem, which formally is just a weak convergence result in probability. The interviewer is probably just interested in the most general and well-known result which is what we focus on here.

This form of the Central Limit theorem involves the average of a sum of independent identically distributed random variables with finite second moment. The theorem states that as the number of random variables increases, the average approaches a normal distribution with known parameters. The remarkable part of this result is that it is independent of the starting distribution of the random variables.

More formally, let $X_1, X_2, \ldots, X_n$ be a sequence of n independent and identically distributed random variables with finite mean μ and variance σ^2. Let S_n denote the sum of the random variables, that is $S_n = X_1 + X_2 + \cdots + X_n$.

The Central Limit theorem states that the random variable

$$Y_n = \frac{S_n - \mu n}{\sigma \sqrt{n}}$$

converges (in distribution) to the standard normal distribution.

As mentioned, other less well-known forms exist. Lindeberg proved a version of the Central Limit theorem for independent random variables which do not have identical distributions.

Here are some possible related questions:

- What is convergence in distribution? What other types of convergence are there in probability theory?
- Using characteristic functions, prove the Central Limit theorem for sums of random variables with finite second moments.
- What is Lindeberg's condition?

$\square$

Solution to Question 3.35. We have to be slightly careful here: the result is actually not true as stated. Interviewers often get it wrong! In fact, covariance matrices are positive semi-definite not positive definite: the difference is that a covariance matrix, C, can have a zero eigenvalue, or equivalently, there can exist a vector x such that

$$x^t C x = 0.$$

The key to this problem is the fact that if the random variables

$$X_1, X_2, \ldots, X_n,$$

have covariance matrix C then if we take a linear combination of them,

$$Y = a_1 X_1 + a_2 X_2 + \cdots + a_n X_n,$$

it has variance

$$a^t C a,$$

where

$$a = (a_1, a_2, \ldots, a_n).$$

Since any random variable has non-negative variance, this is greater than or equal to zero and we are done.

One should really prove that Y has the variance claimed. To see this, observe that it is enough to consider the case where $\mathbb{E}(X_i) = 0$, for all i and then write out the sums.

For further discussion, see [3], pp.80–82.

Here are some possible related questions:

- How can you tell if a matrix is positive definite?
- Give an example of a matrix with positive entries that is not positive semi-definite.
- Show that we did not lose any generality by assuming $\mathbb{E}(X_i) = 0$.

$\square$

Solution to Question 3.36. Change of measure means just that: changing the measure. The measure in question might be simply a distribution (say, of returns), or a measure defining a stochastic process. Changing the measure places different emphasis on different parts of the distribution, by making them more or less likely under the new measure. This might mean emphasising paths of a Brownian motion that have an upwards trend, or making excessive returns more likely. However there are two golden rules: the new measure must assign probabilities to the same subsets, and things that were impossible under the old measure must be impossible under the new measure.

Mathematically a change of measure is can be constructed as follows. Assume we have a probability space $(\Omega, \mathcal{F}, \mathbb{P})$ and a positive random variable on this space with expectation 1, X. We then define the set function $\mathbb{Q} : \mathcal{F} \to [0, 1]$ by

$$\mathbb{Q}(A) = \mathbb{E}[\mathbb{1}_A X] = \int_A X dP,$$

for $A \in \mathcal{F}$. Clearly $\mathbb{Q}$ is absolutely continuous with respect to $\mathbb{P}$, that is

$$\mathbb{P}(A) = 0 \Rightarrow \mathbb{Q}(A) = 0.$$

The random-variable X is called the Radon–Nikodym derivative and is often written $d\mathbb{Q}/d\mathbb{P}$. According to the Radon–Nikodym theorem, for any measure on

$(\Omega, \mathcal{F})$ which is absolutely continuous with respect to $\mathbb{P}$ there exists such a (a.s. unique) derivative so that the new measure may be expressed in this manner.

The measures $\mathbb{P}$ and $\mathbb{Q}$ are said to be equivalent if $\mathbb{P}$ and $\mathbb{Q}$ are absolutely continuous with respect to each other. If $\mathbb{P}$ and $\mathbb{Q}$ are equivalent, then we also have the derivative $d\mathbb{P}/d\mathbb{Q}$, which is

$$\frac{d\mathbb{P}}{d\mathbb{Q}} = \left(\frac{d\mathbb{Q}}{d\mathbb{P}}\right)^{-1}.$$

The biggest use of measure changes in derivatives pricing is Girsanov's theorem, which is used to change the drift of a Brownian motion. Let $(\mathcal{F}_t)$ be the filtration of $(\Omega, \mathcal{F}, \mathbb{P})$, and $\mathbb{P}_t$ the restriction of $\mathbb{P}$ to $\mathcal{F}_t$. Suppose we have a positive martingale X_t, $t \in [0, T]$ with $\mathbb{E}[X_T] = 1$. We then define a new probability measure $\mathbb{Q}_t$ on $\mathcal{F}_t$,

$$\mathbb{Q}_t(A) = \mathbb{E}_{\mathbb{P}_t}[\mathbb{1}_A X(t)],$$

where $A \in \mathcal{F}_t$ and we use the subscript on $\mathbb{E}_{\mathbb{P}_t}$ to denote the measure we are taking the expectation under. This process is then the Radon–Nikodym derivative $d\mathbb{Q}_t/d\mathbb{P}_t$. We now present the idea of Girsanov's Theorem, see [4] p.556 for the details:

(Girsanov theorem) Let γ be an adapted process satisfying certain conditions and define

$$X_t = \exp\left(-\frac{1}{2}\int_0^t |\gamma(u)|^2 du + \int_0^t \gamma(u) dW(u)\right).$$

If $\mathbb{E}_{\mathbb{P}}[X_T] = 1$, then X_t is a martingale and defines a new measure $\mathbb{Q}$ where

$$\frac{d\mathbb{Q}}{d\mathbb{P}} = X(T).$$

Under $\mathbb{Q}$, the process

$$W_t^{\mathbb{Q}} = W_t - \int_0^t \gamma(u) du$$

is a standard Brownian motion.

Hence Girsanov's theorem has defined a new measure under which the Brownian motion with drift $W_t^{\mathbb{Q}}$ is a driftless Brownian motion.

As an application of change of measure to Monte Carlo, we look at *importance sampling*, as discussed in Section 4.6 of [4]. Here our goal is to use change of measure to reduce the variance of a sample. The idea is that some of the paths generated have little impact on the final result (usually an expectation), so time spent generating these paths is essentially wasted. Using importance sampling, we make paths which have more impact more likely.

Let's consider a simple example, which is redundant (the expectation can be calculated simply without using Monte Carlo methods) but provides a good illustration of the point.

Say the final value of a stock (in the appropriate risk-neutral measure, with zero interest rates) is uniformly distributed on the interval $(0, 1)$, that is $S_T \sim U(0, 1)$. Denote this measure by P. Consider a digital option on this stock which pays 1 if the stock at time T is above a level $a \in (0, 1)$ and 0 otherwise. Let C denote the value of this option, so

$$C = \mathbb{E}_{\mathbb{P}}(\mathbb{1}_{\{S_T > a\}}) = \int_0^1 \mathbb{1}_{\{z > a\}} dz.$$

The standard method of Monte Carlo simulation would be to simulate n random variables with a $U(0, 1)$ distribution, count how many are greater than a and divide by n. If $\hat{C}$ is this Monte Carlo estimator, then

$$\hat{C} = \frac{1}{n} \sum_{k=0}^{n} \mathbb{1}_{\{U_k > a\}},$$

where the U_k are independent and identically distributed $U(0, 1)$ random variables.

We can evaluate the variance of this estimator in the standard way (note that $\mathbb{E}(\mathbb{1}_{\{U_k > a\}})^m = \mathbb{P}(U_k > a) = (1 - a)$, $m = 1, 2, \ldots$), and see that $\text{Var}(\hat{C}) = a(1 - a)/n$.

Now consider changing the measure we use. The simulation under the current measure only gives a non-zero result if we finish in the interval $(a, 1)$, so let's change the measure to place more emphasis on the important part of the distribution, where the option has value. Do this by defining the measure with density

$$f(x) = \begin{cases} \frac{\alpha}{a}, & 0 \le x \le a, \\ \frac{1-\alpha}{1-a}, & a \le x \le 1, \end{cases}$$

for $0 < \alpha < 1$. This puts probability $1 - \alpha$ on falling in the area where the option has value. The new measure, $\mathbb{Q}$, has Radon–Nikodym derivative (with respect to

$\mathbb{P}$) $f(x)$, since the old density was 1. Thus

$$C = \mathbb{E}_{\mathbb{P}}(\mathbb{1}_{\{S_T > a\}}) = \mathbb{E}_{\mathbb{Q}}\left(\mathbb{1}_{\{S_T > a\}}\frac{d\mathbb{P}}{d\mathbb{Q}}\right)$$

$$= \frac{1-a}{1-\alpha}\mathbb{E}_{\mathbb{Q}}(\mathbb{1}_{\{S_T > a\}}).$$

When we use this in a simulation, we obtain the estimator

$$\hat{C}_2 = \frac{1-a}{1-\alpha}\frac{1}{n}\sum_{k=0}^{n}\mathbb{1}_{\{U_k^* > a\}},$$

where the U_k^* have density given by $f(x)$. This gives

$$\mathrm{Var}(\hat{C}_2) = \frac{1}{n}\frac{(1-a)^2}{1-\alpha}\alpha,$$

which is smaller than the variance of $\hat{C}$ if

$$\frac{1-a}{a} < \frac{1-\alpha}{\alpha},$$

or for large enough α (Why is this not surprising? Why can't we take $\alpha = 1$?).

As mentioned this is a very simple example, and finding a density to improve the variance is often tricky. Another standard use is to reduce variance when pricing out-of-the-money options. For example, if a call option is stuck at K with K much bigger than S_0, the initial stock price, then most paths will finish out of the money in the Black–Scholes model. We therefore shift measure to make the drift of the log of the stock price equal to

$$\frac{\log K - \log S_0}{\sigma\sqrt{T}}$$

to ensure that half the paths finish in the money. The pay-off for each path is multiplied by the likelihood ratio (i.e. the Radon–Nikodym derivative) to ensure that the expectation does not change.

Here are some possible related questions:

- In the above example, show that the expectation under the new measure still gives the correct result by evaluating it directly.
- Is it possible to perform a change of measure from a normal distribution to a Poisson distribution? Why or why not?

- What is the Radon–Nikodym derivative required to change a normal distribution to a Cauchy distribution?
- Why can change of measure be used only to change the drift, and not the diffusion of an Itô process?
- What is the Radon–Nikodym derivative used to change the stochastic differential equation

$$dX_t = \mu(X_t)dt + \sigma dW_t$$

to

$$dX_t = \alpha(X_t)dt + \sigma dW_t?$$

What conditions are needed on this derivative to ensure the change of measure is applicable to these two processes?

□

Solution to Question 3.37. To calculate $\mathbb{E}(X^2)$, recall that the variance of a random variable, $\text{Var}(X)$, is given by

$$\text{Var}(X) = \mathbb{E}(X^2) - (\mathbb{E}(X))^2.$$

For the random variable in question, we have $\text{Var}(X) = \sigma^2$ and $\mathbb{E}(X) = \mu$. Rearranging the above then gives

$$\mathbb{E}(X^2) = \sigma^2 + \mu^2.$$

In general, the expectation of a function $g(X)$ is given by

$$\mathbb{E}(g(X)) = \int g(x)f(x)dx,$$

where $f(x)$ is the corresponding probability density function (p.d.f.) for X and the integral is taken over all possible values of X. Note that the expectation is only defined if the integral

$$\int |g(x)|f(x)dx$$

converges. For the random variable X with distribution $N(\mu, \sigma)$, the p.d.f. is given by

$$f(x) = \frac{1}{\sqrt{2\pi}\sigma} \exp\left(-\frac{(x-\mu)^2}{2\sigma^2}\right),$$

and so the second part of the problem is to evaluate

$$\mathbb{E}(\exp(\lambda X)) = \int_{-\infty}^{\infty} \exp(\lambda x) \frac{1}{\sqrt{2\pi}\sigma} \exp\left(-\frac{(x-\mu)^2}{2\sigma^2}\right) dx.$$

The important point here is to recognise that this integral can be re-written as the integral of the p.d.f. of another normal random variable, as follows:

$$\mathbb{E}(\exp(\lambda X)) = \int_{-\infty}^{\infty} \frac{1}{\sqrt{2\pi}\sigma} \exp\left(-\frac{1}{2\sigma^2}(x^2 - 2x\mu - 2\sigma^2\lambda x + \mu^2)\right) dx$$

$$= \int_{-\infty}^{\infty} \frac{dx}{\sqrt{2\pi}\sigma} \exp\left(-\frac{(x-(\mu+\sigma^2\lambda))^2}{2\sigma^2} - \frac{\mu^2}{2\sigma^2} + \frac{(\mu+\sigma^2\lambda)^2}{2\sigma^2}\right)$$

$$= \exp\left(\mu\lambda + \frac{\sigma^2\lambda^2}{2}\right) \int_{-\infty}^{\infty} \frac{dx}{\sqrt{2\pi}\sigma} \exp\left(-\frac{(x-(\mu+\sigma^2\lambda))^2}{2\sigma^2}\right).$$

Now the integrand is the p.d.f. of a $N(\mu + \sigma^2\lambda, \sigma)$ random variable, and hence the integral evaluates to 1. This leaves

$$\mathbb{E}(\exp(\lambda X)) = \exp\left(\mu\lambda + \frac{\sigma^2\lambda^2}{2}\right).$$

Note that one can interpret this function is the *moment generating function* of the random variable X.

Here are some possible related questions:

- Calculate the moment generating function for the Poisson random variable with parameter α, that is the random variable Y such that

$$\mathbb{P}(Y = k) = \frac{e^{-\alpha}\alpha^k}{k!}.$$

- Show that if the moment generating function of X is given by $M(\lambda)$, then we can compute moments by

$$\mathbb{E}(X^n) = \left.\frac{d^n M(\lambda)}{d\lambda^n}\right|_{\lambda=0}.$$

- Note that if Y is $N(0,1)$, then $X = \sigma Y + \mu$. Calculate the moment generating function of Y and use this to confirm your previous calculation of the moment generating function of X.

$\square$

Solution to Question 3.38. By '$M(x)$ is the cumulative Gaussian function', the interviewer means that if X is $N(0,1)$, then

$$M(x) = \mathbb{P}(X \le x) = \Phi(x).$$

There are two ways to approach this question: the easy way and the hard way. We'll start with the hard way, which is a bit more brute force but won't fail if you don't notice the subtleties of the question. The problem can be tackled by standard calculation of an expectation by integrating against a density. Let $f(x)$ denote the density of X, that is

$$f(x) = \frac{1}{\sqrt{2\pi}} e^{-\frac{x^2}{2}},$$

then the question is to evaluate

$$\int_{-\infty}^{\infty} M(x)f(x)dx.$$

The easiest way to evaluate this is to observe that $M(x)$ is *almost* an odd function. Recall the definition of an odd function $h(x)$ is one such that $h(-x) = -h(x)$. Then if we set $g(x) = M(x) - \frac{1}{2}$ we have

$$g(-x) = M(-x) - \frac{1}{2}$$
$$= 1 - M(x) - \frac{1}{2}$$
$$= \frac{1}{2} - M(x) = -g(x),$$

using the properties of the cumulative Gaussian. Recalling that the integral from $-\infty$ to ∞ of a product of odd and even ($f(x)$ is clearly even since $f(x) = f(-x)$) functions is zero (see extension questions), we then have

$$\int_{-\infty}^{\infty} M(x)f(x)dx = \int_{-\infty}^{\infty} (M(x) - \frac{1}{2} + \frac{1}{2})f(x)dx$$
$$= \int_{-\infty}^{\infty} g(x)f(x)dx + \frac{1}{2}\int_{-\infty}^{\infty} f(x)dx$$
$$= \frac{1}{2},$$

since $f(x)$ is a density and hence integrates to 1.

Now for the easy way. Clearly $M(X)$ is a random variable on $(0, 1)$, but what is its distribution? For $x \in (0, 1)$, we have

$$\mathbb{P}(M(X) \leq x) = \mathbb{P}(\Phi(X) \leq x)$$
$$= \mathbb{P}(X \leq \Phi^{-1}(x))$$
$$= x,$$

by the definition of the cumulative Gaussian function. Hence $M(X)$ has a uniform distribution on $(0, 1)$, and it thus has expectation of $1/2$.

Here are some possible related questions:

- Use the definition of odd and even functions to show that the integral from $-\infty$ to ∞ of a product of odd and even functions is zero.
- What is the expectation of $f(X)$?
- Suppose X was not normal, will we always have the same answer for $\mathbb{E}(F(X))$ if F is the cumulative distribution function of X?

$\square$

Solution to Question 3.39. This is another question that can be answered using Bayes' theorem (see the solution to Question 3.10 for the definition).

To answer this question let A_1 denote the event that we selected the coin with 10 heads and A_2 denote the event that we selected a normal coin. Denote by B the event that we get 10 heads from 10 tosses.

Clearly $\mathbb{P}(B|A_1) = 1$ since each toss can only give a head. It is also clear that $\mathbb{P}(B|A_2) = 2^{-10}$, since each coin toss has a 1/2 chance of landing heads. The probability of each of A_1 and A_2 are implied by the question.

The question asks us to determine $\mathbb{P}(A_1|B)$, and using Bayes' Theorem this is given by

$$\mathbb{P}(A_1|B) = \frac{\mathbb{P}(B|A_1) \times \mathbb{P}(A_1)}{\mathbb{P}(B|A_1) \times \mathbb{P}(A_1) + \mathbb{P}(B|A_2) \times \mathbb{P}(A_2)}$$
$$= \frac{1/1000}{1/1000 + 2^{-10} \times 999/1000}$$
$$= 1024/2023 \approx 51\%.$$

Here are some possible related questions:

- Generalise to N heads in a row and M coins in the bag.
- Bayes' Theorem uses the concept of a prior distribution, a distribution that is assumed before an event. What is the prior distribution in this question?

□

Solution to Question 3.40. Let X denote the event that the first ball is red, Y the event that the second ball is black, U_A the event that we select our first ball from urn A and U_B the event that we select our first ball from urn B.

We are interested in $\mathbb{P}(X|Y)$, which can be written as

$$\mathbb{P}(X|Y) = \mathbb{P}(X|Y,U_A)\mathbb{P}(U_A|Y) + \mathbb{P}(X|Y,U_B)\mathbb{P}(U_B|Y)$$
$$= \mathbb{P}(X|Y,U_A)\mathbb{P}(U_A) + \mathbb{P}(X|Y,U_B)\mathbb{P}(U_B),$$

since U_A and U_B are independent of Y.

We can assume that $\mathbb{P}(U_A) = \mathbb{P}(U_B) = 0.5$. Since urn A contains no black balls, the probability $\mathbb{P}(X|U_A)$ is independent of the event Y, that is $\mathbb{P}(X|U_A,Y) = \mathbb{P}(X|U_A)$. Clearly from the question $\mathbb{P}(X|U_A) = \frac{2}{7}$. If we know the second ball is black and we are drawing from urn B, that leaves 4 red balls and 3 black balls in urn B for our first draw, so $\mathbb{P}(X|Y,U_B) = \frac{4}{7}$. Hence the answer is

$$\mathbb{P}(X|Y) = \frac{2}{7} \times \frac{1}{2} + \frac{4}{7} \times \frac{1}{2} = \frac{3}{7}.$$

Here are some possible related questions:

- What is the probability that the first ball is white given that the second ball is black?
- What is the probability that the first ball is black given that the second ball is black?

□

Solution to Question 3.41. There are obviously many possible solutions, but the easiest one is just to toss the coin twice and repeat if we get one of the four possible outcomes. So we set $HH = 1, HT = 2, TH = 3$ and if we get TT we start again.

To determine the average number of tosses to do this, consider throwing the coin twice as one 'trial'. This trial has a 0.75 probability of success and a 0.25 probability of failure. Then the number of trials (X) until success has a geometric distribution with parameter 0.75 ($\mathbb{P}(X = k) = 0.75 \times 0.25^{k-1}, k = 1, 2, \ldots$). The expectation of this is therefore $4/3$. Since we need two tosses for one trial, the average number of tosses is $8/3$.

Here are some possible related questions:

- Given a coin, how would you simulate a Bernoulli trial with non-equal probability of success and failure, say $p = 0.3$?
- Derive the mean and variance of the geometric distribution.

$\square$

Solution to Question 3.42. After 3 tosses there are 4 possible outcomes for your total points: $-3, -1, 1$ or 3. These correspond to tossing 0, 1, 2 and 3 heads respectively. Denote the total number of heads by X. Then X has a binomial distribution with $N = 3$ and $p = 0.45$, so

$$\mathbb{P}(X = k) = \binom{3}{k} 0.45^k \times 0.55^{3-k}, k = 0, 1, 2, 3.$$

We win if $X = 2$ or $X = 3$, so

$$\mathbb{P}(win) = 0.42525.$$

This gives an expected value of the game of $42.525.

We can generalise to N tosses by simply stating the probability of a win as the sum of the probability of getting strictly more heads than tails, that is

$$\mathbb{P}(win) = \sum_k \binom{N}{k} 0.45^k \times 0.55^{N-k},$$

where the summation is over $k = \lfloor \frac{N}{2} \rfloor + 1$ to N and $\lfloor x \rfloor$ denotes the largest integer not greater than x.

As N increases we can use the normal approximation for the binomial distribution. If $Y \sim Bi(N, p)$ then Y has mean Np and variance $Np(1-p)$, and can be approximated by a normal random variable with the same first moments. The distribution of X is approximated by a normal distribution with mean $0.45N$ and variance $0.45 \times 0.55N$.

Here are some possible related questions:

- What is the variance of your winnings?
- If you were charged \$42 to play the game, would you prefer to play 1 game with the stakes multiplied by 100 or 100 of the original games?
- What is the continuity correction for the normal approximation to the binomial distribution?

□

Solution to Question 3.43. Let X_i denote the value of selection i. Our goal is to determine

$$\mathbb{E}(X_1 + X_2 + X_3) = \mathbb{E}(X_1) + \mathbb{E}(X_2) + \mathbb{E}(X_3).$$

If we draw the three cards at random, there is no reason for the distribution of the third card drawn to be any different from the distribution of the first, each value is equally likely to appear in any draw. So we have

$$\mathbb{E}(X_1 + X_2 + X_3) = 3\mathbb{E}(X_1).$$

Clearly the mean of the first selection, $\mathbb{E}(X_1)$, is 7 (just consider the mean of one suit, since all suits are identical.) So

$$\mathbb{E}(X_1 + X_2 + X_3) = 3\mathbb{E}(X_1) = 21.$$

Here are some possible related questions:

- Does the above reasoning hold for the distribution of each selection X_i if the probability distribution on the sample is not uniform?
- Repeat the question using blackjack values for the jack, queen and king.
- Sketch some pseudo-code to test your results using simulation.

□

Solution to Question 3.44. We will assume the fourth card is drawn from the deck before the card with the lowest value from the original 3 is placed back into the deck. Hence, using the results and notation of the solution to Question 3.43 (and a straight-forward extension to the fourth draw, X_4), we know that the distribution of each of the four draws is identical.

The key to this problem is to think about it in the correct way. An equivalent way of expressing our draws is to say that we draw 4 cards, and take out the card with the least value from the first 3. Using linearity of expectation the problem is then to calculate

$$\mathbb{E}(X_1 + X_2 + X_3 + X_4) - \mathbb{E}(\min(X_1, X_2, X_3)).$$

Again using the solution to Question 3.43 we know the first term is 28. We then need to determine the expectation of the minimum of the first 3 cards, which we will denote by m. We have

$$\mathbb{P}(m \geq k) = (1 - \mathbb{P}(X_1 \leq k - 1))^3 = \left(1 - \frac{k-1}{13}\right)^3.$$

For a discrete non-negative integer random variable Y we also have that $\mathbb{E}(Y) = \sum_{i=1}^{\infty} \mathbb{P}(Y \geq i)$. Hence

$$\mathbb{E}(m) = \sum_{k=1}^{13} \left(1 - \frac{k-1}{13}\right)^3 = \frac{1}{13^3} \sum_{k=1}^{13} k^3 = \frac{1}{13^3} \left(\sum_{k=1}^{13} k\right)^2,$$

from a relationship for squared triangular numbers (also called Nicomachus's theorem). Using $\sum_{i=1}^{n} i = \frac{1}{2}n(n+1)$ we then have

$$\mathbb{E}(m) = \frac{1}{13^3} (13 \times 7)^2 = \frac{49}{13}.$$

Hence the solution to our original problem is $\frac{315}{13}$.

Here are some possible related questions:

- Derive the distribution of the minimum of n i.i.d. random variables.
- What is the expected value if we replace the highest value card?
- Prove Nicomachus's theorem.

□

Solution to Question 3.45. We need to compute

$$\mathbb{E}(X_1 + X_2 + X_3 + X_4) = \mathbb{E}(X_1) + \mathbb{E}(X_2) + \mathbb{E}(X_3) + \mathbb{E}(X_4) = 4\mathbb{E}(X_1).$$

We compute

$$\mathbb{E}(X_1) = \sum_{j=1}^{13} \frac{4}{54} \times j + \frac{2}{54} \times 100,$$

$$= \frac{2}{27} \sum_{j=1}^{13} j + \frac{1}{27} \times 100,$$

$$= \frac{2}{27} \frac{13(13+1)}{2} + \frac{100}{27},$$

$$= \frac{94}{9}.$$

So the answer is

$$\frac{376}{9}.$$

Here are some possible related questions:

- What is the probability of drawing two or more aces in the sample?
- How many ways can you draw 6 red cards from a sample of 10 using a standard 52 card deck?

$\square$

Solution to Question 3.46. Let T be the number of throws. The easiest way to do this one is to use *first step analysis*. If on the first throw we get a six, we are done and $T = 1$. Otherwise, the expected number of more throws needed is the same as it was before. So

$$\mathbb{E}(T) = \frac{1}{6} \times 1 + \frac{5}{6}(1 + \mathbb{E}(T)).$$

We now solve for $\mathbb{E}(T)$. We get

$$6\mathbb{E}(T) = 1 + 5 + 5\mathbb{E}(T).$$

So $\mathbb{E}(T) = 6$.

Here some possible related questions:

- What if the die had n sides?
- How long to get two sixes in a row?
- What else can first step analysis be used for?

☐

Solution to Question 3.47. This one is easy if we throw the dice first. The key is that on a roulette wheel all numbers are equally likely and so have probability $1/38$. This probability will hold for the number already rolled on the dice and so the answer is $1/38$.

Here are some possible related questions:

- Is it possible to skew the odds in your favour at roulette?
- What's the probability of the same number coming up twice in a row at roulette?
- What's the probability of winning if you bet on a colour at roulette?
- If we had two dice of different colours, and regarded one as the first digit of a number and the other as the second, what would the answer then be?

☐

Solution to Question 3.48. They will not collide if and only if they all travel in the same direction. We can compute this probability in two ways. First method: choose one ant, it moves in some direction. What is the probability that the other two move in the same direction as it? This is clearly

$$\left(\frac{1}{2}\right)^2 = \frac{1}{4}.$$

A second way is to observe that there are eight possible configurations and these are all equally likely. In only two of these do all the ants move in the same direction so the answer is $2/8$.

Here are some possible related questions:

- What if we use n ants on a polygon with n sides?

- What if we use n ants on a polygon with k sides with $k > n$?
- What if 8 ants walk along edges of a cube?

□

Solution to Question 3.49. Let p be the probability. Consider the related question of what is the probability that I have more tails than you. This must have the same probability p of occurring if the coin is fair. However, precisely one of the two events must occur since I have one more coin than you. So

$$2p = 1,$$

and the answer is 0.5.

Here are some possible related questions:

- What is the coin is not fair?
- What if I have $N + 2$ coins?
- If I have a dice what is the probability that I roll 6 more often than you with one more throw?

□

Solution to 3.50. The easy way to do this one is to reverse the order. The question is then what is the probability that a blue ball and a green ball are drawn before the first red ball? Note that once we have drawn a ball of a given colour, we can ignore further draws of that colour as not affecting the problem. So once a blue ball has been drawn, we can assume that all blue balls evaporate, and likewise for green. We now proceed under this assumption.

Let F denote the value of the first draw and S the second. Denote the three colours R, G and B. The probability is therefore

$$\mathbb{P}(F = B)\mathbb{P}(S = G|F = B) + \mathbb{P}(F = G)\mathbb{P}(S = B|F = G).$$

This equals

$$\frac{2}{6} \times \frac{3}{4} + \frac{3}{6} \times \frac{2}{3} = \frac{3}{8} + \frac{1}{3} = \frac{17}{24}.$$

Here are some possible related questions:

- How can you formally show that reversing the order works?
- What is the probability that the last 3 balls contain all 3 colours?
- How would the problem change if there was also 40 purple balls?

☐

Solution to Question 3.51. The possible results are

$$HH, HT, TH, TT.$$

Each of these has probability $1/4$. If we have terminated, one of the first three must have occurred. So the probability of HT or TH is

$$\frac{1}{2} \times \frac{1}{\frac{3}{4}} = \frac{2}{3}.$$

Here are some possible related questions:

- What if the pay-off occurs on two heads?
- What if you retoss on one of each and get 1 on 2H and 0 on 2T?
- What if you retoss on HT but not on TH?

☐

Solution to Question 3.52. It is often easier to compute the probability of an event not happening on either day which is the complement of it happening at least once. The probability of no rain is

$$(1 - 0.6)(1 - 0.7) = 0.4 \times 0.3 = 0.12.$$

So the probability of rain is 0.88.

Here are some possible related questions:

- Is the independence assumption reasonable?
- If there is a probability of 0.2 of rain each day, what is the probability of rain in a week?
- If there is 0.5 probability of rain each day and it never rains on both days, what is the probability of rain on the weekend?

- How would you model a derivative that pays off if there is rain on the weekend?
- Do such derivatives exist?

$\square$

Solution to Question 3.53. There are 2^N possible strings. The answer will be the number of valid strings, G_N, divided by this total number.

Simple counting yields that the first few numbers are

$$G_1 = 2, \ G_2 = 3 \ G_3 = 5.$$

Note that we have

$$G_3 = G_2 + G_1.$$

In general, when computing G_N, consider the first toss. If it is a T then the rest of the string can be any combination of $N - 1$ tosses with no HHs in it. There are G_{N-1} such strings. If the first toss is an H, the second one must be a T and the rest of the string is any combination that has no HH in it. There are G_{N-2} such strings. In conclusion,

$$G_N = G_{N-1} + G_{N-2}.$$

If we set

$$G_{-1} = G_0 = 1$$

then the relations holds for all $N > 0$. We recognise G_N as the Fibonacci numbers with a shifted index. So if F_N is the Nth Fibonacci number then the answer is

$$\frac{F_{N+2}}{2^N}.$$

Here are some possible related questions:

- What about no tosses of the form HHH?
- What about no tosses HT?
- If we roll a dice N times what is the probability of never getting six twice in a row?

$\square$

Solution to 3.54. We begin by considering two independent standard Guassian random variables Z_1 and Z_2. We can see that

$$\mathbb{E}[Z_1 + Z_2 | Z_1 + Z_2] = Z_1 + Z_2.$$

Using the additive property of conditional expectation and the symmetry between Z_1 and Z_2, we see that

$$\mathbb{E}[Z_1 | Z_1 + Z_2] = \frac{Z_1 + Z_2}{2}.$$

Extending this a little further, we consider two independent Gaussian random variables

$$W_1 = aZ_1 \sim N(0, a)$$

and

$$W_2 = bZ \sim N(0, b)$$

with non zero a or b. Using the result from above with $W_1 = aZ_1$, we can show that

$$\mathbb{E}[Z_1 | W_1 + W_2] = \frac{W_1 + W_2}{a + b},$$

and since $W_1 \sim aZ_1$, we have

$$\mathbb{E}[W_1 | W_1 + W_2] = \frac{a(W_1 + W_2)}{a + b}.$$

We now return to our original problem and use the usual trick to build two correlated Guassians from independent Gaussians

$$X \sim aZ_1,$$
$$Y \sim b(\rho Z_1 + \sqrt{1 - \rho^2} Z_2).$$

With the results above we can work out that

$$\mathbb{E}[X | 2X + Y] = \frac{a(2X + Y)}{2a + b(\rho + \sqrt{1 - \rho^2})}.$$

We use the same technique to calculate $\mathbb{E}[Y | 2X + Y]$. We then take the difference of the two results and we are done.

Here are some possible related questions:

- Explain how conditional expectation can be used as a method of model parameter estimation.
- What is the tower property of conditional expectation? Explain it.

□

3.3.2. Stochastic processes.

Solution to Question 3.55. It's hard to put a limit on how much detail you can go into for this question (so perhaps ask the interviewer to do so for you). The basic definition of Brownian motion is (see, for example, [6] p. 92) that W_t, $t \geq 0$, is a *Brownian motion* if $W_0 = 0$ and for all $s < t$ we have that $W_t - W_s$ is normally distributed with mean zero and variance $t - s$, and is independent of W_r for $r \leq s$.

This will probably be sufficient for most interviews, however for completeness we go into further detail on what could possibly define Brownian motion.

Equivalent descriptions are given in [18] Theorem 3.3.2. If we consider any $t_0, t_1, \ldots, t_m$, where $0 = t_0 < t_1 < \cdots < t_m$, then:

(1) The increments

$$W_{t_2} - W_{t_1}, W_{t_3} - W_{t_2}, \ldots, W_{t_m} - W_{t_{m-1}}$$

are independent and the distribution of $W_{t_j} - W_{t_{j-1}}$ is given by

$$W_{t_j} - W_{t_{j-1}} \sim N(0, t_j - t_{j-1}).$$

(2) $W_{t_1}, W_{t_2}, \ldots, W_{t_m}$ are jointly normally distributed random variables with zero mean and covariance matrix

$$\begin{bmatrix} t_1 & t_1 & \cdots & t_1 \\ t_1 & t_2 & \cdots & t_2 \\ \vdots & \vdots & \vdots & \vdots \\ t_1 & t_2 & \cdots & t_m \end{bmatrix}.$$

(3) $W_{t_1}, W_{t_2}, \ldots, W_{t_m}$ have the joint moment-generating function

$$\theta(u_1, u_2, \ldots u_m)$$
$$= \exp\left\{\frac{1}{2}(u_1 + u_2 + \cdots u_m)^2 t_1 + \frac{1}{2}(u_2 + u_3 + \cdots u_m)^2(t_2 - t_1) + \right.$$
$$\left. \cdots + \frac{1}{2}u_m^2(t_m - t_{m-1})\right\}.$$

One way to arrive at a Brownian motion is as a limit of a scaled random walk (see, for example, [18] pp. 83–94). To this end, consider a sequence of coin tosses, and define

$$X_j := \begin{cases} 1 & \text{if the } j\text{th toss is a head,} \\ -1 & \text{if the } j\text{th toss is a tail.} \end{cases}$$

Then define $M_0 = 0$ and for $k = 1, 2, \ldots$

$$M_k = \sum_{j=1}^{k} X_j.$$

This is a random walk, which moves up or down by one for each unit time step. To approximate Brownian motion, we need to speed up time and decrease the distance of each step. Define

$$W_t^{(n)} = \frac{1}{\sqrt{n}} M_{nt},$$

for integer nt, and for non-integer value of nt interpolate linearly between the nearest integer points. As we let $n \to \infty$ we obtain a Brownian motion. Even before this passage to the limit, the scaled random walk has most of the properties of a Brownian motion (check): if we choose s and t such that $0 \leq s \leq t$ and ns and nt are integers then

$$\mathbb{E}\left(W_t^{(n)} - W_s^{(n)}\right) = 0,$$
$$\text{Var}\left(W_t^{(n)} - W_s^{(n)}\right) = t - s,$$

and the quadratic variation (see Question 3.69) of $W_t^{(n)}$ is t.

What are some other interesting properties of Brownian motion? Unlike our scaled random walk, which was linear where we interpolated, Brownian motion is infinitely jagged and has no linear pieces. Related to this is that it is continuous everywhere, but nowhere differentiable. Also, if Brownian motion crosses a level α, then it crosses it infinitely many times in an arbitrarily short interval. (Recall that these properties are said to hold *almost surely*.)

For a bit of history, Brownian motion is named after the botanist Robert Brown, who is regarded as having discovered it in 1827. Brown observed the movement of pollen particles floating in water under a microscope was quite jittery.

Finally, in higher dimensions we define the k-dimensional Brownian motion to be a vector of k independent Brownian motions.

Here are some possible related questions:

- What is a diffusion process?
- Why is Brownian motion useful in finance?

□

Solution to Question 3.56. The crucial observation is that our location is a martingale. Our expected position at any time in the future is our current position. This extends to our current position at a random time provided the random time is a stopping time with finite expectation: this is the optional sampling theorem.

Let X_t be the value at time t. It is a martingale. The time of first hitting the boundary, τ, is a stopping time with finite expectation. So X_t stopped at τ is a martingale. Its expected value is therefore X_0.

Let p the probability of hitting 1000. The expected value at stopping is then

$$1000p.$$

If we start at 80, we immediately have

$$p = 8/100,$$

and the probability of hitting zero first is

$$92/100.$$

(Note: make sure to answer the question asked: the probability of hitting zero.)

To be totally correct we really need to show that the stopping time has finite expectation and so the theorem applies.

The best reference for these sorts of problems is [21].

Here are some possible related questions:

- Solve the general case: we start at k and terminate at 0 or L.
- What if the probability of an up-move is $q \in (0,1)$ instead of 0.5?

□

Solution to Question 3.57. Once we recall the stochastic differential equation for a log-normal Brownian motion, the solution to this question follows immediately from Itô's formula. Recall that if S_t follows a log-normal Brownian motion, then

$$dS_t = \mu S_t dt + \sigma S_t dW_t,$$

for $\mu, \sigma > 0$ and a Brownian motion W_t. To find the process for the square of S_t, let $Y_t = f(S_t)$, where $f(x) = x^2$, and so

$$
\begin{aligned}
d(S_t)^2 = dY_t &= f'(S_t)dS_t + \frac{1}{2}f''(S_t)(dS_t)^2 \\
&= 2S_t dS_t + (dS_t)^2 \\
&= 2\mu(S_t)^2 dt + 2\sigma(S_t)^2 dW_t + \sigma^2(S_t)^2 dt \\
&= (2\mu + \sigma^2)Y_t dt + 2\sigma Y_t dW_t.
\end{aligned}
$$

Notice that this means Y_t is also a log-normal Brownian motion. The process S_t has drift parameter μ and diffusion σ, while the process $(S_t)^2$ has drift parameter $(2\mu + \sigma^2)$ and diffusion 2σ.

The above derivation is the typical way to proceed when faced with this sort of question. However, since we know the exact form of the solution of S_t there is a quicker, and perhaps more intuitive, way to derive the same result. The solution of the stochastic differential equation

$$dS_t = \mu S_t dt + \sigma S_t dW_t,$$

is given by

$$S_t = S_0 \exp\left\{ \left(\mu - \frac{\sigma^2}{2}\right)t + \sigma W_t \right\}$$

(verify this using Itô's formula). From this, it is clear that

$$(S_t)^2 = S_0^2 \exp\left\{\left(2\mu - \sigma^2\right)t + 2\sigma W_t\right\},$$

which immediately shows that $(S_t)^2$ is a log-normal Brownian motion with the mentioned parameters.

Here are some possible related questions:

- Without further work, write down the stochastic differential equation for $(S_t)^k$, for positive integer k.
- If R_t is a d-dimensional (for integer d) Bessel process, that is

$$dR_t = \frac{d-1}{2R_t}dt + dW_t,$$

  what process does the square of R_t follow? Derive this in two ways – first by applying Itô's formula to the above stochastic differential equation, and secondly by starting with the definition of the Bessel process as the distance from the origin of a d-dimensional Brownian motion (see the extension questions for Question 3.64).

□

Solution to Question 3.58. The price still satisfies the Black–Scholes equation. To see this, check the derivation of the Black–Scholes equation. You will notice that the form of the payoff is not important, instead it is only important that the option price is a function of the current time and stock price. Hence for any claim whose payoff satisfies this condition, the price will satisfy the Black–Scholes equation, and the only things that will change are the boundary conditions.

It is very easy to go badly wrong on this sort of question: a very important fact to remember is that S_t^2 is NOT the price process of a traded asset; we cannot treat it the same way we treat S_t in the derivation of the Black–Scholes equation. In particular, S_t^2 will not have drift r in the risk-neutral measure.

Here is a possible related question:

- What about S_T^3?
- Is it possible to have a contract that is *always* worth $\log S_t$?
- What is the process of S_t^2 in the risk-neutral measure?

- What is the process of S_t^3 in the risk-neutral measure?
- What is the process of S_t^2 in the stock measure?

□

Solution to Question 3.59. This process is a *mean-reverting* process. Why? If the stock price is above μ, then the drift term will be negative, making the trend of the process downwards, and toward the level μ. If the stock price is below μ, the drift term is positive and the process again moves toward μ. Thus whatever level the process is at, the general trend is to head back to the level μ, and we call this trait mean reversion (with mean level μ). The size of the parameter α affects the size of the drift when the stock price is a given level away from the mean μ. Thus it affects the rate of the mean reversion.

The drift term of the process has no impact on the price of a call option, since we know that under the correct pricing measure we need the discounted stock price to have zero drift. This is achieved by changing the drift of the original process, rendering any initial drift term irrelevant.

Here are some possible related questions:

- What stochastic differential equation does the process $X_t = S_t^2$ follow?
- For the geometric Brownian motion process Y_t following the stochastic differential equation

$$dY_t = \mu Y_t dt + \sigma Y_t dW_t,$$

  what effect do the parameters μ and σ have?
- The Bessel process R_t of dimension 3 follows the stochastic differential equation

$$dR_t = \frac{1}{R_t} dt + dW_t,$$

  and starts at a position $R_0 = x > 0$. Explain what characteristics mean that this process can never be negative.

□

Solution to Question 3.60. This is a straight-forward application of Itô's formula. Let $X_t = f(S_t)$, where $f(x) = \log(x)$. Then

$$
\begin{aligned}
dX_t &= \left.\frac{\partial f}{\partial x}\right|_{x=S_t}(dS_t) + \frac{1}{2}\left.\frac{\partial^2 f}{\partial x^2}\right|_{x=S_t}(dS_t)^2 \\
&= \frac{1}{S_t}(\mu S_t dt + \sigma S_t dW_t) - \frac{1}{2S_t^2}(\sigma^2 S_t^2 dt) \\
&= \mu dt + \sigma dW_t - \frac{\sigma^2}{2}dt \\
&= \left(\mu - \frac{\sigma^2}{2}\right)dt + \sigma dW_t.
\end{aligned}
$$

The alternative is to realise

$$
S_t = S_0 \exp\left\{\left(\mu - \frac{\sigma^2}{2}\right)t + \sigma W_t\right\},
$$

so

$$
X_t = \log S_0 + \left(\mu - \frac{\sigma^2}{2}\right)t + \sigma W_t,
$$

from which the solution is obvious.

Here are some possible related questions:

- Given the above result, write down the solution of X_t, and hence S_t.
- What is the SDE for $(S_t)^2$?

$\square$

Solution to Question 3.61. Odds are the interviewer wants you to show X_t is a process with zero drift component, by a simple application of Itô's formula. There are some more technical aspects to the question, but we'll ignore those for the moment and just address this issue.

To show X_t has zero drift, we calculate its stochastic differential equation. We have $X_t = g(t, W_t)$, where

$$
g(t, x) = \cosh(\lambda x)\exp(-\lambda^2 t/2).
$$

This gives

$$\frac{\partial g}{\partial t} = -\frac{\lambda^2}{2}g(t,x),$$

$$\frac{\partial g}{\partial x} = \lambda \sinh(\lambda x)\exp(-\lambda^2 t/2),$$

and

$$\frac{\partial^2 g}{\partial x^2} = \lambda^2 \cosh(\lambda x)\exp(-\lambda^2 t/2).$$

Applying Itô's formula we find

$$dX_t = dg(t,W_t)$$

$$= g_t(t,W_t)dt + g_x(t,x)|_{x=W_t}dW_t + \frac{1}{2}g_{xx}(t,x)|_{x=W_t}(dW_t)^2$$

$$= -\frac{\lambda^2}{2}X_t dt + \lambda \sinh(\lambda W_t)\exp(-\lambda^2 t/2)dW_t + \frac{\lambda^2}{2}X_t dt$$

$$= \lambda \sinh(\lambda W_t)\exp(-\lambda^2 t/2)dW_t,$$

which shows X_t is a process with zero drift (all of the 'dt' terms canceled). Hopefully, this is all that is required of you from this question.

However technically this is not the complete story, and we address the additional requirement here. If X_t is a martingale, it must satisfy the properties

(1) $\mathbb{E}(X_s|\mathcal{F}_t) = X_t$,
(2) $\mathbb{E}(|X_t|) < \infty$ for all t,

where $\mathcal{F}_t$ is the filtration generated by the Brownian motion W_t. These are known to be satisfied (see for example [12] p.33) if

$$X_t = X_0 + \int_0^t f(t,W_t)dW_t,$$

and

$$\mathbb{E}\left(\int_0^T f(t,W_t)^2 dt\right) < \infty.$$

We have already seen X_t satisfies

$$X_t = X_0 + \int_0^t f(t,W_t)dW_t,$$

where $f(t, W_t) = \lambda \sinh(\lambda W_t) \exp(-\lambda^2 t/2)$. We need to confirm the second condition. Substituting the expression for $f(t, W_t)$ we see

$$\mathbb{E}\left(\int_0^T f(t, W_t)^2 dt\right) = \frac{\lambda^2}{4}\mathbb{E}\left(\int_0^T \left(e^{2\lambda W_t} - 2 + e^{-2\lambda W_t}\right)e^{-\lambda^2 t}dt\right)$$

$$\leq \frac{\lambda^2}{4}\int_0^T \mathbb{E}\left(e^{2\lambda W_t} + e^{-2\lambda W_t}\right)dt$$

$$= \frac{\lambda^2}{4}\int_0^T 2e^{2t\lambda^2}dt,$$

using the result from Question 3.37. Evaluating this integral confirms the required condition, and we are done.

Here are some possible related questions:

- Show that the following processes are martingales:
  (1) $X_t = W_t^2 - t$;
  (2) $Y_t = W_t^3 - 3tW_t$;
  (3) $Z_t = \exp\left(\sigma W_t - \frac{1}{2}\sigma^2 t\right)$.

$\square$

Solution to Question 3.62. There are some further technical considerations, but in general if such a process is a martingale then the stochastic differential equation it satisfies will only have a diffusion (dW_t) term. The technical considerations are only necessary if this condition is satisfied, so we begin by applying Itô's formula to

$$X_t = W_t^3.$$

This gives

$$dX_t = 3W_t^2 dW_t + 3W_t(dW_t)^2$$

$$= 3W_t dt + 3W_t^2 dW_t.$$

Since there is a drift term $(3W_t)$ we can conclude that W_t^3 is not a martingale.

Here are some possible related questions:

- What other condition do you need to check if the process has zero drift?
- Write down two simple martingales involving Brownian motion.

- Show that $W_t^2 - t$ is a martingale, both by the method used here and the 'standard' method (that is, show $\mathbb{E}[W_t^2 - t|\mathcal{F}_s] = W_s^2 - s, s < t$).
- Is any power of Brownian motion a martingale?
- How could you make W_t^3 into a martingale?

□

Solution to Question 3.63. To apply Itô's lemma, we first need to determine first and second derivatives of the function $f(x) = 2^x$. This is straightforward once you observe

$$f(x) = 2^x = e^{x \log 2}.$$

From here, it is clear we have

$$f'(x) = \log(2)e^{x \log 2} = \log(2)2^x,$$
$$f''(x) = (\log(2))^2 e^{x \log 2} = (\log(2))^2 2^x.$$

If we set $Y_t = 2^{W_t}$, this immediately gives

$$dY_t = \log(2)2^{W_t}dW_t + \frac{1}{2}(\log(2))^2 2^{W_t}(dW_t)^2$$
$$= \log(2)Y_t dW_t + \frac{1}{2}(\log(2))^2 Y_t dt.$$

Since the stochastic differential equation for Y_t has a non-zero drift term, the process cannot be a martingale.

Here are some possible related questions:

- Define a new process by $X_t = 2^{W_t}g(W_t)$. Prove that in order for X_t to be a martingale, it is necessary for the function g to satisfy

$$(\log(2))^2 g(x) + 2\log(2)g'(x) + g''(x) = 0.$$

- Can you explain in words why 2^{W_t} will not be a martingale?

□

Solution to Question 3.64. Each of W_t and Z_t are distributed normally with mean zero and variance t. Hence we can simplify the first part of this question by considering the case $t = 1$, the general case is a straight-forward extension.

Each of W_1 and Z_1 are normally distributed random variables with mean zero and variance one which we denote by W and Z respectively.

We begin by conditioning on the value of Z in the expression for the distribution of the ratio:

$$
\begin{aligned}
\mathbb{P}\left(\frac{W}{Z} \leq u\right) &= \int_{-\infty}^{\infty} \mathbb{P}\left(\frac{W}{Z} \leq u \middle| Z = z\right) \mathbb{P}(Z \in dz) \\
&= \int_{-\infty}^{0} \mathbb{P}\left(W \geq zu\right) \mathbb{P}(Z \in dz) + \int_{0}^{\infty} \mathbb{P}\left(W \leq zu\right) \mathbb{P}(Z \in dz) \\
&= \int_{-\infty}^{0} \left(1 - \mathbb{P}\left(W \leq zu\right)\right) \mathbb{P}(Z \in dz) \\
&\quad + \int_{0}^{\infty} \mathbb{P}\left(W \leq zu\right) \mathbb{P}(Z \in dz).
\end{aligned}
$$

We then differentiate the above expression with respect to u to find the probability density function for the ratio, denoting the density of W by ϕ,

$$
\begin{aligned}
\mathbb{P}\left(\frac{W}{Z} \in du\right) &= \int_{-\infty}^{0} -z\phi(zu)\mathbb{P}(Z \in dz) \\
&\quad + \int_{0}^{\infty} z\phi(zu)\mathbb{P}(Z \in dz) \\
&= \int_{-\infty}^{\infty} |z|\phi(zu)\mathbb{P}(Z \in dz).
\end{aligned}
$$

This final expression, which gives the density of a ratio of two independent random variables as an integral of their densities, is often (unimaginatively) called the *ratio distribution*. From here we use the form of ϕ,

$$
\begin{aligned}
\mathbb{P}\left(\frac{W}{Z} \in du\right) &= \frac{1}{2\pi} \int_{-\infty}^{\infty} |z| \exp\left\{-\frac{(zu)^2}{2} - \frac{z^2}{2}\right\} dz \\
&= \frac{1}{\pi} \int_{0}^{\infty} z \exp\left\{-\frac{(zu)^2}{2} - \frac{z^2}{2}\right\} dz \\
&= \frac{1}{\pi} \int_{0}^{\infty} z \exp\left\{-z^2 \left(\frac{u^2}{2} + \frac{1}{2}\right)\right\} dz,
\end{aligned}
$$

the second equality due to the even integrand. We then use the observation that for $c > 0$,

$$\int_0^\infty z e^{-cz^2} dz = \int_0^\infty \frac{1}{2} e^{-cy} dy$$

$$= \frac{-1}{2c} \left[e^{-cy} \right]_0^\infty = \frac{1}{2c}.$$

This gives

$$\mathbb{P}\left(\frac{W}{Z} \in du \right) = \frac{1}{\pi} \frac{1}{u^2 + 1}.$$

Thus we have that $\frac{W}{Z}$ has a standard Cauchy distribution.

The second part of this question is answered by using the product rule for stochastic processes: the differential of the product of two stochastic processes is given by

$$d(X_t Y_t) = X_t dY_t + Y_t dX_t + dX_t dY_t.$$

Before we can apply this rule we need to deduce the differential for $(Z_t)^{-1}$. Using Itô's formula for $f(Z_t)$, where $f(x) = x^{-1}$ gives

$$df(Z_t) = f'(Z_t) dZ_t + \frac{1}{2} f''(Z_t)(dZ_t)^2$$

$$= -\frac{1}{Z_t^2} dZ_t + \frac{1}{Z_t^3} dt.$$

Then, applying the product rule to $\frac{W_t}{Z_t} = W_t(Z_t)^{-1}$, we obtain

$$d\left(\frac{W_t}{Z_t} \right) = \frac{1}{Z_t} dW_t + W_t d\left(\frac{1}{Z_t} \right) + dW_t d\left(\frac{1}{Z_t} \right)$$

$$= \frac{1}{Z_t} dW_t + W_t \left(-\frac{1}{Z_t^2} dZ_t + \frac{1}{Z_t^3} dt \right)$$

$$+ dW_t \left(-\frac{1}{Z_t^2} dZ_t + \frac{1}{Z_t^3} dt \right)$$

$$= \frac{1}{Z_t} dW_t - \frac{W_t}{Z_t^2} dZ_t + \frac{W_t}{Z_t^3} dt,$$

using $dZ_t dW_t = 0$ since the two Brownian motions are independent.

Here are some possible related questions:

- Prove the first part of the question for general t.

- If instead we are concerned with the product $W_t Z_t$, derive the equivalent of the ratio distribution.
- Repeat the second question assuming W_t and Z_t have correlation ρ, that is

$$dW_t dZ_t = \rho dt.$$

What happens as $\rho \to 1$?

- (Bessel processes). Let $W_t^1, \ldots, W_t^d$ be independent Brownian motions. Define

$$R_t = \sqrt{\left(W_t^1\right)^2 + \cdots + \left(W_t^d\right)^2}.$$

Show that R_t satisfies the stochastic differential equation

$$dR_t = \frac{d-1}{2R_t}dt + dW_t,$$

for some Brownian motion W_t.

□

Solution to Question 3.65. The most general form of the Ornstein-Uhlenbeck process is the mean-reverting process evolving according to the SDE

$$dX_t = \theta(\mu - X_t)dt + \sigma dW_t.$$

The SDE is solved by introducing the integrating factor $e^{\theta t}$, and evaluating the differential $d\left(e^{\theta t}X_t\right)$:

$$\begin{aligned}
d\left(e^{\theta t}X_t\right) &= \theta e^{\theta t}X_t dt + e^{\theta t}dX_t \\
&= \theta e^{\theta t}X_t dt + e^{\theta t}\theta(\mu - X_t)dt + e^{\theta t}\sigma dW_t \\
&= e^{\theta t}\theta\mu dt + e^{\theta t}\sigma dW_t.
\end{aligned}$$

The stochastic differential written above is just shorthand for the equation

$$e^{\theta t}X_t = X_0 + \int_0^t \theta\mu e^{\theta s}ds + \int_0^t e^{\theta s}\sigma dW_s,$$

and evaluating the first integral gives the solution

$$X_t = X_0 e^{-\theta t} + \mu\left(1 - e^{-\theta t}\right) + \int_0^t \sigma e^{\theta(s-t)}dW_s.$$

Here are some possible related questions:

- Show that $\mathbb{E}(X_t) = X_0 e^{-\theta t} + \mu(1 - e^{-\theta t})$.
- Show that $\mathrm{Var}(X_t) = \mathbb{E}(X_t^2) - (\mathbb{E}(X_t))^2 = \frac{\sigma^2}{2\theta}(1 - e^{-2\theta t})$.

$\square$

Solution to Question 3.66. This question uses one of the most frequently used and simplest tricks in mathematics: $x = x + y - y$. We assume without loss of generality that $s \leq t$. One of the important properties of Brownian motion is independence of increments: for any $t_1 \leq t_2 \leq t_3$, $W_{t_2} - W_{t_1}$ is independent of $W_{t_3} - W_{t_2}$. Then:

$$\mathbb{E}(W_s W_t) = \mathbb{E}\left(W_s(W_s + (W_t - W_s))\right)$$
$$= \mathbb{E}\left(W_s^2\right) + \mathbb{E}\left(W_s(W_t - W_s)\right)$$
$$= s + \mathbb{E}(W_s)\mathbb{E}(W_t - W_s),$$

where the final line uses the independence of increments. Since $W_{t_2} - W_{t_1}$ is normally distributed with mean zero

$$\mathbb{E}(W_s W_t) = s.$$

Given that we initially assumed $s \leq t$, we conclude

$$\mathbb{E}(W_s W_t) = \min(s, t).$$

Here is a possible related question:

- What is $\mathbb{E}\left(\exp\{\lambda W_t\}\right)$?

$\square$

Solution to Question 3.67. The crucial aspect of such problems is to think about the symmetries. Here we have two time steps of equal length. The distribution of $X(2) - X(1)$ is equal to that of $X(1) - X(0)$ and it is a Brownian motion, so they are independent.

We must have that the sign of $X(2) - X(1)$ is negative which occurs with probability $1/2$. We must also have that

$$|X(2) - X(1)| > |X(1)| = |X(1) - X(0)|.$$

Since they have the same distribution, this occurs with probability $1/2$, and the answer is $1/4$.

Here are some possible related questions:

- What properties of Brownian motion make this answer work?
- If a Brownian motion starts at zero, what is the probability that it is positive at both time 1 and 2?

$\square$

Solution to Question 3.68. The question asks us to calculate the conditional probability density

$$\mathbb{P}(W_s \in dy | W_t = x),$$

with $W_0 = 0$. We proceed in the usual way when dealing with conditional probabilities, that is we write the above as

$$\mathbb{P}(W_s \in dy | W_t = x) = \frac{\mathbb{P}(W_s \in dy, W_t \in dx)}{\mathbb{P}(W_t \in dx)}.$$

We are familiar with probabilities for Brownian motion if we are moving forward, for example we know $\mathbb{P}(W_s \in dx | W_u = y)$, by the independence of increments for Brownian motion. We therefore try to express the above in this way, continuing from the above:

$$\mathbb{P}(W_s \in dy | W_t = x) = \frac{\mathbb{P}(W_s \in dy)\mathbb{P}(W_t \in dx | W_s = y)}{\mathbb{P}(W_t \in dx)}.$$

As mentioned, we know

$$\mathbb{P}(W_t \in dx | W_s = y) = \frac{1}{\sqrt{2\pi(t-s)}} \exp\left\{-\frac{(x-y)^2}{2(t-s)}\right\} dx,$$

hence

$$\mathbb{P}(W_s \in dy | W_t = x) = \frac{1}{\sqrt{2\pi s}} \exp\left\{-\frac{y^2}{2s}\right\} \frac{1}{\sqrt{2\pi(t-s)}} \exp\left\{-\frac{(x-y)^2}{2(t-s)}\right\}$$

$$\times \sqrt{2\pi t} \exp\left\{\frac{x^2}{2t}\right\}$$

$$= t\frac{1}{\sqrt{2\pi ts(t-s)}} \exp\left\{-\frac{(yt-sx)^2}{ts(t-s)}\right\}.$$

This shows that W_s is normally distributed with mean $(s/t)W_t$ and variance $s(t-s)$.

Here are some possible related questions:

- Suppose the original Brownian motion has drift μ, then what is the distribution of W_s?
- Generalise this to a Brownian motion constrained such that $W_0 = z$.
- Derive the stochastic differential equation that is satisfied by the Brownian bridge process?

$\square$

Solution to Question 3.69. The interviewer is looking for evidence you understand the fundamental relations in stochastic calculus. The statement $dt = (dW_t)^2$ expresses the idea that the square of increments of Brownian motion are sizable even in the limit, so that when doing Taylor expansion they cannot be discarded.

We begin by considering the statement as a statement related to the informal derivation of Itô's lemma using a Taylor series expansion (see e.g. [5] pp. 243-244). If we consider the non-random function $F(x)$, then the Taylor series for a small change in F, ΔF, is given by

$$\Delta F = \frac{dF}{dx}\Delta x + \frac{1}{2}\frac{d^2 F}{dx^2}(\Delta x)^2 + \cdots$$

In the limit as $\Delta x \to 0$, all terms of order greater than Δx can be ignored and we get the (rather obvious) differential for F,

$$dF = \frac{dF}{dx}dx.$$

Now let X_t satisfy the stochastic differential equation

$$dX_t = \mu(t, X_t)dt + \sigma(t, X_t)dW_t,$$

and consider the function $F(X_t)$. We proceed as above, and have the same Taylor series for a small change in F,

$$\Delta F = \frac{dF}{dx}\Delta X_t + \frac{1}{2}\frac{d^2 F}{dx^2}(\Delta X_t)^2 + \cdots$$

Dropping the arguments for μ and σ, we can write a discrete version of the differential for X_t,

$$\Delta X_t = \mu\Delta t + \sigma Z\sqrt{\Delta t},$$

where Z is a standard normal random variable. This implies that

$$(\Delta X_t)^2 = \sigma^2 Z^2\Delta t + \cdots,$$

where the extra terms are of order great than Δt. Since $\mathbb{E}(Z^2) = 1$ and it can be shown (see below) that the variance of $Z^2\Delta t$ approaches zero as Δt goes to zero, as we move to the limit as $\Delta \to 0$ the $Z^2\Delta t$ term becomes constant at Δt. This is essentially what is meant by the statement: the contribution in the expansion from the square of small changes in W_t is like a small change in t.

Another way of viewing the statement is that it is an informal way of saying (see, for example, [18] pp. 101– 105):

The quadratic variation of Brownian motion grows at the rate one per unit time.

What does this mean? The quadratic variation of a function $f(t)$ over the interval $0 \le t \le T$ is defined as

$$[f, f](T) = \lim_{||\Pi||\to 0} \sum_{j=0}^{n-1}[f(t_{j+1}) - f(t_j)]^2,$$

where $0 = t_0 < t_1 < \cdots < t_n = T$, $\Pi = \{t_0, t_1, \ldots, t_n\}$ and $||\Pi|| = \max_{j=0,\ldots,n-1}(t_{j+1} - t_j)$ is the largest of the partitions. For any two functions f, g, we can define the *cross-variation* via

$$[f, g](T) = \lim_{||\Pi||\to 0} \sum_{j=0}^{n-1}(f(t_{j+1}) - f(t_j))(g(t_{j+1}) - g(t_j)).$$

For a function f with a continuous derivative, the quadratic variation $[f, f](T)$ is zero, so the quadratic variation is not usually considered in ordinary calculus. However with probability 1, Brownian motion is nowhere differentiable and the quadratic variation is important.

Our original statement can be rephrased as $[W, W](T) = T$. We have to be a little careful in that with the standard definition of quadratic variation, this statement is NOT true. It is true, however, if we restrict to certain partitions, for a detailed discussion see [16], page 21.

We prove a related result that the expectation of the variation across a partition is always t and that the variance goes to zero as the size of the partition goes to zero. Let

$$H_\Pi = \sum_{j=0}^{n-1}(W_{t_{j+1}} - W_{t_j})^2,$$

for a partition Π.

This is clearly a random variable, and our goal is to show this converges to a random variable with mean T and zero variance as $||\Pi|| \to 0$. By the properties of Brownian motion, we have

$$\mathbb{E}\left((W_{t_{j+1}} - W_{t_j})^2\right) = t_{j+1} - t_j,$$

and so

$$\mathbb{E}\left(H_\Pi\right) = T$$

as desired. The centralised fourth moment of a random variable with a $N(\mu, \sigma)$ distribution is $3\sigma^2$. This gives

$$\begin{aligned}
\mathrm{Var}\left((W_{t_{j+1}} - W_{t_j})^2\right) =& \mathbb{E}\left(\left((W_{t_{j+1}} - W_{t_j})^2 - (t_{j+1} - t_j)\right)^2\right) \\
=& \mathbb{E}\left((W_{t_{j+1}} - W_{t_j})^4\right) \\
& - 2(t_{j+1} - t_j)\mathbb{E}\left((W_{t_{j+1}} - W_{t_j})^2\right) + (t_{j+1} - t_j)^2 \\
=& 2(t_{j+1} - t_j)^2.
\end{aligned}$$

Combining gives

$$\text{Var}\left(H_\Pi\right) = \sum_{j=0}^{n-1} 2(t_{j+1} - t_j)^2$$

$$\leq \sum_{j=0}^{n-1} 2||\Pi||(t_{j+1} - t_j)$$

$$= 2||\Pi||T,$$

which converges to zero as $||\Pi|| \to 0$.

Here are some possible related questions:

- Show that for a $N(0, \sigma)$ random variable the third moment is zero and the fourth is $3\sigma^2$.
- Use the same ideas to show $[W, t](T) = 0$ and $[t, t](T) = 0$. How do we typically record these facts?
- Show that the first variation of Brownian motion, defined as

$$\sum_{j=0}^{n-1} |W_{t_{j+1}} - W_{t_j}|,$$

as the maximum partition interval approaches zero, is infinite.
- Show that a continuously differentiable function f has zero quadratic variation.
- Show that a continuous function with finite first variation has zero quadratic variation on an interval $[0, T]$.

$\square$

Solution to Question 3.70. Potentially, this is a very involved question with much high-level mathematics in stochastic theory. However the interviewer is probably not interested in these details, and so we present here an informal version of the proof of Itô's lemma.

We begin by giving a statement of the lemma. Let X_t be an Itô process satisfying the stochastic differential equation

$$dX_t = \mu(t, X_t)dt + \sigma(t, X_t)dW_t,$$

where W_t is a Brownian motion or Wiener process. Let $f(t, x)$ be a function which has a continuous first derivative in t and a continuous second derivative in x (note this can be extended to functions with an absolutely continuous second derivative). Then the stochastic differential equation for the process $Y_t = f(t, X_t)$ is given by

$$(3.1) \qquad dY_t = \frac{\partial f}{\partial t}(t, X_t)dt + \frac{\partial f}{\partial x}(t, X_t)dX_t + \frac{1}{2}\frac{\partial^2 f}{\partial x^2}(t, X_t)(dX_t)^2.$$

Using the rules of stochastic calculus

$$(dW_t)^2 = dt, \qquad (dt)^2 = dW_t dt = 0,$$

this becomes

$$dY_t = \left(\frac{\partial f}{\partial t}(t, X_t) + \mu(t, X_t)\frac{\partial f}{\partial x}(t, X_t) + \frac{1}{2}\sigma^2(t, X_t)\frac{\partial^2 f}{\partial x^2}(t, X_t)\right) dt$$
$$+ \sigma(t, X_t)\frac{\partial f}{\partial x}(t, X_t)dW_t.$$

We proceed to answer the question by giving an informal derivation of the proof of this statement, using Taylor's theorem. The arguments of the functions have been dropped for clarity. Writing $f(t, x)$ as its Taylor series in t and x gives

$$df = \frac{\partial f}{\partial t}dt + \frac{\partial f}{\partial x}dx + \frac{1}{2}\frac{\partial^2 f}{\partial x^2}(dx)^2 + \mathcal{O}\left((dt)^2\right) + \mathcal{O}\left((dx)^3\right).$$

We then replace the dx terms with the differential for X_t, noting that this will result in the higher order terms being zero according to the rules of stochastic calculus mentioned above. This immediately gives the result stated in (3.1).

The interviewer is likely to ask for justifications of the rules of stochastic calculus. See Question 3.69 for more discussion of these.

As mentioned this 'proof' omits many details of a more technical nature, however it does give a flavour of the idea which is probably what the interviewer is looking for. For more detail, see [12] Section 4.1 or [6] Chapter 5.

Here are some possible related questions:

- What is the Itô isometry? Prove that the relationship holds for piece-wise constant functions and continuous functions.
- What are some other properties of the Itô integral?

□

Solution to Question 3.71. The Poisson process has independent increments, that is the distribution of $N_{t_3} - N_{t_2}$ is independent of N_{t_1} for all $0 \le t_1 \le t_2 \le t_3$. We can write

$$\mathbb{E}\left(N_{t_2}|N_{t_1} = k\right) = \mathbb{E}\left(N_{t_2} - N_{t_1} + N_{t_1}|N_{t_1} = k\right)$$
$$= \mathbb{E}\left(N_{t_2} - N_{t_1}|N_{t_1} = k\right) + \mathbb{E}\left(N_{t_1}|N_{t_1} = k\right).$$

The second term is clearly k and we can use the independence of increments to write the first term as $\mathbb{E}\left(N_{t_2} - N_{t_1}\right)$. Since the increment between t_n and t_{n-1} ($t_n \ge t_{n-1}$) of a Poisson process with parameter λ has a Poisson distribution with parameter $\lambda(t_n - t_{n-1})$ we have

$$\mathbb{E}\left(N_{t_2}|N_{t_1} = k\right) = \lambda(t_2 - t_1) + k.$$

Here are some possible related questions:

- Derive the mean and variance of the Poisson process from first principles.
- What is a non-homogeneous Poisson process? What is its expectation at time t?
- Repeat the original question if $0 < t_2 < t_1$.

$\square$

Solution to Question 3.72. There are at least two ways to approach this problem.

The first is generally applicable to sums or products of random variables with given distributions. We are interested in the distribution of $X + Y$. Begin by conditioning on the value of Y:

$$\mathbb{P}(X + Y = n) = \sum_{k=0}^{n} \mathbb{P}(X + Y = n|Y = k)\mathbb{P}(Y = k)$$
$$= \sum_{k=0}^{n} \mathbb{P}(X = n - k)\mathbb{P}(Y = k),$$

where the limits of the summation are determined by the range of values X and Y can take (here each of X and Y is a non-negative integer). Using the probability distribution function of the Poisson random variable gives

$$\mathbb{P}(X + Y = n) = \sum_{k=0}^{n} \frac{e^{-\lambda}\lambda^k}{k!} \frac{e^{-\mu}\mu^{n-k}}{(n-k)!}.$$

At this point you hopefully recognise that this is starting to look like another Poisson distribution function, and manipulate the summation accordingly:

$$\mathbb{P}(X + Y = n) = \frac{e^{-(\mu+\lambda)}}{n!} \sum_{k=0}^{n} \frac{n!\lambda^k\mu^{n-k}}{k!(n-k)!}$$

$$= \frac{e^{-(\mu+\lambda)}}{n!} \sum_{k=0}^{n} \binom{n}{k} \lambda^k\mu^{n-k}$$

$$= \frac{e^{-(\mu+\lambda)}}{n!}(\lambda+\mu)^n.$$

From here it is clear that $X + Y$ also has a Poisson distribution, with parameter $\lambda + \mu$.

The second approach uses probability generating functions (PGFs). The PGF of a discrete random variable V taking values in the non-negative integers is given by $G(z) = \mathbb{E}(z^V)$. Hence the PGF of a Poisson random variable with parameter λ is given by $G_\lambda(z) = \exp(\lambda(z - 1))$. In addition, the sum of two random variables has a PGF given by the product of the PGFs of each of the individual random variables. Hence the PGF of $X + Y$ is given by

$$H(z) = G_\lambda(z)G_\mu(z)$$
$$= \exp\big((\lambda + \mu)(z - 1)\big),$$

which is clearly the PGF of another Poisson random variable with parameter $\lambda + \mu$.

Here are some possible related questions:

- Derive the PGF of the Poisson distribution.
- Show how to recover the probability distribution function of a discrete random variable from its PGF.
- Prove that the sum of two normal random variables is normal. Use integration and moment generating functions.

□

Solution to Question 3.73. To answer this question we need to know the distribution of the maximum of a Brownian motion to time t,

$$M_t = \max_{0 \le s \le t} W_t.$$

The derivation of this distribution uses the *reflection principle* (see, for example, [6] p. 192).

Consider the probability $\mathbb{P}(W_t \ge x)$. Clearly we have

$$\mathbb{P}(W_t \ge x) = \mathbb{P}(W_t \ge x, M_t \ge x) + \mathbb{P}(W_t \ge x, M_t < x).$$
$$= \mathbb{P}(W_t \ge x, M_t \ge x)$$
$$= \mathbb{P}(W_t \ge x | M_t \ge x)\mathbb{P}(M_t \ge x),$$

since the event $\mathbb{P}(W_t \ge x, M_t < x)$ can not occur.

To derive the probability $\mathbb{P}(W_t \ge x | M_t \ge x)$ consider the first time τ that $W_s = x$. The event $M_t \ge x$ is equivalent to the event $\tau = t_0$ for some $t_0 \le t$, and we also have

$$\mathbb{P}(W_t \ge x | W_{t_0} = x) = \mathbb{P}(W_{t-t_0} \ge 0) = 1/2$$

for all $t_0 \le t$. Hence $\mathbb{P}(W_t \ge x | M_t \ge x) = 1/2$ and

$$\mathbb{P}(M_t \ge x) = 2\mathbb{P}(W_t \ge x).$$

Substituting $x = 1$ gives the answer to the original problem.

Here are some possible related questions:

- Use the reflection principle to derive the joint distribution of the maximum and the terminal value of the Brownian motion.
- What is the probability that a Brownian motion will eventually cross the level 1 (that is, the limit as $T \to \infty$)?
- Derive the distribution of the maximum of a Brownian motion with drift μ.
- What is the probability that a Brownian motion will be above the line $a + bt$ ($a, b \in \mathbb{R}$) before time 1? Consider all appropriate conbinatinos of positive and negative a and b.

□

Solution to Question 3.74. These problems can be solved by using either martingale techniques or a PDE approach. Here we present the solution using the martingale approach.

Initially consider the process W_t. Let τ be the first time W_t reaches either 1 or -2, i.e.:

$$\tau := \inf\{t \geq 0 : W_t = 1 \text{ or } W_t = -2\}.$$

For completeness, we show τ is a finite stopping time with respect to the filtration generated by the Brownian motion, $\mathcal{F}_t$, although this would most likely not be required in an interview. Clearly τ is $\mathcal{F}_t$ measurable. To show that $\mathbb{P}(\tau < \infty) = 1$, we have that

$$
\begin{aligned}
\mathbb{P}(\tau < t) \geq & \mathbb{P}(|W_t| > 2), \\
= & 1 - \mathbb{P}(|W_t| \leq 2) \\
\geq & 1 - 4 \left. \frac{d}{dt}\mathbb{P}(W_t \leq t)\right|_{t=0}, \\
= & 1 - \frac{4}{\sqrt{2\pi t}}, \\
\to & 1 \text{ as } t \to \infty.
\end{aligned}
$$

We then apply the optional sampling theorem (OST), which says that for finite stopping times

$$\mathbb{E}(W_\tau) = \mathbb{E}(W_0) = 0.$$

Hence

$$
\begin{aligned}
0 = \mathbb{E}(W_\tau) = & \mathbb{P}(W_\tau = 1) - 2\mathbb{P}(W_\tau = -2) \\
= & \mathbb{P}(W_\tau = 1) - 2(1 - \mathbb{P}(W_\tau = 1)).
\end{aligned}
$$

Solving for $\mathbb{P}(W_\tau = 1)$ gives

$$\mathbb{P}(W_\tau = 1) = \frac{2}{3}.$$

To determine $\mathbb{E}(\tau)$, note that the process $Y_t := W_t^2 - t$ is a martingale. Again using the OST,

$$0 = \mathbb{E}(Y_\tau) = \mathbb{E}(W_\tau^2) - \mathbb{E}(\tau).$$

Using the previous result then gives

$$\mathbb{E}(\tau) = \frac{2}{3} + 4\frac{1}{3} = 2.$$

Now consider the process $X_t = \mu t + W_t$. We introduce the exponential martingale

$$Z_t^\lambda := \exp\left\{\lambda X_t - \lambda(\mu + \frac{1}{2}\lambda)t\right\},$$

which is a martingale for any $\lambda \in \mathbb{R}$. In particular, if we take $\lambda = -2\mu$ we have that $Z_t^{-2\mu} = \exp\{-2\mu X_t\}$ is a martingale. Again we can use the OST (how do we justify its use?) which gives

$$1 = \mathbb{E}(Z_0^{-2\mu}) = \mathbb{E}(Z_\tau^{-2\mu}) = e^{-2\mu}\mathbb{P}(X_\tau = 1) + e^{4\mu}(1 - \mathbb{P}(X_\tau = 1)),$$

with the slight abuse of notation that τ now represents the first time the process X_t hits the level 1 or -2. Solving for $\mathbb{P}(X_\tau = 1)$ gives

$$\mathbb{P}(X_\tau = 1) = \frac{1 - e^{4\mu}}{e^{-2\mu} - e^{4\mu}}.$$

Finally, to determine $\mathbb{E}(\tau)$ in this case note that the process

$$V_t := X_t - \mu t$$

is again a martingale. Hence $0 = \mathbb{E}(V_\tau)$ which gives

$$\begin{aligned}
\mathbb{E}(\tau) &= \frac{1}{\mu}\mathbb{E}(X_\tau) \\
&= \frac{1}{\mu}\left(\frac{1 - e^{4\mu}}{e^{-2\mu} - e^{4\mu}} - 2\left(1 - \frac{1 - e^{4\mu}}{e^{-2\mu} - e^{4\mu}}\right)\right) \\
&= \frac{1}{\mu}\left(\frac{3(1 - e^{4\mu})}{e^{-2\mu} - e^{4\mu}} - 2\right).
\end{aligned}$$

Clearly we could have used this approach from the start for the standard Brownian motion, taking the limit as $\mu \to 0$. It is always good to have a few possible ideas up your sleeve.

Here are some possible related questions:

- Prove $Z_t^{-2\mu}$ is a martingale.
- Generalise to the probability W_t hits the level a before b, $a > 0$ and $b < 0$.

- Check that taking the limit as $\mu \to 0$ in the X_t case gives the same results as for the standard Brownian motion.
- Reconcile your answers in this question with the solution to Question 3.73.
- Complete the problem using the PDE approach.
- What are the necessary conditions to apply the OST?

$\square$

Solution to Question 3.75. There are many ways to do this one. It is important to realise that since W_s is continuous as a function of s, the integral is benign and can be regarded as an ordinary Riemann integral on each path. First, note that we are essentially adding together a bunch of normals of zero mean so we get a normal of zero mean. We need to find its variance. We can write

$$I(t)^2 = \left(\int_0^t W_s ds \right)^2 ,$$

$$= \left(\int_0^t W_s ds \right) \left(\int_0^t W_r dr \right) ,$$

$$= \int_0^t \int_0^t W_s W_r dr ds.$$

We want the expectation of this quantity, we can take the expectation through the integral.

$$\mathbb{E}(I(t)^2) = \int_0^t \int_0^t \mathbb{E}(W_s W_r) dr ds.$$

Now,

$$\mathbb{E}(W_s W_r) = \min(r, s).$$

To see this, take $s > r$ and write

$$W_s = W_r + (W_s - W_r).$$

So

$$\mathbb{E}(I(t)^2) = \int\limits_{0}^{t} \int\limits_{0}^{t} \min(r, s) dr ds = \frac{t^3}{3}.$$

Since we have zero mean, this is the variance.

Here are some possible related questions:

- What is the joint distribution of W_t and $I(t)$?
- What about the average of W_s from time zero to time t?
- Deduce the above result from basic definitions.
- When is it valid to interchange orders of integration?

$\square$

Solution to Question 3.76. Take $t_1 \leq t_2$. The variances of the normals are t_1 and t_2. To compute the covariance, observe that the increments of the second Brownian motion after t_1 are independent of behaviour up to time t_1. The covariance is therefore the same for t_2 bigger than t_1 and so we can take $t_2 = t_1$ when computing it. It is therefore just ρt_1. The correlation is therefore

$$\frac{\rho t_1}{\sqrt{t_1}\sqrt{t_2}} = \rho \sqrt{\frac{t_1}{t_2}}.$$

This expression only holds for $t_1 \leq t_2$. In general, using symmetry we can write

$$\rho \sqrt{\frac{\min(t_1, t_2)}{\max(t_1, t_2)}}.$$

Here are some possible related questions:

- Is it possible for two Brownian motions to have non-zero correlation without being jointly normal?
- What is the covariance between a Brownian motion and itself at different times?
- Suppose the two Brownian motions had different volatilities, how would this affect the result? What if the volatilities were time-dependent?

$\square$

CHAPTER 4

Interest rates

4.1. Introduction

The area of interest rates, specifically interest rate options, usually requires the most complicated quant work. The main reason for this is that an interest rate derivative depends on the yield curve, which is a one-dimensional object, as opposed to an equity or FX option which depends on a zero-dimensional object: the stock price or FX rate.

Since these options are fairly complex, for entry-level jobs detailed knowledge of interest rate pricing is rarely expected. However, if the job you are applying for is on an interest rate options desk, you would be expected to demonstrate some real interest and understanding of the topic.

It is therefore worth taking the time to understand the most common interest rates (e.g. forward and swap rates) and also the most commonly used model, the LIBOR market model (LMM or BGM).

The LIBOR market model is not too difficult to understand, but there are many subtleties regarding implementation. One of the best ways to understand the model is therefore to implement it yourself. A good place to start is by trying Computer Project 11 in [6].

Some introductory books containing chapters on interest rates models are

- "The Concepts and Practice of Mathematical Finance" by Mark Joshi, [6]. This contains a chapter on forward rate agreements and swaps and a chapter on the LMM but does not discuss short rate models.
- "Financial Calculus," by M. Baxter and A. Rennie, [1]. This contains an overview of the main short rate models.

- "Interest Rate Models - Theory and Practice," by D. Brigo and F. Mercurio, [2], has a good broad discussion of interest rate modelling.
- "Interest Rate Models: An Introduction," by A. Cairns is a good book at the introductory level.

4.2. Questions

QUESTION 4.1. If the six-month forward rate is 5% and the one-year forward rate is 10%. What is the forward rate from six months to one year?

QUESTION 4.2. Given a savings account with continuously compounded interest rate r, why is the time for the money to double approximately equal to $70/r$?

QUESTION 4.3. How do you go about pricing an interest rate swap?

QUESTION 4.4. Why does it matter whether interest rates follow a mean reversion process?

QUESTION 4.5. A bond has annual coupon payments. Derive the formula to convert yield volatility into price volatility.

QUESTION 4.6. What are the two main classes of interest rate models? Explain the difference between them.

QUESTION 4.7. Under what conditions is the LIBOR market model (LMM or BGM) Markovian?

QUESTION 4.8. Could you tell us briefly about Vasicek model?

4.3. Solutions

Solution to Question 4.1. To answer this question we only need to remember the formula for a forward rate. From Section 13.2.2 of [6] we have

$$f(t_1, t_2) = \frac{\frac{P(t_1)}{P(t_2)} - 1}{t_2 - t_1},$$

where $f(t_1, t_2)$ represents the forward rate from time t_1 to t_2. Similarly $P(t_1)$ is the value today of the zero-coupon bond expiring at time t_1. Using the given interest rates we can work out the value of the bonds

$$P(t_1) = \frac{1}{1 + 0.5 \times 0.05} = 0.976,$$

$$P(t_2) = \frac{1}{1 + 1 \times 0.10} = 0.909.$$

The forward rate from time 0.5 to 1 is

$$f(0.5, 1) = \frac{\frac{0.976}{0.909} - 1}{1 - 0.5}$$
$$= 14.6\%.$$

Here are some possible related questions:

- If the six-month rate is 6% and the one-year rate is 5%, what is the forward rate from six months to one year?
- What relationship on zero-coupon bond prices must be enforced to avoid negative forward rates?

□

Solution to Question 4.2. The answer to this question becomes clear once it is in mathematical form. Our bank account starts with $1, how long will it take to have $2? Using the continuously compounded interest rate r

$$2 = 1 \exp\left(\frac{r}{100}t\right).$$

We rearrange to find

$$t = 100 \ln(2)/r.$$

Recall that $\ln(2) \approx 0.7$ and we have the approximation.

Here is a possible related question:

- Derive the rule using an annually compounding interest rate. For what values of r will the approximation be accurate?

□

Solution to Question 4.3. An interest rate swap allows one investor to swap floating interest rates to fixed rates. Its price is entirely model-independent and can be calculated by simply present valuing the future payments.

Take a set of dates $T_0 < T_1 < \ldots < T_n$. The fixed part of the swap involves making n payments at times $T_1, \ldots, T_n$ based on a pre-agreed swap rate SR. The present value of these payments is

$$\sum_{i=0}^{n-1} \mathrm{SR}\, \tau_i P(T_{i+1}),$$

where $\tau_i = T_{i+1} - T_i$, which is usually 0.25 or 0.5 years, and $P(T_i)$ is the value today of the zero-coupon bond expiring at time T_i. For the floating side we have payments on the same dates based on the forward rate f_i for the period; its present value is

$$\sum_{i=0}^{n-1} f_i \tau_i P(T_{i+1}).$$

To calculate the swap rate, SR, we simply equate the two payment streams so that the swap will have zero initial value. The swap rate is

$$\mathrm{SR} = \sum_{i=0}^{n-1} w_i f_i,$$

where

$$w_i = \frac{\tau_i P(T_{i+1})}{\sum_{i=0}^{n-1} \tau_i P(T_{i+1})}.$$

Here are some possible related questions:

- What is $\sum_{i=0}^{n-1} w_i$ equal to? What interpretation of the swap rate does this suggest?
- Would a quant ever price a swap using an interest rate model such as the LIBOR market model?

□

Solution to Question 4.4. There is strong economic theory and evidence that interest rates follow a mean reverting process. If interest rates are high the economy slows down and the demand for money decreases, pushing interest rates back down. As interest rates decrease the economy becomes more active and the demand for money increases, pushing interest rates back up. A rule of thumb regarding whether a quantity is mean-reverting is whether you expect it to be in the same range roughly 100 years from now, if you do, then it must have some sort of mean reversion. Financial models are designed to capture market behavior, so if the market behaves in a mean reverting way then we would expect a good model to capture this feature.

A big difference between the interest rate models known as short rate models and models for the equity market is that in a short rate model the drift matters. The reason for this is that the short rate is NOT a tradeable asset so if the drift is mean-reverting it will affect derivative prices. However, if the drift of a stock is mean-reverting it will not affect derivative prices since drift never affects prices of equity options; see Question 2.29.

Here are some possible related questions:

- Which do you think is more important, a model which returns current market prices or one which captures the market's dynamics? Discuss.
- What are the advantages and disadvantages of modelling interest rates as normally distributed rather than log-normally distributed?

□

Solution to Question 4.5. As the volatility for a bond is often quoted as yield volatility instead of price volatility, it is necessary to be able to convert from one to the other. To derive the formula we start with the price, P, of a bond, which is simply the sum of all future coupons C_i and the principal A returned at the end suitably discounted

$$P = \sum_{i=1}^{n} \frac{C_i}{(1+y_n)^i} + \frac{A}{(1+y_n)^n},$$

where y_n is the bond's yield to maturity. We can differentiate the price with respect to the yield, obtaining

$$dP = \left[\frac{-1}{1+y_n} \left(\sum_{i=1}^{n} \frac{iC_i}{(1+y_n)^i} + \frac{nA}{(1+y_n)^n} \right) \right] dy_n.$$

The term inside the round brackets divided by P is known as the *duration* of the bond, D, which is a measure of how long on average the bond owner needs to wait to receive cash flows. Substituting this in we have

$$\frac{dP}{P} = \frac{-D}{1+y_n} dy_n.$$

We can make a further simplification by using the modified duration $D^* = D/(1+y_n)$, giving

$$\frac{dP}{P} = -D^* dy_n.$$

Assuming that the yield is log-normally distributed it will follow a process similar to

$$\frac{dy_n}{y_n} = \sigma_y dW_t.$$

Using this we can substitute it into the equation above obtaining

$$\frac{dP}{P} = D^* \sigma_y y_n dW_t.$$

Therefore the price volatility of a bond will be given by the modified duration multiplied by the yield volatility multiplied by the yield to maturity

$$\sigma_P = D^* \sigma_y y_n.$$

Here are some possible related questions:

- What is the duration of a zero-coupon bond?
- What bounds hold on the duration of a bond for sensible market values?

$\square$

Solution to Question 4.6. There are arguably three main classes of interest rate models, the two most common are short rate models and market models with the third being Markov functional models.

Short rate models specify a process for the unobservable continuously compounding interest rate r, for example

$$dr = \alpha(r, t)dt + \beta(r, t)dW_t,$$

which then implies dynamics for the money market account

$$B(t) = \exp\left(\int_0^t r(s)ds\right).$$

Prices of market instruments such as caplets are then derived from the money market account.

One of the main issues with short rate models is that the dynamics are not compatible with the standard market prices from Black's formula. This makes calibrating the model, fitting α and β, to the market very difficult. Usually one has to calibrate to only a portion of instruments and then minimise the error of the other instruments.

Another issue is that at a particular point in time the set of attainable yield curves is one dimensional (however, two-factor models do exist). This can simply be too limiting for most exotic interest rate derivatives. For example, products which derive their value from the changing shape of the yield curve will not be priced very well using a short rate model.

An advantage of short rate models lies in their implementation, which is often done on a lattice resulting in fast pricing. Lattice methods are ideally suited for early exercise products (see question 2.65), giving short rate models an advantage over the necessary Monte Carlo implementation of a market model.

For more details on short rate models see [2].

Market models specify a process for observable quantities (unlike short rate models) such as forward rates or swap rates. For example in the forward LIBOR market model, dynamics for the forward rates f_j are

(4.1) $$\frac{df_j}{f_j} = \mu_j dt + \sigma_j dW_t^{(j)}.$$

The volatility σ_j is chosen to price the caplet on the jth forward rate correctly. So calibration to the current yield curve and the at-the-money caplet market is automatic as the model is consistent with Black's formula.

The set of attainable yield curves is high dimensional, depending on the chosen dimension of the Brownian motion W_t, which makes market models more suited to exotic products. The high dimensionality comes at a cost, market models need to be implemented using Monte Carlo, which makes them much slower than short rate models.

For more details on market models see [6].

Markov functional models were designed to incorporate some of the good features of both short rate models and market models. The idea is to have market rates and instruments as a function of a low-dimensional Markov process x where

$$dx(t) = \lambda(t)dW_t.$$

To obtain option prices using a Markov functional model it is only necessary to keep track of this underlying Markov process, meaning they can be priced using a lattice. They also allow for easy calibration to market prices as there is freedom to chose the functional form of the model.

Similarly with short rate models, the assumption that the space of yield curves attainable at a given time is expressed by one or two random factors can be too simplistic to give good prices for exotic instruments. See [13] for more details on Markov functional models.

Here are some possible related questions:

- Explain how you would implement a short rate model.
- Under the terminal measure, explain why the drift in equation (4.1) is not equal to zero for all j. Derive the expression for the drift.
- Give an outline of the main steps in pricing an interest rate derivative using the LIBOR market model.

$\square$

Solution to Question 4.7. This is a difficult question and would only be asked to experienced quants. However, below is a brief explanation of the main idea.

If we ignore drifts, a sufficient condition for the LIBOR market model to be Markovian in the underlying Brownian motion is that the volatility function is *separable*. Let $\sigma_i(t)$ denote the volatility function for a particular LIBOR rate. If the volatility can be written as

$$\sigma_i(t) = v_i \times \nu(t),$$

then it is said to be separable. We have that v_i is a LIBOR specific scalar and $\nu(t)$ is a deterministic function of time that is common to all LIBOR rates.

The LIBOR market model is never truly Markovian in the Brownian motions since it contains state-dependent drifts. However, these can be approximated using schemes such as predictor-corrector to make the rates functions of the underlying increments only across a single step.

Note that the question is poorly worded in that asking whether something is Markovian only makes in terms of what it is allowed to be a function of. The LIBOR market model is always Markovian as a function of the underlying rates.

Here are some possible related questions:

- Why is separability of the volatility function important for the LIBOR market model to be Markovian?
- Is stochastic vol BGM Markovian?

□

Solution to Question 4.8. Your answer to this question will depend on the job you're applying for and your level of experience. If you are claiming to be an expert interest rate quant, then you will obviously have to provide much more detail than someone with little or no interest rate modelling experience. A good place to start is to mention that it is a short rate model (see Question 4.6), where the short rate follows the mean reverting diffusion process

$$dr(t) = k[\theta - r(t)]dt + \sigma dW(t)$$

for constant values of k, θ and σ.

The Vasicek model is an example of an affine model, which produces tractable bond pricing formulas. One drawback of the model, however, is that the diffusion implies that $r(t)$ has a normal distribution meaning the short rate can become negative with positive probability.

The Vasicek model has only three parameters so it cannot be used to calibrate to the discount curve. This makes it be of limited use in derivatives pricing. Typically, the parameters are made to be time dependent to get over this problem. It is then called the Hull–White extended Vasicek model. For more details on the Vasicek model, see [2].

Here are some possible related questions:

- Derive the mean and variance of the short rate at time t in the Vasicek model, conditional on information up to time $s < t$.
- Outline how you would price a Bermudan swaption under the Vasicek model. Is this sensible?
- Suggest a way to improve the model so that it better calibrates to swaption implied volatilities.

□

CHAPTER 5

Numerical techniques and algorithms

5.1. Introduction

In this chapter, we look at programming-style questions which are not tied to a specific language. These tend to be of three main sorts:

(1) algorithms for organising and sampling data, for example, questions about sorting are of this type;
(2) questions around computing a specific number; a routine to write a numerical integrator is typical;
(3) brainteasers related to programming; make two robots crash together using a limited language.

Some questions are, of course, a mix of types.

The problems in this chapter are unlikely to go away even if the relative trendiness of computer languages does change. We present most of the solutions in C++, since it appears to be the language in most common use for quant roles at the time of writing.

5.2. Questions

QUESTION 5.1. Write an algorithm to carry out numerical integration. How might you optimise the algorithm?

QUESTION 5.2. Suppose an asset takes values from a discrete set v_j and the probability of v_j is p_j. Write an algorithm that produces the random variable for this asset from a uniformly distributed random variable.

QUESTION 5.3. Write a program to compute Fibonacci numbers.

QUESTION 5.4. Given 9999 of the first 10,000 numbers, write a routine that is efficient in memory and computation time to find which number is missing.

QUESTION 5.5. Write an algorithm to increment the date by n days. (Robust against leap years and non-leap year centuries.)

QUESTION 5.6. How can we efficiently exponentiate a matrix?

QUESTION 5.7. Code up a histogram maker.

QUESTION 5.8. Let $f(x) = \sin(x)/x$. Write code that returns the value of $f(x)$. I want it to be well behaved - everywhere!

QUESTION 5.9. The Grandma problem is that if the first of 100 passengers sits randomly on a plane, and every other passenger sits in their seat if it's free, and at random otherwise, what is the probability that the last passenger sits in his own seat? Write C++ code (or pseudo but as C++ as you can) to run a Monte Carlo simulation that finds the probability.

QUESTION 5.10. Write an algorithm which, when given an array of random real numbers (positive or negative), finds the subarray whose sum of elements is maximal.

QUESTION 5.11. Suppose I claim I have a routine that can sort n numbers in $\mathcal{O}(n)$ time. Prove me wrong.

QUESTION 5.12. Use the `rand()` function to randomly permute the integers between 1 and 100.

QUESTION 5.13. Write a routine to calculate n factorial.

QUESTION 5.14. You are given a matrix with the property that every row is increasing and every column is increasing. A number, x, is known to lie within the matrix, give an efficient algorithm to locate it.

QUESTION 5.15. A vector v of integers has N elements. Every element is in the (closed) range 0 to $N - 1$. Write an algorithm that determines whether any number is duplicated. You do not need to preserve the array. The algorithm can be sketched rather than written in code.

QUESTION 5.16. Write a routine to do linear interpolation.

QUESTION 5.17. A submarine starts at some point on the integer line; it moves a constant number of integers each turn. Once a turn you can lob a missile at some point on the integer line. Can you give an algorithm that will hit the submarine in a finite number of turns?

QUESTION 5.18. Two robots are parachuted on the integer line at the same time. When they land, they each drop their parachutes, then execute the code programmed by you. Each robot must have identical code. Each line of code takes one second to execute. Each line of code can say

- Go 1 unit left
- Go 1 unit right
- GOTO line XXX
- If there is a parachute at your current location, GOTO line XXX.

Write code to make them collide.

QUESTION 5.19. Write a routine that sums the numbers in the nodes of a tree. Nodes can have two branches, one, or none.

QUESTION 5.20. Given that a stock price at time T is $N(100, 1)$, you want to price a digital call struck at 110 by Monte Carlo simulation. What will happen if you do this? Improve the method.

QUESTION 5.21. Describe an algorithm that could be used to generate exponential random variables.

QUESTION 5.22. What techniques can be used to improve the convergence of Monte Carlo simulations?

QUESTION 5.23. Given a uniform random number generator, how can you simulate standard normal random variables?

QUESTION 5.24. Exactly how many operations are needed to find the largest element out of n elements? How about to find both the biggest and the smallest?

QUESTION 5.25. You have a sequence of cards, write an algorithm to find the longest subsequence of increasing numbers.

5.3. Solutions

Solution to Question 5.1. We present a solution in C++. We integrate a given fixed function F.

```cpp
double F(double x)
{
  // put your function here

  return x*x;
}


double IntegrateF(double a, double b, int N)
{
  double result=0.0;
  double length= (b-a)/N;

  for (int i=0; i < N; ++i)
    result +=F(a+(i+0.5)*length);

  result *= length;

  return result;
}
```

This routine implements one of the simplest possible numerical integrators. We divide the interval into N pieces of equal size, take the value at the mid-point of each sub-interval, sum them and then multiply by the length of the interval.

Note that we have multiplied by the length once at the end, rather than on every iteration of the loop. In general, when optimising we want to do as many computations outside the loop as possible. This routine could be further optimised by simplifying the expression a+(i+0.5)*length using more pre-computations.

Here are some possible related questions:

- What is the order of convergence?
- How could you tell if the routine has converged?
- What functions would it fail on?
- Implement the trapezium rule.
- What is your favourite integration procedure and how does it work?
- How would you design the code so that the function name is not hard-coded?

□

Solution to Question 5.2. We present a solution in C++. We use a simple array class from the xlw project but you could use any reasonable `vector` class.

```cpp
double Simulate(const MyArray& p,
                const MyArray& v,
                double u)
{
    int i=0;

    while ( u > p[i])
    {
      u-= p[i];
      ++i;
    }

    return v[i];
}
```

Essentially, we want to find the first i such that the cumulative probability up to i is bigger than u. Rather than computing all the cumulatives, we instead subtract the probability of each event until we get something sufficiently small.

Note that the timing of this algorithm is $O(N)$ where N is the number of possible events. The memory usage is constant.

Here are some possible related questions:

- Suppose N is very big, how would you get a faster algorithm?
- How would you test this algorithm?
- Give an algorithm to generate a uniformly distributed random variable from an integer random number generator.
- What is your favourite integer random number generator?
- What problems can arise when using random number generators?

$\square$

Solution to Question 5.3. The first and quickest way to implement Fibonacci numbers is by recursion.

```
int Fib1(int N)
{
   if (N <=1)
      return 1;

   return Fib1(N-1) + Fib1(N-2);
}
```

This is a terrible solution! Why?

If we run this with a reasonable value of N, it will take forever to return. The reason is that we compute the same Fibonacci number over and over again. For example, Fib(30) computes Fib(29) and Fib(28), but then Fib(29) computes it again. This gets worse and worse as we get further below 30. In this case, recursion is an attractive trap.

How can we avoid all this recomputation? One solution is simply to compute upwards, storing the numbers as we go.

```
int Fib2(int N)
{

    std::vector<int> v(N+1);
    v[0] = 1;
    v[1] = 1;

    for (int j=2; j <=N; ++j)
      v[j] = v[j-1] + v[j-2];

    return v[N];
}
```

The main downside of this is that we use more memory; in fact, the program
is linear in memory usage. Since Fibonacci numbers grow exponentially this is
a small problem – the number will be huge long before we use much memory.
However, we can achieve constant memory usage by realising that it is only the
previous two numbers that matter:

```
int Fib3(int N)
{
    std::vector<int> v(3);
    v[0] = 1;
    v[1] = 1;

    for (int j=0; j <=N-2; ++j)
      v[(j+2) % 3 ] = v[(j+1) % 3 ] + v[j % 3];

    return v[N % 3];
}
```

Here are some possible related questions:

- Do you think that recursion is a useful technique?

- Is it possible to compute Fibonacci numbers in constant time?
- How could we avoid reallocating the memory for an array each time the routine was called?

☐

Solution to Question 5.4. Clearly, there are many ways to do this. One easy way is to sort the array and then scan through until a gap is found. However, sorting is an $O(n \log n)$ operation so this will not be fast. A second approach is to define a second array of booleans all set to false. We then set each element to true using its index in the array as a number is found. We then scan through and find the one false one. This is $O(n)$ in time but also $O(n)$ in memory.

A method which is $O(n)$, but efficient in memory, is to add all the numbers together. The sum will be too low by the missing number.

```
int FindMissingInt(const std::vector<int>& numbers)
{
    int N = numbers.size()+1;
    int total = N*(N+1)/2;

    int x=0;

    for (unsigned long j=0; j < numbers.size(); ++j)
        x += numbers[j];

    int r= total-x;

    return r;

}
```

Here are some possible related questions:

- How do you prove the formula for the sum of the first N numbers? (Gauss could do this when he was five.)
- How big can N get before this routine breaks?
- What about the other approaches?

□

Solution to Question 5.5. It is worth checking whether they want an efficient routine or just something that works. For this one, they probably will not care about efficiency. They sometimes do, however.

The problem is fiddly because of the rules regarding the 29th of February. These are:

- It exists in leap years.
- A year is a leap year if the year is divisible by four, unless it is divisible by 100, in which case it must be divisible by 400.

So 2000 was a leap year, but 2100 is not.

Since we are not required to be efficient, we add one day, n times. If we are not on the last day of a month that is easy. If we are on the last day of a month, we need to check for leap years. If we go over the end of a month, we increment the month, and the year if necessary.

```
bool IsLeapDayNext(int y, int m, int d)
{
    if (m!=2)
        return false;

    if (d!=28)
        return false;

    if (y % 4 > 0)
        return false;
```

```
  if (y % 100 > 0)
     return true;

  if (y % 400 == 0)
     return true;

  return false;
}

void AddOneToDate(int &y, int &m, int& d)
{

    static double lengths[] = { 31, 28, 31, 30, 31, 30, 31, 31,
        30, 31, 30, 31 };

    if (d < lengths[m-1]) { ++d; return; }

    if (IsLeapDayNext(y,m,d))
    {
      ++d;
      return;
    }

    d=1;
    ++m;

    y = y + (m /12);
    m =m % 12;

}

void AddToDate(int &y, int &m, int& d, int N)
{
  for (int i=0; i < N; ++i)
```

```
    AddOneToDate(y,m,d);
}
```

Here are some possible related questions:

- Suppose we need a faster routine. What changes would you make?
- Suppose we needed a fast routine, but we could use as much memory as we liked, how would we do it?

□

Solution to Question 5.6. This one is nastier than it looks in that the problem is still an area of active research. There is even a paper entitled "Nineteen dubious ways to compute the exponential of a matrix," which was republished and updated after 25 years, [10]. We therefore content ourselves with some discussion of the problem.

First, let's define the problem. Analytic functions of matrices are defined via power series. For a matrix A, this means

$$\exp(A) = \sum_{j=0}^{\infty} \frac{A^j}{j!}.$$

This will always converge; the easiest way to see this is that we can estimate using the operator norm, $||A||$,

$$\left\| \sum_{j=M}^{N} \frac{A^j}{j!} \right\| \leq \sum_{j=M}^{N} \frac{||A||^j}{j!}.$$

The sum for $\exp(||A||)$ exists so the sequence is Cauchy and so must converge. All norms are equivalent in finite-dimensional Banach spaces, so the sum converges in any norm.

We therefore have a simple way to compute, just keep taking powers of A and add until things get small. We can use the error for $||A||$ to bound the operator norm of the error. The main problems with this approach are inefficiency and problems with round-off error. If the entries of A are initially large, the powers may results in very large numbers being divided by other very large ones and the result may converge to the wrong answer.

How else can we proceed? If the matrix is diagonalisable, then we can write

$$A = PDP^t$$

with P the matrix of orthonormal eigenvectors and D diagonal. This means that $PP^t = I$. So

$$A^j = PD^j P^t,$$

and

$$\exp(A) = P\exp(D)P^t.$$

The exponential of D is easy, we just take the exponential of diagonal elements and we are done. Unfortunately not all matrices are diagonalisable, although all real symmetric matrices are. If the matrix is known to be diagonalisable then this method is fine.

What else can we do? One solution is to use the Cayley–Hamilton theorem. This states that a matrix always satisfies its own characteristic polynomial, p. The characteristic polynomial is defined via

$$p(\lambda) = \det(\lambda I - A),$$

and is an nth order polynomial, by definition the eigenvalues of the matrix are its roots. One solution is therefore to compute the polynomial and since $p(A) = 0$, we must have

$$A^n = \sum_{j<n} c_j A^j.$$

An immediate consequence is that $\exp(A)$ can be written as a polynomial in A where the coefficients of the polynomial depend only on A's eigenvalues. Once one has these it is easy.

Here are some possible related questions:

- What is the minimal polynomial, and how is it related to the characteristic polynomial?
- How would you compute $\sin(A)$?
- If A is a general matrix, prove $\cos^2(A) + \sin^2(A) = I$.

□

Solution to Question 5.7. Here's a simple solution in C++:

```cpp
void MakeHistogram(std::vector<double>& BucketLefts,
      std::vector<int>& BucketContents,
      const std::vector<double>& values,
      int numberOfBuckets)
{
  double minValue =
    *std::min_element(values.begin(), values.end());
  double maxValue = *std::max_element(values.begin(),
                                      values.end());

  double bucketSize = (maxValue - minValue)
                                /(numberOfBuckets-1);

  BucketLefts.resize(numberOfBuckets);
  for (int i=0; i < numberOfBuckets; ++i)
    BucketLefts[i] = minValue + bucketSize*i;

  BucketContents.resize(numberOfBuckets);

  for (int i=0; i < values.size(); ++i)
  {
    int k =
      static_cast<int>(floor((values[i]
                              - minValue)/bucketSize));

    ++BucketContents[k];
  }

}
```

The main subtleties are in choosing where to place the buckets. This is done by taking the leftmost point to be the minimum value and the left-hand-side of the rightmost bucket to be the maximum value.

We assign a given value to a bucket simply by dividing its distance from the minimum by the size of a bucket. Note that this is a constant time algorithm but relies heavily on the fact that the buckets are of uniform size.

Here are some possible related questions:

- Can you suggest more sophisticated algorithms for bucket locations?
- If we allow non-uniform buckets, how would you assign a number to a bucket?
- Modify the routine so its stores the mean value of numbers in a bucket as well as the number of items in a bucket.
- Do a two-dimensional analogue.

□

Solution to Question 5.8. The issue here is that f has a removable singularity at zero. In particular, we have

$$\sin(x) = \sum_{j=0}^{\infty} (-1)^j \frac{x^{2j+1}}{(2j+1)!}.$$

So

$$f(x) = \sum_{j=0}^{\infty} (-1)^j \frac{x^{2j}}{(2j+1)!}.$$

This is a well-behaved convergent power series. One solution is therefore simply to use this power series.

The main issue is that for x large, you may need a large number of terms and floating point round-off problems may destroy the accuracy of the answer. A solution is to use the power series for x small, for example for $|x|$ less than $1e - 4$, since powers beyond 4 will then be too small to contribute, and the usual sin function from the standard library, otherwise. The main issue is that then you may get a discontinuity at the transition point: this will reflect the inaccuracies inherent in any floating point implementation.

A standard way to transit between two functions is to use a bump function ϕ. This a smooth function which is 1 near some point (in this case zero), always between zero and one, and zero more than some chosen distance from that point.

We then take

$$\phi(x)f(x) + (1 - \phi(x))\frac{\sin(x)}{x}.$$

This begs the question of how to construct such a ϕ. It can be built up from simpler functions. Let

$$y(x) = \begin{cases} e^{-1/x}, & \text{for } x > 0, \\ 0, & \text{otherwise.} \end{cases}$$

The function g is smooth, positive for $x > 0$ and zero for $x < 0$. With a few simple manipulations ϕ can be constructed from g.

Here are some possible related questions:

- Complete the construction of ϕ.
- How would you compute $(\cos(x) - 1)/x^2$?
- How do you think sin is implemented in computers?

□

Solution to Question 5.9. Here's a simple solution:

```cpp
#include <cstdlib>
#include <cmath>
#include <vector>

double GetUniform()
{
   return rand()/static_cast<double>(RAND_MAX);
}

double SimulateGrandma(int NumberOfPassengers,
                       int NumberOfSimulations)
{
```

```cpp
int numberSuccesses =0;
std::vector<bool> seatTaken(NumberOfPassengers);

for (int j=0; j < NumberOfSimulations; ++j)
{
  for (int k=0; k < NumberOfPassengers; ++k)
    seatTaken[k] = false;

    int firstSeat = static_cast<int>(GetUniform()
                                     *NumberOfPassengers);
    seatTaken[firstSeat] = true;

    for (int l=1; l < NumberOfPassengers-1; ++l)
    {
      if (!seatTaken[l])
          seatTaken[l] = true;
      else
      {
        int seatNumber = static_cast<int>(
                                 (NumberOfPassengers-1)
                                     *GetUniform());
        int m=0;

        for (int n=0; n<seatNumber; ++n, ++m)
        {
          while (seatTaken[m]) ++m;
        }

        while (seatTaken[m])
            ++m;
        seatTaken[m] = true;
      }
    }

    if (!seatTaken[NumberOfPassengers-1])
```

```
        ++numberSuccesses;
    }

    return static_cast<double>(numberSuccesses)
                        /NumberOfSimulations;
}
```

Note the extensive use of static_cast: if we divide integers fractional parts will be discarded; we also do not want warnings about converting doubles into integers.

The algorithm is pretty simple. We put passenger zero in a random seat. For each subsequent passenger, we test to see if his seat is taken, if it is not we fill it, otherwise, we draw a seat number at random from the number of vacant seats. We then scan through until we have found the number of empty seats equal to the random draw and then fill it.

Here are some possible related questions:

- What do you think the computational complexity of this solution is?
- Can you find an algorithm with lower complexity?
- How would you assess how well converged your simulation is?
- How might you test the routine to be sure that it worked correctly?

□

Solution to Question 5.10. The key to this one is to observe that if you can scan from the left and reach a cluster of numbers that makes the running sum negative then that cluster will never be part of the maximal subarray. This means that you can start anew after it. So we can scan from the left, summing as we go, keeping a note of the maximal sum so far and its location. If we ever go negative, we start again.

This is called *Kadane's* algorithm. If you are asked this question in an interview and decide to admit to having seen it before, you will gain by being able to name the algorithm.

We present C++ code using classes from the xlw project.

```cpp
MyArray Kadane(const MyArray& input)
{
    double maximum = -1e100;
    double left = 0;
    double right = 0;

    double currentMax =0;
    unsigned long currentLeft=0;

    for (unsigned long currentRight = 0;
            currentRight < input.size();
            ++currentRight
    {
        currentMax += input[currentRight];
        if (currentMax > maximum)
        {
            maximum = currentMax;
            left = currentLeft;
            right = currentRight;
        }

        if (currentMax < 0)
        {
            currentMax =0;
            currentLeft = currentRight+1;
        }

    }

    MyArray results(3);
    results[0] = maximum;
    results[1] = left;
    results[2] = right;
```

```
    return results;
}
```

Here are some possible related questions:

- What will happen if all entries are negative?
- What do you think should happen if all entries are negative?

□

Solution to Question 5.11. There are two operations to consider: swapping elements and comparing elements. We will show that at least $\mathcal{O}(n \log n)$ comparisons are required.

The key is to observe how many different starting configurations are possible and then look at how many of these can be eliminated by a single comparison. If we have elements that can be in any order initially then clearly there are $n!$ possible configurations.

Using a comparison on a set of k possible configurations can divide it into two subsets one of which must have at least $k/2$ elements. This means after M comparisons, there must always be one of at least

$$\frac{n!}{2^M}$$

elements. We need this number to be less than or equal to 1. Taking logs

$$\log(n!) - M \log 2 \leq \log 1 = 0.$$

Rearranging,

$$M \geq \frac{\log(n!)}{\log 2}.$$

To finish we need an approximation to $\log(n!)$. The standard approximation is Stirling's series:

$$\log \Gamma(z) \sim \frac{1}{2} \log(2\pi) + \left(z - \frac{1}{2}\right) \log z - z + \mathcal{O}(z^{-1}).$$

The Γ function is related to factorial via

$$\Gamma(n + 1) = n!.$$

The biggest term in the expansion for large n is clearly $n \frac{\log n}{\log 2}$, so an order n algorithm cannot exist and we are done.

Here are some possible related questions:

- Do you know an $\mathcal{O}(n \log n)$ algorithm to do sorting?
- What other algorithms can you prove lower bounds on complexity for?
- What is a heap? How would you represent it in memory? What do heaps have to do with sorting?

$\square$

Solution to 5.12. There are multiple ways to do this. For example, one could generate 100 distinct random numbers and then sort them whilst keeping track of their original positions. However, that would take $\mathcal{O}(n)$ extra memory and $\mathcal{O}(n \log n)$ extra time since that is the complexity of sort.

In fact, it is possible to solve the problem without using any extra memory in linear time. We present a simple solution sometimes called the "Knuth shuffle," which has also been attributed to Durstenfeld and to Fisher and Yates. We loop through the array backwards exchanging each element with a random one that is no bigger in initial index than it. We do allow exchange with itself, since a permutation may fix some elements.

```
#include <cstdlib>
#include <vector>
#include <ctime>
```

```
std::vector<int> randomPermutation(int n)
{
  // initialise vector
  std::vector<int> data(n);
  for (int i=0; i < n; ++i)
    data[i] = i;

  while (--n > 0)
  {
    int k = rand() % (n+1);
    int temp = data[n];
    data[n] = data[k];
    data[k] = temp;
  }

  return data;

}
```

Note that we generate a random number in the range 0 to n by taking rand()
modulo $n + 1$. This is almost correct but not precisely so. The reason being that
unless RAND_MAX is divisible by $n + 1$, the numbers in the range 0 to RAND_MAX
modulo $n+1$ will occur one more time than those which are not. For n small, this is
not really an issue but to be strictly correct, we should discard returns from rand()
which are in the range RAND_MAX $-n*$ RAND_MAX $/n$ (using integer division) and
then redraw.

The algorithm relies rather heavily on the fact that rand() is truly random
which is a dubious assumption for many implementations of C++. This is doubly
the case since it is the lowest bits, which we are using, that are often the most
unreliable. Most people therefore implement their own random number generator.

We should really show that the algorithm is correct: it must generate all possible
permutations and they must all be equally likely. Recall that there are $n!$ possible
permutations. It will therefore be enough to show that the algorithm generates $n!$
different permutations with equal likelihood.

To see this, observe that our first draw random draw is from the range 0 to $n - 1$, the second from 0 to $n - 2$ and so on. The total vector of random draws therefore has $n!$ different values and they are all equal likely. We need to show that each of these leads to a different permutation and we are done. Suppose two sequences are equal for the first k draws and different in draw $k + 1$. Draw $k + 1$ will determine the $n - k$ element of the array and this will be fixed by the remainder of the algorithm. Since the two sequences agree up to draw k and differ in $k + 1$, this means that the two permutations will differ in this entry, and are distinct.

Here are some possible related questions:

- How would you test correctness?
- How would we randomly arrange objects of an arbitrary type?
- Implement the method that uses sorting.
- Adapt the code so it works even when n is a large fraction of RAND_MAX.
- Suppose we had a random number generator that returned numbers in the range $[0, 1)$, what difference would that make?

□

Solution to Question 5.13. We present two solutions

```
double FactorialLoop(int n)
{
  double answer =1.0;
  for (int j=2; j <=n; ++j)
    answer*=j;

  return answer;
}


double FactorialRecursion(int n)
{
  if (n ==0)
    return 1.0;
```

```
    return n*FactorialRecursion(n-1);
}
```

The first is a simple naive loop. The second uses recursion which is neat but not necessarily fast.

Note that we have made the return type `double` rather than `int`: the largest `int` is generally around $2E9$, and it does not take a very large n for the factorial function to be bigger than that.

If one wanted a truly fast factorial function, a good solution would be to create a class that stored the values for n from 0 to say 69, and then simply passed back the value requested. Note that 70 factorial is bigger than $1E100$, so it is a reasonable cut-off point, or one could compute the cached values up to the largest number that does not give a float overflow for `doubles`.

Here are some possible related questions:

- How would you compute binomial coefficients efficiently? (Pascal's triangle)
- Do you prefer recursion or loops?
- Which would run faster?
- What is Stirling's formula?
- Suppose we want the answer exactly but it is bigger than the largest `int`, what would you do?

□

Solution to 5.14. The key to this one is to note that if an element is bigger than x, then all elements to the right or below are also bigger than x. Similarly, if an element is less than x, all elements to the left or above are also smaller than x.

We therefore scan the top row from the top right to eliminate right hand columns. We then proceed similarly for the bottom row, the right hand column and the left hand column. We keep on going until there is only one element left. Note that the algorithm is order n where n is the number of rows.

We present C++ code using classes from the xlw project.

```cpp
MyArray FindNumber(const NEMatrix& input, double x)
{
        unsigned long top =0;
        unsigned long bottom = input.rows()-1;
        unsigned long left = 0;
        unsigned long right = input.columns()-1;

        while ( top != bottom || left != right)
        {
                // first scan top row to see
                // how many columns can be removed at right
                while ( input(top,right) > x)
                        --right;

                // scan bottom row to see
                // how many columns can be removed at left
                while ( input(bottom,left) < x)
                        ++left;

                // scan right column to see
                // how many rows can be removed at top
                while ( input(top,right) < x)
                        ++top;

                // scan left column to see
                // many how rows can be removed at bottom
                while ( input(bottom,left) > x)
                        --bottom;

        }

        MyArray result(2);
```

```
      result[0] = top;
      result[1] = left;

      return result;
}
```

Here are some possible related questions:

- What will your routine do if the number is not present? How would you robustify?
- Do you think this algorithm is optimal?

□

Solution to Question 5.15. There are a number of ways to do this one. Each solution will have different pros and cons. Generally, the question is whether to optimise memory or speed, and also whether the solution is robust for large N.

The easiest way to do this is simply to sort the array and then check that the element in place i is i. However, using a general sorting algorithm is overkill since it does not use any of the special structure of the problem, and it is of $\mathcal{O}(N \log N)$ complexity which is higher than we need.

Another simple algorithm is to allocate a vector of booleans and set them all to false. You then loop through setting the value for each number you find to true. If there are no duplicates every element will be true. This is $\mathcal{O}(N)$ in both time and memory.

Here is a simple solution which is fast and uses no extra memory other than a couple of ints. It relies very heavily on the special structure of the problem, however.

```
bool rearrange(std::vector<int>& input)
{
  for (size_t i=0; i< input.size(); ++i)
    while (input[i]!= i)
    {
```

```
    int tmp = input[i];
    if (input[tmp] == tmp)
      return false;
    input[i]=input[tmp];
    input[tmp]=tmp;


  }


  return true;
}
```

We loop through. If the element in place i is wrong, we swap it with the element in the place where it should have been. If that element is already correct, there is a duplicate and we are done. We keep on doing this until the element in place i is correct. This algorithm is $\mathcal{O}(N)$ in terms of computational time. To see this observe that after each swap operation carried out, another element is in the correct place. This means that only N of these operations can be carried out. If there are no duplicates then at the end, the array will be sorted.

Since there are N elements in the array, it is impossible to do better than $\mathcal{O}(N)$ complexity in time.

Here are some possible related questions:

- What if the elements were in the range 0 to M with $M > N$?
- Do you think that time or memory is more important?

□

Solution to Question 5.16. We will assume that we are given two arrays which tell us the value of a function f on a collection of points x. We shall assume that the two arrays are of the same size and that the x coordinates are strictly increasing. We also have to decide what to do if the desired point lies outside the range; for our solution we extrapolate.

There are really two parts to the problem. We first need to identify which two x values straddle the point. Second, we need to interpolate the values at those two points. The standard way to find the appropriate x values is to use binary search, since this has $\log$ complexity for a sorted array.

We present a solution in C++ using STL algorithms and classes:

```cpp
#include <vector>
#include <algorithm>

double Interpolate(const std::vector<double>& xs,
                   const std::vector<double>& fofx,
                   double x)
{
    std::vector<double>::const_iterator it
                = std::lower_bound(xs.begin()+1
                                        ,xs.end(),x);

    if (it == xs.end())
        --it;

    --it;

    std::vector<double>::const_iterator
        it2 = fofx.begin()+(it-xs.begin());

    double xl = *it;
    double fxl = *it2;
    ++it;
    ++it2;
    double xr = *it;
    double fxr = *it2;

    double theta = (x-xl)/(xr-xl);
    double fx = (1.0-theta)*fxl+ theta*fxr;
```

```
    return fx;
}
```

The STL algorithm `lower_bound` returns an iterator pointing to the first element of a sorted range which is greater than or equal to a given element. It uses binary search. Since we want a pair of neighbouring elements, the first smaller than x, and the second bigger than it, we start our search one past the beginning and then decrement the answer. If x is bigger than the entire vector, we will get the end of the vector, that is one after the last element, so we decrement an extra time.

Once the two elements have been found, we compute the fractional distance, θ, and use this to interpolate the function values.

Here are some possible related questions:

- How would you implement the lower bound algorithm yourself?
- If the x values were evenly spaced, could you do this faster?
- Do you think extrapolation is the right solution if x is outside the range?
- Do a bilinear interpolation algorithm.

$\square$

Solution to Question 5.17. We first rephrase the question more mathematically. For some pair of integers a and b, the position after n turns is

$$a + nb.$$

The set of all possible pairs (a, b) is $\mathbb{Z} \times \mathbb{Z}$ which is a countable set. We can therefore find a sequence of pairs (a_n, b_n) which visit all the points on this set. (For example, go clockwise around squares centred at the origin.)

Now suppose at time n, we lob a missile at

$$a_n + nb_n.$$

If $a_n = a$ and $b_n = b$, then this will hit the submarine. Since we are trying all possible pairs, this will eventually happen.

Here are some possible related questions:

- What if a, b are required to be rationals but not integers?
- What if a, b are allowed to be reals but the missile has a blast radius of size $\epsilon > 0$?

☐

Solution to Question 5.18. There are many variants of this floating around; it seems to be more popular in coding interviews, for example at Microsoft, than at quant interviews. It reputedly originated with the Israeli defense force. The idea here is to move slowly until you realise the other robot is ahead of you and then move quickly. We can go slowly by taking one step back for every two steps forward. We arbitrarily start by going left.

```
0 left
1 right
2 left
3 if (parachute) goto 5
4 goto 0
5 left
6 goto 5
```

Here are some possible related questions:

- The code above assumes that the two robots have the same orientation, that is they agree on the leftwards direction. Is the problem solvable if they might not?
- What if the robot's parachute lands separately? You can assume that its parachute is closer than the other robot and its parachute.
- Is the two-dimensional analogue of this problem solvable? What about more than two dimensions?
- Relate this problem to testing a linked list to see if it contains any loops.

☐

Solution to Question 5.19. The easiest way to do this is by recursion. Clearly, the solution will depend on how we represent the tree. One simple solution is that it is a collection of nodes which contain a piece of data, and pointers to two other nodes. If a node is not present then the pointer points to zero instead.

Here is a typical header file for a tree node class

```
#ifndef TREE_NODE_H
#define TREE_NODE_H

class TreeNode
{
public:
  TreeNode* Left;
  TreeNode* Right;
  double data;

};

double GetSum(const TreeNode& top);

#endif
```

Note, however, that we would really need a lot of ancillary code to handle creation and destruction of nodes, but here we present a minimalist solution that would suffice for answering this question.

Our solution does not handle the null case that the tree is empty, but that could be dealt with by having the tree live inside a class which takes care of emptiness.

The easiest way to traverse the entire tree is to use recursion. The sum will be the value at the top plus the sum of the values for each of the two nodes below it if they exist.

```
double GetSum(const TreeNode& top)
{
  double value = top.data;

  if (top.Left !=0)
    value += GetSum(*top.Left);

  if (top.Right !=0)
    value += GetSum(*top.Right);

  return value;
}
```

Here are some possible related questions:

- Modify the solution so it handles the empty case.
- The solution above uses recursion, can you do it without?
- Write a full tree class that includes all the creation, destruction and assignments.
- What is a red-black tree?

□

Solution to Question 5.20. The fundamental problem here is that virtually all paths finish out of the money. The probability of a ten standard deviation move is tiny; according to EXCEL, it is $7E - 24$. The value of this option is therefore almost zero, and run a naive Monte Carlo simulation for any reasonable number of paths and you will get zero.

However, there are techniques to cope with such problems. The simplest is importance sampling. We want to evaluate the integral

$$\int f(S_0 + z)\phi(z)dz$$

and f is zero for $z < 10$. We therefore let ψ be the density of a normal random variable with mean 10, and write the integral as

$$\int f(S_0 + z)\frac{\phi(z)}{\psi(z)}\psi(z)dz.$$

We now draw z from the distribution of $N(10, 1)$, and multiply the pay-off on each path by

$$\frac{\phi(z)}{\psi(z)}.$$

It is useful to compute the value of this:

$$\frac{e^{-\frac{z^2}{2}}}{e^{-\frac{(z-\mu)^2}{2}}} = e^{\frac{\mu^2}{2}-\mu z}$$

with $\mu = 10$.

Here are some possible related questions:

- Do you think $\mu = 10$ is optimal?
- Can you get an analytic formula for the price?
- Could you use stratified sampling here?

$\square$

Solution to Question 5.21. An easy way to tackle this problem is to use inverse transform sampling. You can assume you have a random generator for a uniform random variable U. The idea is that samples from U correspond to values from the cdf of the variable you wish to sample.

Mathematically, suppose we want to sample a random variable X with distribution function $F(x)$. Then we generate a uniform random variable, U, and set $U = F(X)$ or $X = F^{-1}(U)$. Then

$$\mathbb{P}(X \leq x) = \mathbb{P}(F^{-1}(U) \leq x) = \mathbb{P}(U \leq F(x)) = F(x),$$

by definition of the uniform distribution, so X has the distribution of the random variable we wish to sample.

In the case of the exponential random variable, $F(x) = 1 - \exp(-\lambda x)$, so

$$F^{-1}(x) = \frac{-\ln(1 - x)}{\lambda}.$$

Sampling uniform random variables and using this transform will generate exponential random variables.

Here are some possible related questions:

- Prove that the variable X above has an exponential distribution.
- Write pseudo-code to implement the above solution.
- What are some other methods to generate exponential random variables?
- Describe a general technique to generate discrete random variables.

$\square$

Solution to Question 5.22. There are several possible methods to improve the convergence of Monte Carlo simulations, which is essentially an exercise in reducing the variance of the simulated values. We will consider possible approaches in the context of sampling using a normal random variable.

Anti-thetic sampling uses the property that if x has a standard normal distribution then so does $-x$. During the simulation, when one normal random variable is simulated its negative is also used in the simulation. Thus one random draw (or path of draws if the simulation requires it) generates two random outcomes. The advantage of this approach is that the samples are guaranteed to have a mean of zero, achieving the symmetry of the normal distribution.

This idea can be taken further in a method called *moment matching*. Using antithetic sampling we already have that all odd moments of our random numbers are zero (matching the standard normal distribution). Moment matching re-scales the variables to ensure that a given number of even moments also match the standard normal distribution.

Another method that is sometimes applicable is *importance sampling*. This is useful when a large number of the random draws will generate uninteresting results, such as a deep out-of-the-money option where most simulations give an option value of zero. This method is discussed in more detail in Question 3.36.

One of the most powerful methods is using *low discrepancy numbers*. The reason Monte-Carlo simulation works is that eventually you will cover all points (at least, get arbitrarily close to all points) in the sample space (say the unit interval) in a uniform way. However in the short term values will tend to cluster which slows convergence. The idea of low discrepancy numbers is to cover this space in a deterministic and efficient manner, to avoid clustering and other problems associated with standard Monte Carlo. The rate of convergence of the simulation is closer to $\mathcal{O}(N)$. This method is also called *quasi-Monte Carlo*. Note that since the individual draws are no longer independent variance is no longer an accurate measure of the convergence of the simulation, however.

For more information and further references, see [6] pp. 176–181 and [8] for detailed discussion of low discrepancy numbers.

Here are some possible related questions:

- What is the rate of convergence for standard Monte Carlo simulation?
- What are the Sobol and Van der Corput sequences?
- Describe a situation when importance sampling may be useful and how you would use it.

$\square$

Solution to Question 5.23. There are many possible methods to simulate normal random variables. A very simple idea is to use the central limit theorem. Recall that, under appropriate conditions, if a sequence of i.i.d random variables X_i has mean μ and variance σ^2 then

$$\sqrt{n}\left(\left(\frac{1}{n}\sum_{i=1}^{n}X_i\right) - \mu\right) \xrightarrow{d} N\left(0, \sigma^2\right).$$

Thus adding 12 uniform random numbers together and subtracting 6 gives a random number that is (very) approximately normal. This is quick and easy to use, but is not suitable if greater precision is necessary.

An alternative approach is to use the Box-Muller transform. If we take two uniform random variables U_1 and U_2, then the random variables Z_1 and Z_2 defined by

$$Z_1 = \sqrt{-2\ln(U_1)}\cos(2\pi U_2)$$

and

$$Z_2 = \sqrt{-2\ln(U_1)}\sin(2\pi U_2)$$

are independent standard normal random variables.

Another idea is to use the inverse cumulative distribution function (see the solution to Question 5.21 for how this works). However, there is no easy way to calculate the inverse cumulative normal distribution function. Several approximations have been developed, in particular the Moro algorithm. The absolute error of this algorithm is less than 1.15×10^{-9} for any point in the unit interval.

See Appendix B of [6] for more detail on the Moro algorithm.

Here are some possible related questions:

- Prove that the first method above has the correct mean, variance and third moment.
- What is acceptance-rejection sampling?
- Explain the composition approach to simulating random variables.
- Name some other methods for simulating normal random variables.

□

Solution to Question 5.24. One approach to finding the largest element is to simply sort the array, but this is an $\mathcal{O}(n \log n)$ operation. A quicker approach is to iterate through all n elements and update a single variable which stores the largest element so far. To find the smallest number we can use the same procedure, instead updating a variable storing the smallest element. These two operations are $\mathcal{O}(n)$. Note that we have to increment a counter, perform a comparison, and possibly perform an update to the largest element so need at least $3n$.

Here are some possible related questions:

- Present a routine to find the k largest elements.
- Present a routine to find the kth largest element.

□

Solution to Question 5.25. An efficient way to find the longest subsequence of cards in a deck is to use *patience sorting*. Consider a deck of n cards simply labeled 1 through to n. For example we might have 10 cards in the following order

$$\mathbf{1}, 8, \mathbf{5}, \mathbf{6}, 3, \mathbf{7}, \mathbf{10}, 4, 2, 9$$

and one longest subsequence is shown in bold: $1, 5, 6, 7, 10$.

To find the longest subsequence using patience sorting we draw out cards one by one and place them in piles of decreasing order. If we draw a card that cannot be placed on a pile, we start a new pile to the right of the current pile. When we start a new pile we simply mark the card on the top of the previous pile. The longest subsequence of increasing numbers is then the marked cards read from left to right.

Applying this to our example above, we place the 1 card creating the first pile. 8 is bigger than 1, so we start a new pile to the right and mark the 1 card. The 5 card can go on the 8 and we then place the 6 on a new pile to the right and mark the 5. The 3 can go on the pile showing the 5, but 7 is bigger than any cards showing, so we start a new pile and mark the 6. We continue on through all cards until we have our marked subsequence.

Here are some possible related questions:

- What is the order of this algorithm?
- Write this algorithm in C++.

□

CHAPTER 6

Mathematics

6.1. Introduction

Ultimately, a quant is an applied mathematician. It is therefore common to ask general mathematics questions to test those skills. In this chapter, we present such questions which do not fit naturally into the chapters on probability, option pricing and numerical analysis. Often very basic high-school-type questions are asked: if you get these wrong then the interview is over. Others are more subtle and may require a trick or simply high level mathematics. You will certainly be expected to be comfortable with complex analysis, including Fourier transforms, and linear algebra.

We have divided the chapter into general questions and calculus questions. We include detailed references for the tougher problems.

6.2. Questions

6.2.1. General.

QUESTION 6.1. A lighthouse x miles off the coast of a straight, infinitely long beach revolves at one revolution per minute. How fast is the beam moving along the beach when the beam is y miles from the point on the beach nearest the lighthouse?

QUESTION 6.2. What is

$$\lim_{x \to +\infty} \left(\sqrt{x^2 + 5x} - x \right)?$$

QUESTION 6.3. Find the closed-form solution of the Fibonacci sequence.

QUESTION 6.4. How would you determine π by Monte Carlo simulation?

QUESTION 6.5. Show

$$\frac{e^a + e^b}{2} > e^{\frac{a+b}{2}}.$$

QUESTION 6.6. What is greater: e^π or π^e? Prove it, mathematically.

QUESTION 6.7. What is

$$2 + \cfrac{2}{2 + \cfrac{2}{2 + \cfrac{2}{2 + \cfrac{2}{\cdots}}}}?$$

QUESTION 6.8. What is an inflection point? What is the coordinate of the inflection point of the cumulative distribution function of a $N(\mu, \sigma)$ random variable?

QUESTION 6.9. What is a positive-definite matrix? What properties does a positive-definite matrix have?

QUESTION 6.10. Given the matrix

$$A = \begin{bmatrix} 5 & -3 \\ -3 & 5 \end{bmatrix}.$$

find a matrix M, such that $A = M^2$. Now find a matrix C such that $A = C^T C$.

QUESTION 6.11. Let $A_1, A_2, \ldots, A_n$ denote a permutation of $1, 2, \ldots, n$. Show that the product $(A_1 - 1)(A_2 - 2) \ldots (A_n - n)$ is even when n is odd.

QUESTION 6.12. Prove Liouville's theorem – that is that a function which is differentiable and bounded on the whole complex plane is constant.

QUESTION 6.13. What is the Fourier transform of $\sin(x)$, $\cos(x)$?

QUESTION 6.14. If $f(z)$ is analytical and bounded, prove that f is constant

QUESTION 6.15. How do you approximate $\exp(x)$ and $\ln(x)$? How big is the error of the approximation?

QUESTION 6.16. Does $\sum_{n=1}^{\infty} n^{-1}$ converge? Why not?

QUESTION 6.17. Transform the Black–Scholes equation into the heat equation.

QUESTION 6.18. Which is greater, $2^{1/2}$ or $3^{1/3}$?

QUESTION 6.19. How many zeros at the end of 200!?

QUESTION 6.20. What is the rank of a matrix?

QUESTION 6.21. If the correlation of A and B is 0.5 and the correlation of A and C is 0.8, what is the correlation of B and C?

QUESTION 6.22. Define $g(x)$ by

$$g(x) = \int_0^{F(x)} h(x, y)dy.$$

What is $g'(x)$?

QUESTION 6.23. It is now 6.45pm, what is the angle between the hour and the minute hands (you must do this in your head)?

QUESTION 6.24. What is the Taylor series expansion of $\exp(x)$?

QUESTION 6.25. Consider 2^{42}:

(1) What is the leading term in the decimal representation?
(2) What is the order of magnitude?
(3) What is the next significant figure after the leading term?

QUESTION 6.26. Say you can buy chicken nuggets in lots of 6, 9 or 20. What is the largest integer number of nuggets you cannot buy? Prove it.

QUESTION 6.27. Given $a \in [0, 1]$, what is $\sum\limits_{n=0}^{\infty} n^2 a^n$?

QUESTION 6.28. Differentiate $\ln(x)^2$.

QUESTION 6.29. You have a bus, $3/4$ of people get off, 7 get in, $3/4$ get off, 7 get in, $3/4$ get off, 7 get in. What is the smallest number of people that can have been in the bus in the beginning?

QUESTION 6.30. There are 13 chairs in a row and 13 people ordered 1 to 13. Each person enters the room one at a time and must sit next to someone else apart from the first person who chooses his seat randomly. How many possible combinations are there?

QUESTION 6.31. What is the rank of AA^T, where A is an $n \times m$ matrix?

QUESTION 6.32. Find two positive integers, $x \neq y$, such that $x^y = y^x$.

6.2.2. Integration and differentiation.

QUESTION 6.33. What is the derivative of $f(x) = x^x$?

QUESTION 6.34. Compute

$$\frac{\partial}{\partial f} \left(\frac{1}{1 + f\tau} \right)^n,$$

and

$$\frac{\partial}{\partial f_j} \prod_{i=1}^{n} \frac{1}{1 + f_i \tau_i}$$

QUESTION 6.35. Derive, from first principles, the derivative of

$$g(x) = e^{\cos(x)}.$$

QUESTION 6.36. Differentiate $f(x) = x \log(x)$.

QUESTION 6.37. What is $\int \log(x) dx$?

QUESTION 6.38. Evaluate

$$\int \log^n x \, dx.$$

QUESTION 6.39. What is

$$2 \int_0^{1/2} dx \int_{1/2}^{1/2+x} dy?$$

QUESTION 6.40. What is the value of $\int_{-\infty}^{\infty} e^{-x^2} dx$?

QUESTION 6.41. Evaluate

$$\int_0^{\infty} \frac{\log(x)}{(1 + x + x^2)} dx.$$

(Hint: use contour integration.)

QUESTION 6.42. Show that the normal density integrates to one.

6.3. Solutions

6.3.1. General.

Solution to Question 6.1. Let y denote the position of the beam on the beach from the point on the beach nearest the lighthouse. Let θ denote the angle the beam makes with the straight line connecting the lighthouse and the point on the beach nearest it. The question asks us to find $\dot{y} = \frac{dy}{dt}$, where t is time in minutes. From ordinary calculus, we have

$$\frac{dy}{dt} = \frac{dy}{d\theta}\frac{d\theta}{dt}.$$

We are told the lighthouse does one revolution per minute, and can make the obvious assumption that it is rotating at a constant speed. This gives

$$\frac{d\theta}{dt} = 2\pi.$$

From the description, it is clear we have $y = x\tan(\theta)$ and $\theta = \arctan(y/x)$. Thus

$$\frac{dy}{d\theta} = x\sec^2(\theta),$$

and hence finally

$$\frac{dy}{dt} = 2\pi x\sec^2(\theta)$$
$$= 2\pi x\sec^2\left(\arctan\left(\frac{y}{x}\right)\right)$$
$$= 2\pi\frac{x^2 + y^2}{x},$$

using $\sec^2(\eta) = 1 + \tan^2(\eta)$.

Here are some possible related questions:

- How fast is the velocity changing when the beam is y miles along the beach?
- Assume now the light is on top of a ship moving parallel to the beach at a constant speed s. How fast is the beam moving along the beach now?

$\square$

Solution to Question 6.2. To solve this problem, we manipulate the limit with the goal in mind of expanding the square root as a Taylor series:

$$\lim_{x \to +\infty} \left(\sqrt{x^2 + 5x} - x \right) = \lim_{x \to +\infty} \left(x\sqrt{1 + \frac{5}{x}} - x \right)$$

$$= \lim_{x \to +\infty} \left(x \left(\sqrt{1 + \frac{5}{x}} - 1 \right) \right)$$

$$= \lim_{y \to 0} \left(\frac{1}{y} \left(\sqrt{1 + 5y} - 1 \right) \right).$$

Now consider the Taylor series about $x = 0$ for the function $f(x) = \sqrt{1 + ax}$. We have

$$f'(x) = \frac{1}{2}a(1 + ax)^{-1/2}, \qquad f''(x) = \frac{-1}{4}a^2(1 + ax)^{-3/2},$$

which gives

$$f(x) = 1 + \frac{1}{2}ax + \mathcal{O}(x^2)$$

as a Taylor expansion about $x = 0$. Applying this to our limit we see that

$$\lim_{x \to +\infty} \left(\sqrt{x^2 + 5x} - x \right) = \lim_{y \to 0} \left(\frac{1}{y} \left(1 + \frac{5}{2}y + \mathcal{O}(y^2) - 1 \right) \right)$$

$$= \lim_{y \to 0} \left(\frac{5}{2} + \mathcal{O}(y) \right) = \frac{5}{2}.$$

Here are some possible related questions:

- State l'Hôpitals rule.
- Prove the following limits:

(1) $\displaystyle \lim_{x \to 0} \frac{\sin(x)}{x} = 1.$

(2) $\displaystyle \lim_{|x| \to \infty} \left(x \sin \left(\frac{1}{x} \right) \right) = 1.$

(3) $\displaystyle \lim_{x \to \infty} \left(x^n e^{-x} \right) = 0,$ for positive integer n.

□

Solution to Question 6.3. The Fibonacci sequence, $f(n)$ is defined by

$$f(n) := \begin{cases} 1, & \text{for } n = 1, \\ 1, & \text{for } n = 2, \\ f(n-1) + f(n-2), & \text{for } n \geq 3. \end{cases}$$

As it stands, this is a tough question. You need to recognise this is an example of a linear recurrence equation $f(n) = Af(n-1) + Bf(n-2)$, $n \geq 2$. These equations have solutions of the form

$$f(n) = \frac{x_1^n - x_2^n}{x_1 - x_2},$$

where x_1 and x_2 solve $x^2 = Ax + B$. Since in our case $A = B = 1$, we have

$$x_1 = \frac{1 + \sqrt{5}}{2} \quad \text{and} \quad x_2 = \frac{1 - \sqrt{5}}{2}.$$

This gives the closed form of the sequence as

$$f(n) = \frac{1}{\sqrt{5}}(x_1^n - x_2^n) = \frac{(1 + \sqrt{5})^n - (1 - \sqrt{5})^n}{2^n \sqrt{5}}.$$

This is known as *Binet's formula*, and the value x_1 is sometimes referred to as the *golden ratio*.

Fingers crossed you won't be asked this question directly, as it requires quite specific knowledge about linear recurrence equations. If instead you are given the closed form and asked to verify if satisfies the definition of the Fibonacci sequence, how should you proceed? Induction is the easiest way. First verify the base cases for $n = 0$ and $n = 1$. Now assume the relationship holds for all $n < k$, does it hold for $n = k$?

$$\begin{aligned} f(k) &= f(k-1) + f(k-2) \\ &= \frac{1}{\sqrt{5}}(x_1^{n-1} - x_2^{n-1}) + \frac{1}{\sqrt{5}}(x_1^{n-2} - x_2^{n-2}) \\ &= \frac{1}{\sqrt{5}}x_1^{n-2}(1 + x_1) - \frac{1}{\sqrt{5}}x_2^{n-2}(1 + x_2) \\ &= \frac{1}{\sqrt{5}}(x_1^n - x_2^n), \end{aligned}$$

where the last equality is justified since x_1 and x_2 solve $x^2 = x + 1$, which can easily be checked. This concludes the inductive proof.

Here are some possible related questions:

- Show

$$\lim_{n\to\infty} \frac{f(n+1)}{f(n)} = \frac{1+\sqrt{5}}{2}.$$

- The *Lucas numbers* satisfy the relationship

$$L(n) := \begin{cases} 1 & \text{for } n = 1, \\ 3 & \text{for } n = 2, \\ L(n-1) + L(n-2) & \text{for } n \geq 3. \end{cases}$$

Verify by induction that the closed form solution is given by

$$L(n) = \left(\frac{1+\sqrt{5}}{2}\right)^n + \left(\frac{1-\sqrt{5}}{2}\right)^n.$$

□

Solution to Question 6.4. The general principle here is that we can find the area of any set by computing the expectation of the indicator function of the set after enclosing it in a square (or cube). That is we find what proportion of points drawn from the square at random lie in the set.

We compute the area of a circle with radius $1/2$ centred at $(1/2, 1/2)$ and multiply by 4, since the area is given by $A = \pi r^2$. To compute the area, repeatedly draw pairs of independent uniforms from $[0, 1] \times [0, 1]$, and measure what fraction land inside the circle (that is, if your uniforms are U_1 and U_2, check that $(U_1 - 1/2)^2 + (U_2 - 1/2)^2 \leq 1$). This will converge to $\pi/4$ at a rate of $n^{-1/2}$ by the Central Limit theorem.

Here are some possible related questions:

- Do you think this a good way to numerically approximate π?
- Prove that the rate of convergence is $n^{-1/2}$.
- What is Monte Carlo good for?
- How would you approximate π if you had to find it to 100 decimal places?

□

Solution to Question 6.5. The key to this question is to recognise that it is a statement about convexity. A function is strictly convex if and only if the second derivative is positive, equivalently if and only if the chord between two points on the graph lies above the graph. We are asked to prove the latter condition for the special case that the point is the midpoint of the interval.

We check the second derivative. Let $f(x) = e^x$ so $f''(x) > 0$ and the answer is immediate.

Here are some possible related questions:

- Are convex functions always differentiable?
- Are convex functions always continuous?
- If the mid-point of every chord is above the graph, does this make the function convex?
- Do the problem using the inequality of arithmetic and geometric means.

□

Solution to Question 6.6. This is a nasty transcendental equation. Our best hope is to find a way of rearranging it so that e only appears on one side and π on the other. When confronted with nasty powers, taking logs to simplify is often a good plan.

Taking logs and rearranging, $e^\pi \geq \pi^e$ if and only if

$$\pi \log e \geq e \log \pi,$$

or

$$\frac{\log e}{e} \geq \frac{\log \pi}{\pi}.$$

It is now a statement about the function

$$f(x) = (\log x)/x.$$

We need to show that it is decreasing, so check its derivative:

$$f'(x) = \frac{1 - \log x}{x^2}.$$

This is equal to zero for $x = e$, and less than zero for $x > e$. So f is a decreasing function on (e, ∞) and e^π is bigger.

Here are some possible related questions:

- What is $e^{i\pi}$?
- What is the value of e?

☐

Solution to Question 6.7. This is an example of a *continued fraction*. The key to this problem is to recognise the repetition in the equation. In other words, if we set

$$y = 2 + \cfrac{2}{2 + \cfrac{2}{2 + \cfrac{2}{\cdots}}},$$

then what we really have is

$$y = 2 + \frac{2}{y}.$$

Multiplying through by y gives the equation $y^2 - 2y - 2 = 0$, and applying the quadratic formula gives the possible solutions $y = 1 \pm \sqrt{3}$. Clearly the original equation has only one solution (think of the intersection of the graphs $f(y) = y$ and $g(y) = 2 + \frac{2}{y}$), which one do we choose? From the definition of y we can see $y > 2$, and so we conclude $y = 1 + \sqrt{3}$. The extra solution occurred because we multiplied by y to create the quadratic form.

Here is a possible related question:

- What is

$$1 + \cfrac{1}{1 + \cfrac{1}{1 + \cfrac{1}{\cdots}}}?$$

☐

Solution to Question 6.8. An inflection point, or point of inflection, is a point on a curve where the sign of the curvature (concavity) changes. To find inflection points of a function $f(x)$, note that it is necessary to have $f''(x) = 0$. However this condition is not sufficient, and we must further check that the second derivative has changed sign at this point, rather than just touching zero.

Recall the cumulative distribution function of the $N(\mu, \sigma)$ random variable is given by

$$F(x) = \int_{-\infty}^{x} \frac{1}{\sqrt{2\pi}\sigma} \exp\left(-\frac{(y-\mu)^2}{2\sigma^2}\right) dy.$$

This gives

$$F'(x) = \frac{1}{\sqrt{2\pi}\sigma} \exp\left(-\frac{(x-\mu)^2}{2\sigma^2}\right),$$

and

$$F''(x) = \frac{1}{\sqrt{2\pi}\sigma} \exp\left(-\frac{(x-\mu)^2}{2\sigma^2}\right) \left(-\frac{(x-\mu)}{\sigma^2}\right).$$

Clearly $F''(x) = 0$ if and only if

$$\left(-\frac{(x-\mu)}{\sigma^2}\right) = 0,$$

or

$$x = \mu.$$

We need to check the second derivative changes sign at $x = \mu$. The exponential term is always positive, so the only term affecting the sign of the second derivative is $(x - \mu)$. This is positive for $x > \mu$ and negative for $x < \mu$, so the second derivative changes sign and we are done.

Here are some possible related questions:

- What are the inflection points of the $N(\mu, \sigma)$ density function (trick question)?
- What are the inflection points of $g(x) = \sin(kx)$?

$\square$

Solution to Question 6.9. There are several equivalent definitions for a positive-definite matrix, which must be a square matrix. We will state the most common definition, and note a couple of useful equivalent properties. For a matrix A, we will denote by A^T its transpose and by A^* its conjugate transpose. Recall that if A has entries A_{ij}, $1 \le i \le n$, $1 \le j \le n$, then its transpose has entries $A_{ij}^T = A_{ji}$ and the conjugate transpose is formed by first taking the transpose and then the complex conjugate of each entry.

Let M be a $n \times n$ matrix. Then M is positive definite if for all non-zero vectors $\mathbf{z} \in \mathbb{C}^n$ we have

$$\mathbf{z}^* M \mathbf{z} > 0.$$

This is the most common definition of a positive definite matrix. However it may be useful to use an alternative, equivalent, definition. If M is a Hermitian matrix (a matrix is Hermitian if it is square and equal to its own conjugate transpose – for a matrix with only real entries, this is equivalent to being square and symmetric), then M is positive definite if and only if either

- M has only positive eigenvalues; or
- All the following matrices have positive determinant:
    - The upper-left 1-by-1 corner of M
    - The upper-left 2-by-2 corner of M
    - ...
    - M.

Most often in quantitative finance, we are only concerned with the case where the matrix is a covariance matrix, in which case the matrix is real and symmetric.

A real symmetric matrix is a covariance matrix for some set of random variables if and only if it is *positive semi-definite*. The "semi" refers to the fact that zero eigenvalues are allowed, and thus there are vectors such that

$$x^T M x = 0,$$

but non-negativity is still required.

Here are some possible related questions:

- Are the following matrices positive definite?

$$\begin{pmatrix} 1 & 0 \\ 0 & 1 \end{pmatrix} \quad \begin{pmatrix} \cos(\theta) & -\sin(\theta) \\ \sin(\theta) & \cos(\theta) \end{pmatrix}$$

$\square$

Solution to Question 6.10. Denote our matrix M by

$$M = \begin{bmatrix} a & b \\ c & d \end{bmatrix}.$$

We then have that M^2 is given by

$$M^2 = \begin{bmatrix} a^2 + bc & ab + bd \\ ac + cd & bc + d^2 \end{bmatrix}.$$

Setting $M^2 = A$ gives the four equations

$$a^2 + bc = 5, \qquad\qquad ab + bd = -3,$$
$$ac + cd = -3, \qquad\qquad bc + d^2 = 5.$$

The second and third equations give $-3 = b(a+d)$ and $-3 = c(a+d)$ respectively, which gives $b = c$. This reduces the problem to the three equations

$$5 = a^2 + b^2, \qquad -3 = ab + bd, \qquad 5 = b^2 + d^2.$$

The first and third give $a^2 = d^2$, so we take $a = d = \sqrt{5 - b^2}$. Inserting this into the second gives

$$-\frac{3}{2} = b\sqrt{5 - b^2},$$

so we see b must be negative. This is an important observation, since to solve the above equation we will square both sides, creating a second positive solution. Squaring the above and using the quadratic formula gives

$$b^2 = \frac{5 \pm 4}{2}.$$

To keep a and d real, we take $b^2 = \frac{1}{2}$, so $b = -\frac{1}{\sqrt{2}}$. Thus the solution is

$$M = \begin{bmatrix} \frac{3}{\sqrt{2}} & -\frac{1}{\sqrt{2}} \\ -\frac{1}{\sqrt{2}} & \frac{3}{\sqrt{2}} \end{bmatrix}.$$

We now consider the second part of the problem, finding a matrix C such that $A = C^T C$. Let the matrix C be given by

$$C = \begin{bmatrix} e & f \\ g & h \end{bmatrix}.$$

The matrix $C^T C$ is then given by

$$C^T C = \begin{bmatrix} e^2 + f^2 & eg + fh \\ eg + fh & g^2 + h^2 \end{bmatrix}.$$

This time setting $C^T C = A$ gives only the three unique equations

$$e^2 + f^2 = 5,$$
$$eg + fh = -3,$$
$$g^2 + h^2 = 5.$$

With three equations and four unknowns we clearly do not have a unique solution. This means we will have one free variable, which the value of the others will be expressed in terms of. However there is no need to go to this length of generality. The question asks us to find a matrix C, so we can assign any value to one of the variables and see if we can find an appropriate matrix.

Clearly the easiest way to do this is to set one of the variables equal to zero, so we choose $f = 0$. Immediately we have $e = \pm\sqrt{5}$, and again with the theme of only needing one solution we take $e = \sqrt{5}$. The second equation then gives $g = \frac{-3}{\sqrt{5}}$, and the final equation gives $h = \pm\frac{4}{\sqrt{5}}$. Thus our matrix C is

$$\begin{bmatrix} \sqrt{5} & 0 \\ \frac{-3}{\sqrt{5}} & \frac{4}{\sqrt{5}} \end{bmatrix}.$$

Here are some possible related questions:

- Is there more than one solution to the first part of this problem?
- How do you define the eigenvalues and eigenvectors of a matrix?
- There is a second, more elegant way to find the square root of a matrix involving the eigenvalues and eigenvectors of the matrix. Look this up and apply it to this example.

□

Solution to Question 6.11. We begin by recalling some rules regarding subtraction and multiplication of odd and even integers:

odd − odd = even,	odd − even = odd,	even − even = even,
odd × odd = odd,	odd × even = even,	even × even = even.

Observing this, we can see that the statement $B_1 \times B_2 \times \cdots \times B_n$ is even is equivalent to saying that at least one of the B_i's is even, $1 \le i \le n$. In other words our task is to show that one of the terms

$$(A_i - i), \ 1 \leq i \leq n,$$

is even when n is odd.

When n is odd, we have $(n+1)/2$ odd numbers and $(n-1)/2$ even numbers amongst the A_i's (and hence amongst the numbers $1, 2, \ldots, n$ which we subtract from them). However to avoid having any even numbers, we must subtract from each odd number an even number (and from each even an odd, but we can ignore this). This is clearly not possible since there are more odd A_i's than there are even numbers in $1, 2, \ldots, n$.

Here are some possible related questions:

- What conclusions can you draw when n is even?
- Does the problem change if instead of writing $(A_i - i)$ we write $(A_i + i)$?
- If instead we look at the product of factors $(A_i - 2i)$ the result is always even, why is this?

$\square$

Solution to Question 6.12. The following is based on the proof in [19], pp. 184–185.

Let f be the function in question, that is we assume $f(z)$ is differentiable on the whole complex plane and $|f(z)| \leq M$ for some constant M.

We then need Cauchy's estimate. Cauchy's estimate states that if f is differentiable on the open disc $|z - z_0| < R$, and $|f(z)| \leq M$ for $|z - z_0| \leq r, 0 < r < R$, then

$$|f^{(n)}(z_0)| \leq \frac{Mn!}{r^n},$$

for all integers $n \geq 0$.

For us this gives, with r arbitrary,

$$|f'(z_0)| \leq \frac{M}{r}.$$

However since f is differentiable on the whole plane and r is arbitrary, we can let $r \to \infty$. With $f'(z_0)$ independent of r this gives

$$|f'(z_0)| = 0.$$

This holds for all z_0 and hence $f'(z) = 0$ on the complex plane — f is constant.

Here are some possible related questions:

- Define holomorphic and entire functions.
- What are the Cauchy–Riemann equations, and what is their significance?
- What is Cauchy's integral formula?
- Prove Cauchy's estimate (use a generalisation of Cauchy's integral formula).
- State Cauchy's residue theorem.

□

Solution to Question 6.13. Taking the Fourier transform of a function is essentially an exercise in integration, however this problem is not as easy as it first seems. For a function $f(x)$, we define the Fourier transform, $F(s)$, as

$$F(t) = \frac{1}{\sqrt{2\pi}} \int_{-\infty}^{\infty} e^{-itx} f(x) dx,$$

since this definition is closely related to the *characteristic function* in probability theory. Note that other definitions exist, however these only differ by constant factors and so do not impose any real changes on what follows.

Hence our problem is to evaluate

$$F_s(t) = \frac{1}{\sqrt{2\pi}} \int_{-\infty}^{\infty} e^{-itx} \sin(x) dx,$$

where we use the s subscript to denote the Fourier transform of the $\sin(x)$ function. The key to proceeding from here is to write the $\sin(x)$ function as a linear combination of complex exponentials:

$$\sin(x) = \frac{e^{ix} - e^{-ix}}{2i}.$$

This gives

$$F_s(t) = \frac{1}{2i\sqrt{2\pi}} \int_{-\infty}^{\infty} \left(e^{-ix(t-1)} - e^{-ix(t+1)} \right) dx.$$

To evaluate this expression, we need to step back a bit to some Fourier transforms of simple functions. Firstly, the Fourier transform of 1 is

$$F_1(t) = \sqrt{2\pi}\delta(t),$$

where $\delta(t)$ is the *Dirac delta function*. How do we know this? The defining characteristic of the Dirac delta function is that for a function $f(x)$,

$$\int_{-\infty}^{\infty} f(x)\delta(x)dx = f(0).$$

For a Fourier transform $F(t)$, the original function $f(x)$ can be recovered by inversion,

$$f(x) = \frac{1}{\sqrt{2\pi}} \int_{-\infty}^{\infty} e^{itx} F(t)dt.$$

Thus if we invert $\sqrt{2\pi}\delta(t)$ to obtain the original function, we see

$$f(x) = \frac{1}{\sqrt{2\pi}} \int_{-\infty}^{\infty} e^{itx} \sqrt{2\pi}\delta(t)dt$$
$$= 1,$$

and hence $\sqrt{2\pi}\delta(t)$ is the Fourier transform of 1. The second property of Fourier transforms we need is the shift operator. That is, suppose $f(x)$ has Fourier transform $F(t)$. What is the Fourier transform of $e^{iax}f(x)$, $G(t)$?

$$G(t) = \frac{1}{\sqrt{2\pi}} \int_{-\infty}^{\infty} e^{-itx} e^{iax} f(x)dx$$
$$= \int_{-\infty}^{\infty} e^{-ix(t-a)} f(x)dx$$
$$= F(t-a).$$

When we write $\sin(x)$ as a sum of exponentials, they essentially become shifts of the function $f(x) = 1$. Hence combining these results gives

$$F_s(t) = i\sqrt{2\pi}\frac{\delta(t+1) - \delta(t-1)}{2}.$$

Proceeding in the same way gives

$$F_c(t) = \sqrt{2\pi} \frac{\delta(t-1) + \delta(t+1)}{2},$$

where $F_c(t)$ denotes the Fourier transform of $\cos(x)$.

Here are some possible related questions:

- How is the Fourier transform related to the characteristic function in probability theory?
- Show the Fourier transform of $e^{-\alpha x^2}$, $\alpha > 0$, is

$$\frac{1}{\sqrt{2\alpha}} e^{-\frac{t^2}{4\alpha}}.$$

- Under a couple of assumptions, if the Fourier transform of $f(x)$ is $F(t)$, show that the Fourier transform of $\frac{d^n}{dx^n} f(x)$ is

$$(it)^n F(t).$$

  What are the assumptions?
- Let the Fourier transforms of $f_1(x)$ and $f_2(x)$ be $F_1(t)$ and $F_2(t)$ respectively. The *convolution* of f_1 and f_2 is defined by

$$g(x) = (f_1 \star f_2)(x) = \int_{-\infty}^{\infty} f_1(s) f_2(x-s) ds.$$

  Show that the Fourier transform of $g(x)$ is

$$G(t) = \sqrt{2\pi} F_1(t) F_2(t).$$

  □

Solution to Question 6.14. Just making sure you were paying attention! This is just a re-wording of Liouville's theorem, see the solution to Question 6.12 for the proof.   □

Solution to Question 6.15. In general, if you are asked to approximate a function you should think of using the Taylor series expansion for the function. The Taylor series of a function $f(x)$ expresses the function as a sum of polynomials.

Technically, if the function $f(x)$ is infinitely differentiable in a neighbourhood of a real or complex number z, then we can approximate the function via

$$f(x) \sim \sum_{n=0}^{\infty} \frac{f^{(n)}(z)}{n!}(x-z)^n,$$

where $f^{(n)}(z)$ is the nth derivative of the function evaluated at z. This sum may or may not converge. If it converges to the function $f(x)$ then the function is said to be *analytic*. Whether or not the function is analytic, we always have

$$f(x) - \sum_{n=0}^{N} \frac{f^{(n)}(z)}{n!}(x-z)^n = \mathcal{O}\left((x-z)^{N+1}\right).$$

To approximate the function, we want to use the first N terms. A natural question is then what is the error of this approximation? The Lagrange form of the remainder term R_N, the error after taking the first N terms, states that there exists a number ζ between x and z such that

$$R_N = \frac{f^{(N+1)}(\zeta)}{(N+1)!}(x-z)^{N+1}.$$

Usually we are interested in bounds on the error, and in this case we would take

$$|R_N| \leq \sup_{\zeta \in (x,z)} \frac{|f^{(N+1)}(\zeta)|}{(N+1)!}|x-z|^{N+1}.$$

Let's look at applying this to the two given functions. For $f(x) = \exp(x)$, the easiest point to expand about is $z = 0$. We have

$$f^{(n)}(x) = \exp(x)$$

for all $n = 0, 1, 2, \ldots$ and hence $f^{(n)}(0) = 1$. This gives the Taylor series

$$\exp(x) = \sum_{n=0}^{\infty} \frac{1}{n!}x^n.$$

The error term after using N terms to approximate $f(x)$ is

$$\frac{e^{\zeta}}{(N+1)!}x^{N+1},$$

for ζ between x and z. This will converge rapidly for x small but slowly for x large. One solution is to write

$$e^x = \left(e^{x/N}\right)^N,$$

where N is an integer larger than x.

For the function $g(x) = \ln(x)$ we can not expand about $z = 0$ as $g(x)$, and its derivatives, are not defined there. Typically we would expand about $z = 1$. The derivatives are given by

$$g^{(n)}(x) = \frac{(-1)^{n+1}(n-1)!}{x^n},$$

for $n = 1, 2, \ldots$ hence

$$g^{(n)}(1) = (-1)^{n+1}(n-1)!.$$

This gives the Taylor series

$$\ln(x) = \sum_{n=1}^{\infty} \frac{(-1)^{n+1}}{n}(x-1)^n,$$

and the error term after N steps of

$$\frac{(-1)^{N+2}}{\zeta^{N+1}(N+1)}(x-1)^{N+1},$$

for ζ between x and z.

Here are some possible related questions:

- What is the Taylor series for $\sqrt{x}$? What is the error term?
- Use the above Taylor series to integrate $\sqrt{x}$.
- What is a Maclaurin series?

$\square$

Solution to Question 6.16. The short, and perhaps obvious answer from the way the question is posed, is no. This is perhaps one of the most commonly used examples of a divergent series and there's a good chance you know the answer off the top of your head. Let's look at how to prove it.

First consider the function

$$g(x) = \frac{1}{\lfloor x \rfloor}, \qquad x > 1,$$

where $\lfloor x \rfloor$ denotes the largest integer less than or equal to x. The integral over $(1, \infty)$ of this function clearly gives the desired sum,

$$\int_1^\infty g(x)dx = \sum_{n=1}^\infty \frac{1}{n}.$$

In addition, $g(x)$ dominates the function $f(x) = \frac{1}{x}, x > 1$, that is $g(x) \geq f(x)$ for $x > 1$. Hence we have

$$\int_1^\infty g(x)dx \geq \int_1^\infty \frac{1}{x}dx$$
$$= [\log(x)]_1^\infty = \infty,$$

proving that the original sum is unbounded (please note that we have been a little sloppy on notation here, but the idea is solid.)

Here are some possible related questions:

- Prove $\sum_{n=1}^\infty 1/n^2$ converges.
- What is the alternating series test for convergence? Use it to prove $\sum_{n=1}^\infty (-1)^n 1/n$ converges. Does this series converge absolutely?
- What is the ratio test for convergence? Use it to prove $\sum_{n=1}^\infty \frac{n}{e^n}$ converges.

□

Solution to Question 6.17. Let C denote the price of the call option on a stock with current price S at time t, where the stock price satisfies the stochastic differential equation

$$dS_t = \mu S_t dt + \sigma S_t dW_t,$$

for a Brownian motion W_t. If r is the constant interest rate, then the Black–Scholes equation is given by

$$\frac{\partial C}{\partial t} + rS\frac{\partial C}{\partial S} + \frac{1}{2}\sigma^2 S^2 \frac{\partial^2 C}{\partial S^2} = rC,$$

where it is understood that C and its partial derivatives are functions of S and t. To transform this equation into the heat equation, we follow the method outlined in [6],

p. 109. To begin, observe that the solution to the stochastic differential equation for S_t is an exponential function (it's a geometric Brownian motion). This motivates writing $S = e^Z$, or $Z = \log(S)$. We then have

$$\frac{\partial C}{\partial S} = \frac{\partial C}{\partial Z} \cdot \frac{\partial Z}{\partial S}$$
$$= \frac{\partial C}{\partial Z} \cdot \frac{1}{S},$$

and

$$\frac{\partial^2 C}{\partial S^2} = \frac{\partial}{\partial S}\left(\frac{\partial C}{\partial S}\right) = \frac{\partial}{\partial S}\left(\frac{\partial C}{\partial Z} \cdot \frac{1}{S}\right)$$
$$= \frac{1}{S^2}\left(\frac{\partial^2 C}{\partial Z^2} - \frac{\partial C}{\partial Z}\right).$$

Substituting this into the original equation gives

$$\frac{\partial C}{\partial t} + \left(r - \frac{1}{2}\sigma^2\right)\frac{\partial C}{\partial Z} + \frac{1}{2}\sigma^2\frac{\partial^2 C}{\partial Z^2} = rC.$$

We now have a constant coefficient equation. The next step is to notice that it is not really the current time, t, that is important in pricing the option, but rather the time until expiry, $\tau = T - t$. Making this substitution gives

$$\frac{\partial C}{\partial \tau} - \left(r - \frac{1}{2}\sigma^2\right)\frac{\partial C}{\partial Z} - \frac{1}{2}\sigma^2\frac{\partial^2 C}{\partial Z^2} = -rC.$$

Further, we know that the call option is a discounted value of a possible future cash flow. We call this cash flow D, and express this by writing $C = e^{-r\tau}D$. This gives

$$\frac{\partial D}{\partial \tau} - \left(r - \frac{1}{2}\sigma^2\right)\frac{\partial D}{\partial Z} - \frac{1}{2}\sigma^2\frac{\partial^2 D}{\partial Z^2} = 0.$$

The final step is to note that the mean value of Z at time t is $Z_0 + (r - \frac{1}{2}\sigma^2)t$. We shift coordinates to take this into account, by letting $y = Z + \left(r - \frac{1}{2}\sigma^2\right)\tau$. Evaluating the new derivatives gives

$$\frac{\partial D}{\partial \tau} = \frac{1}{2}\sigma^2\frac{\partial^2 D}{\partial y^2},$$

which is none other than the one-dimensional heat equation.

Here are some possible related questions:

- What are the boundary conditions for the original Black–Scholes equation?
- Follow the transformations used in the above derivation to arrive at the boundary conditions for the problem expressed as the heat equation.
- Solve the heat equation using the new boundary conditions, and then reverse the transformations to obtain the solution to the Black–Scholes equation.

□

Solution to Question 6.18. One *tempting* approach to answer this question is to consider the more general case of the function

$$f(x) = x^{1/x},$$

and look at where the function is an increasing function of x and where it is a decreasing function of x.

To differentiate, write

$$f(x) = \exp\left\{\log(x^{1/x})\right\} = \exp\left\{\frac{1}{x}\log(x)\right\}.$$

Then using the standard rules of differentiation we have

$$f'(x) = \frac{f(x)}{x^2}\left(1 - \log(x)\right).$$

Since $f(x)/x^2$ is positive for $x > 0$ the sign of $f'(x)$ changes at the zeros of $1 - \log(x)$, or at $x = e$. Unfortunately at this point you realise why this approach is *tempting* but not helpful – the derivative changes signs between the two points we are interested in (2 and 3).

The solution is simple once you know it: since for positive a and b we have $a > b \Leftrightarrow a^2 > b^2$ and $a > b \Leftrightarrow a^3 > b^3$ we have

$$2^{1/2} < 3^{1/3} \Leftrightarrow 2 < 3^{2/3} \Leftrightarrow 2^3 < 3^2,$$

and clearly the final inequality is true. Hence $2^{1/2} < 3^{1/3}$.

Here are some possible related questions:

- For what values of x is the function $f(x)$ defined?
- What is the derivative of $g(x) = 2^x$?

☐

Solution to Question 6.19. Consider the following algorithm applied to an integer n: any integer n ending in a zero is equal to $5 \times 2 \times n_1$, where n_1 is an integer with all digits prior to the zero of n preserved but with the zero removed. The resulting integer, n_1, may or may not end in a zero. If it does, we can repeat the process, otherwise we are finished. At the end of the process we have written n as $n = (5 \times 2)^k \times n_k$, where n_k does not end in a zero.

Hence the key to this question is to consider the prime decomposition of 200! and see how many 5s and 2s there are: since we are interested in *pairs* of 5s and 2s, the solution to this problem will be the minimum of these numbers.

A number has a 5 in its prime decomposition if and only if it ends in a 5 or a 0. There is at least one factor of 5 in each of $5, 10, 15, \ldots, 200$, of which there are 40 numbers. However, $25, 50, 75, \ldots, 200$ all contain two factors, except for 125 which contains 3 factors. Thus the total number of 5s is 49.

Clearly there are more than 49 2s, since as a minimum every even number has 2 in its prime decomposition.

Hence the answer is 49.

Here are some possible related questions:

- How do you approximate factorials using the natural logarithm and its integral?
- What are some bounds on the above approximation?
- What is Stirling's approximation?
- What is the gamma function?

☐

Solution to Question 6.20. To define the rank of a matrix, we first define the column and row rank. The column rank of a matrix is the number of linearly independent column vectors in the matrix (for completeness, a vector c is linearly independent of the vectors $v_1, v_2, \ldots, v_n$ if there are no scalars $a_1, a_2, \ldots, a_n$ such that $c = a_1 v_1 + a_2 v_2 + \cdots + a_n v_n$). The row rank is similar, being the number of linearly independent row vectors in the matrix.

One can prove that the row rank and column rank of a matrix are equal, and this is called the rank of the matrix.

There are many important properties of a matrix, for example:

- A square matrix is non-singular if and only if it has full rank (a matrix of size $n \times n$ has full rank if its rank is n).
- The rank of an $m \times n$ matrix is less than or equal to the minimum of n and m.
- If you consider the $m \times n$ matrix A as a mapping from F^n to F^m then the rank of A is also the dimension of the image.
- $rank(AB) \leq \min(rank(A), rank(B))$.

Here are some possible related questions:

- What is the Gaussian elimination method to determine the rank of a matrix?
- What are some other methods to determine the rank of a matrix?
- How do you use the rank of a matrix to determine the number of solutions to a system of linear equations?
- What is the kernel of a matrix?
- What is the rank-nullity theorem?

$\square$

Solution to Question 6.21. There may be more than one possible value, and to determine the possible range we need to look at the resulting correlation matrices. We know from Question 3.35 that a correlation matrix must be positive semi-definite. If we let the correlation between B and C be x, then we will have the following correlation matrix

$$M = \begin{pmatrix} 1 & 0.5 & 0.8 \\ 0.5 & 1 & x \\ 0.8 & x & 1 \end{pmatrix}$$

From the solution to Question 6.9, we know that this matrix is positive semi-definite if and only if the determinant of its upper left 1×1 matrix, upper left 2×2 matrix and the entire matrix are positive.

Clearly the determinants of the upper left 1×1 matrix and upper left 2×2 matrix are positive. The determinant of the entire matrix is given by the equation $-x^2 + 0.8x + 0.11$. Since we need this to be positive we find the roots of this equation. This shows that x must lie in the range

$$0.4 - \frac{1}{2}\sqrt{1.08} < x < 0.4 + \frac{1}{2}\sqrt{1.08},$$

which is the solution to the problem.

Here is a possible related question:

- Is there a bound on the correlation between A and B such that there is a possible correlation between B and C?

□

Solution to Question 6.22. This is a straight-forward question if you remember the Leibniz integration rule: assume $h(x, y)$ is such that $h_x(x, y)$ is continuous (where we use the subscript to denote the partial derivative), then

$$\frac{d}{dx} \left(\int_{V(x)}^{W(x)} h(x,y)dy \right)$$

$$= \left(\int_{V(x)}^{W(x)} h_x(x,y)dy \right) + h(x, W(x))W'(x) - h(x, V(x))V'(x).$$

Using this rule, we then have

$$g'(x) = \int_0^{F(x)} h_x(x,y)dy + h(x, F(x))F'(x).$$

Here are some possible related questions:

- Find $f'(x)$ in the following examples:
  (1)
  $$f(x) = \int_0^{x^2} (1 + x + xy)dy.$$
  (2)
  $$f(x) = \int_{\sin x}^{\cos x} (1 + y^2)dy.$$

- Use first principles to prove the Leibniz integral rule for the simple case $f(x) = \int_w^u h(x, y)dy$, where u and w are constants.

□

Solution to Question 6.23. At 6:45 the big hand will be pointing straight at the 9 on the clock dial. The little hand will be three quarters of the way between the 6 and the 7. Since there are 12 number on the clock face, the angle between each number is 30 degrees. Three quarters of this means the little hand has traveled another 22.5 degrees towards the 9 (and the big hand). There are 90 degrees in total between the 6 and the 9, so the remaining angle is 67.5 degrees.

Here is a possible related question:

- What is the angle at 7:23?

□

Solution to Question 6.24. The Taylor series expansion of a function $f(x)$ at a point a is given by

$$\sum_{n=0}^{\infty} \frac{f^{(n)}(a)}{n!}(x - a)^n.$$

Since for the exponential function $f(x) = e^x$ we have $f^{(n)}(x) = e^x$, the Taylor series function for $\exp(x)$ about the point a is given by

$$\sum_{n=0}^{\infty} \frac{e^a}{n!}(x - a)^n.$$

Here are some possible related questions:

- What is a Maclaurin series?
- What is the Maclaurin series expansion of $\sin(x)$ and $\cos(x)$?
- What is the Taylor series expansion of $\ln(x)$ about the point $x = 1$?
- Give a bound on the error when the Maclaurin series is used to approximate the value of $\exp(1)$ using the first three terms.

$\square$

Solution to Question 6.25. You need to be able to quickly approximate 2^{42} and identify which terms are important and in what way.

One approximation that you should keep in mind is $2^{10} \approx 1000 = 10^3$ (you should really know $2^{10} = 1024$, but the approximation is what's important initially). Now we have

$$2^{42} = 2^2 \times 2^{10} \times 2^{10} \times 2^{10} \times 2^{10} \approx 4 \times 10^{12}.$$

This gives the solution to the first two problems: the leading term is 4 and the order of magnitude of the number is 10^{12}.

To get the next significant figure we need to consider the approximation we used in more detail. Really what we said was

$$2^{42} = 4 \times 10^{12} \times 1.024^4,$$

since $2^{10} = 1024 = 10^3 \times 1.024$. To determine the next significant figure we need to expand the value of 1.024^4.

There are at least two approaches to this problem. The first is quick and rough, using some basic finance. The value of 1.024^4 is the value of an investment of \$1 for four periods at a compounding rate of 2.4% per period. At low rates and for a small number of periods the value of compounding and simple interest do not diverge too greatly, so the value of the interest is approximately $2.4\% \times 4 \approx 0.1$. Thus $1.024^4 \approx 1.1$ so our next significant figure is 4 ($1.1 \times 4 = 4.4$).

While the previous approach works quickly (and it's always good to relate questions back to finance), the interviewer is probably expecting you to use the binomial theorem. We can rewrite the required value as

$$1.024^4 = (1 + 0.024)^4.$$

The first term in this expansion is clearly 1 (which gave our first significant figure), while the second term is given by $0.024 \times 4 \approx 0.1$ (see expansion questions below). This, thankfully, gives the same answer as the previous approach.

Here are some possible related questions:

- What is the next significant figure?
- Write $(x + y)^n$ as a series for positive integer n.
- Repeat the original question for 8^7.

□

Solution to Question 6.26. Note that if we can make an odd number n using a combination of 6, 9 and 20 nugget lots, then we must be able to make the even number $n - 9$ using just the 6 and 20 packages (any number we construct with more than one lot of 9 nuggets can be replaced by some multiple of the 6 nugget lots and one or none 9 nugget lot, since $3 \times 6 = 2 \times 9$). Following the same logic, any constructible even number can be constructed using just the 6 and 20 nugget containers.

So what even numbers can we construct using 6 and 20 nugget lots? Clearly any such number n satisfies

$$6a + 20b = n,$$

for some positive integer a and b. Since n is even we can divide by 2 and still have an equation with all unknowns integers,

$$3a + 10b = n/2.$$

This is a more manageable question: what positive integers can we construct using integer multiples of 3 and 10? Writing it down it is clear we can construct 3, 6, 9, 10, 12, 13, 15, 16, 18, 19, 20. Once we have three consecutive numbers we know we can construct every number greater than them, since we can just add three to this series.

Hence using 3 and 10 we can construct every number over 18. Using our initial logic this corresponds to all even numbers greater than 36 and all odd numbers greater than 45. So the highest possible number we cannot construct using the full set is 43. To check this is the correct answer note that if we could construct 43, we could also construct 34 using just 6 and 20. This is equivalent to constructing 17 using 3 and 10, which we have seen we cannot do.

Here are some possible related questions:

- What is the highest number you can not construct using 7 and 10?
- Will there be a highest number you can not construct using two numbers that are not co-prime?
- What are Frobenius numbers? What is the explicit solution for the Frobenius number of two co-prime integers? Can you use them to solve the original problem?

□

Solution to Question 6.27. With these sorts of questions, a good place to start is the fact that

$$\sum_{n=0}^{\infty} a^n = \frac{1}{1-a}$$

for $|a| < 1$. It is also true that one can take derivatives and integrals through the summation. Differentiating, we have

$$\sum_{n=1}^{\infty} na^{n-1} = \frac{1}{(1-a)^2}.$$

Repeating, we get

$$\sum_{n=2}^{\infty} n(n-1)a^{n-2} = \frac{2}{(1-a)^3}.$$

We can rewrite this as

$$\sum_{n=0}^{\infty} (n+2)(n+1)a^n = \frac{2}{(1-a)^3}.$$

We also have

$$\sum_{n=0}^{\infty} (n+1)a^n = \frac{1}{(1-a)^2}.$$

The coefficient of a^n should be n^2. From the second derivative, we have

$$n^2 + 3n + 2.$$

We therefore subtract 3 times the first derivative, and add the original to get the desired coefficient. The answer is thus

$$\frac{2}{(1-a)^3} - \frac{3}{(1-a)^2} + \frac{1}{1-a}.$$

Note that if $a = 1$, the sum does not converge and the answer is ∞.

Here are some possible related questions:

- Why it is OK to differentiate through the summation sign?
- What is the power series expansion for $\log$? How do you derive it?
- What is $\sum n^3 a^n$?

☐

Solution to Question 6.28. The ln here stands for $\log_e$. Mathematicians often just write $\log$. However, different areas have different conventions so it is worth being careful. Really simple questions like this are asked and do knock out candidates so make sure you remember how to differentiate.

So we have $f(x) = (\ln(x))^2$. We have to compute $f'(x)$. Using the chain rule, we get

$$2\ln(x)x^{-1}.$$

Here are some possible related questions:

- What if we use $\log$ base 10?
- What is the integral of $\log x$?
- Is it possible to write a computer program to do symbolic differentiation?
- Is it possible to write a computer program to do symbolic integration?

☐

Solution to Question 6.29. The key here is that after each time $3/4$ get off, we still have an integer. If we start with $4k$ then our sequence is

$$x_0 = 4k,$$
$$x_1 = k + 7,$$
$$x_2 = k/4 + 7/4,$$
$$x_3 = k/4 + 7/4 + 7,$$
$$x_4 = k/16 + 7/16 + 7/4,$$
$$x_5 = k/16 + 7/16 + 7/4 + 7.$$

The final value can be written as

$$x_5 = k/16 + 3/16 + 9.$$

So we must that $k + 3$ is a multiple of 16. The smallest such value is therefore $k = 13$. It is easily checked that this makes all the values integers as required.

Here are some possible related questions:

- What if the same happens again?
- Can you do this using modular arithmetic?
- What if 8 people get on? What if 9? What if 10?

□

Solution to Question 6.30. The first person has 13 choices. If he chooses 1 or 13, then everyone after him has a unique choice of seat so there is only one corresponding seating arrangement. If he sits in 2 then the only flexibility is who sits in seat 1 so we get 12 possible combinations, and similarly for 12. In general, we can see that we get the same number of combinations for the first sitting in n and $14 - n$ since we can just reverse the ordering. All these properties are consistent with binomial coefficients.

It is easier if we work with a numbering from 0 to 12 for seats and people. If the person sits in seat k then there are k seats lower numbered. The only choice is which subset of the other 12 sit in these. So the number of possibilities is

$$\binom{12}{k}.$$

The total number of combinations is

$$\sum_{k=0}^{12} \binom{12}{k} = 2^{12}.$$

The last equality follows from taking the binomial expansion of $(1+1)^{12}$.

Here are some possible related questions:

- What if there are N seats?
- What if the seats are in a circle?
- If everyone sits at random within these constraints, what's the probability that two given people sit next to each other?

□

Solution to Question 6.31. The answer is not unique since A could be zero and then the answer would be zero. So the question is really what is the maximal rank of such a matrix? Note that $B = AA^T$ is square of size n. So an upper bound on the rank is n. If $m < n$, we can do better, however. The rank is the dimension of the image of B as a linear map from $\mathbb{R}^n$ to $\mathbb{R}^n$. However, B has been factored to pass through $\mathbb{R}^m$. So its image is at most as big as that of A applied to $\mathbb{R}^m$ which can be at most m.

In conclusion, the rank is at most $\min(m, n)$.

Here are some possible related questions:

- What about $A^T A$?
- Show that AA^T is symmetric.
- Suppose B is of rank m and square. Show that that there exists an A as in the question such that $B = AA^T$.

□

Solution to Question 6.32. The easiest way to do this one is to guess the answer. However, if we can't what can we do? Take $x < y$. We can simplify by taking logs,

$$y \log x = x \log y.$$

So

$$\frac{\log x}{x} = \frac{\log y}{y}.$$

Let

$$f(x) = \frac{\log x}{x}.$$

We compute

$$f'(x) = \frac{1 - \log x}{x^2}.$$

So $f'(x) < 0$ for $x > e$. We must therefore have $x < 3$. If $x = 1$, $f(x) = 0$, which is no good so we must have $x = 2$. So y satisfies

$$\frac{\log y}{y} = \frac{\log 2}{2}.$$

The other solution of this is $y = 4$. We have

$$2^4 = 4^2.$$

Here are some possible related questions:

- Are there any solutions to $x^{2y} = y^{2x}$?
- What if we allow real values of x and y?
- What if we allow rational values of x and y?

□

6.3.2. Integration and differentiation.

Solution to Question 6.33. If you haven't seen this question before, it can look a little daunting. We can't immediately apply any of the usual 'rules' for differentiation. However, we do know how to differentiate e^x, and this is in a similar form. In fact, the key to this question is to realise

$$f(x) = e^{x \log(x)},$$

which can easily be seen using log and index laws. From here we can apply the product rule, giving

$$\frac{d}{dx} f(x) = e^{x \log(x)} \frac{d}{dx}(x \log(x))$$
$$= x^x (\log(x) + 1).$$

Here are some possible related questions:

- Differentiate $g(x) = \alpha^x$ with respect to x.
- Differentiate $g(x)$ with respect to α.

□

Solution to Question 6.34. Each of these is just a straightforward application of the chain and product rule. For the first, we have

$$\frac{\partial}{\partial f}\left(\frac{1}{1+f\tau}\right)^n = \frac{\partial}{\partial f}(1+f\tau)^{-n}$$

$$= -n\tau\left(\frac{1}{1+f\tau}\right)^{n+1}.$$

For the second, we assume that the values f_j are independent of all other values f_i, $i \neq j$. Then

$$\frac{\partial}{\partial f_j}\prod_{i=1}^n \frac{1}{1+f_i\tau_i} = \left(\prod_{\substack{i=1 \\ i\neq j}}^n \frac{1}{1+f_i\tau_i}\right)\left(-\tau_j\frac{1}{(1+f_j\tau_j)^2}\right)$$

$$= \frac{-\tau_j}{1+f_j\tau_j}\prod_{i=1}^n \frac{1}{1+f_i\tau_i}.$$

Here are some possible related questions:

- What financial interpretation do the two functions we are differentiating have?
- How do you interpret the derivatives?

□

Solution to Question 6.35. Deriving from first principles means that we must use the definition of the derivative of a function $f(x)$ as the limit

$$f'(x) = \lim_{h\to 0}\frac{f(x+h) - f(x)}{h}.$$

To begin with, it is good to have an idea of what we're aiming for. While the question asks us to determine the derivative from first principles, evaluating it by the standard methods first might help by giving you some guidance, a way of seeing the correct solution through whatever mess you create. So, applying the standard chain rule we have

$$g'(x) = -\sin(x)e^{\cos(x)}.$$

Even if you have the impression that your interviewer would not be impressed if you did this calculation first, it is a quick one line of mental mathematics that can be done without pen and paper and may aid you.

Let's return to the original problem. Our task is to evaluate

$$g'(x) = \lim_{h \to 0} \frac{e^{\cos(x+h)} - e^{\cos(x)}}{h}.$$

Begin by re-writing the numerator as

$$e^{\cos(x+h)} - e^{\cos(x)} = e^{\cos(x)}\left(e^{\cos(x+h)-\cos(x)} - 1\right).$$

Then recall that the series expansion of e^x is given by

$$e^x = 1 + x + \frac{x^2}{2!} + \mathcal{O}(x^3),$$

and the series expansion of $\cos(x)$ is given by

$$\cos(x) = 1 - \frac{x^2}{2!} + \frac{x^4}{4!} + \mathcal{O}(x^6),$$

hence

$$\cos(x+h) - \cos(x) = \mathcal{O}(h),$$

and thus

$$e^{\cos(x+h)-\cos(x)} - 1 = \cos(x+h) - \cos(x) + \mathcal{O}(h^2).$$

This gives the derivative as

$$g'(x) = e^{\cos(x)} \lim_{h \to 0} \frac{\cos(x+h) - \cos(x) + \mathcal{O}(h^2)}{h}$$

$$= e^{\cos(x)} \lim_{h \to 0} \frac{\cos(x+h) - \cos(x)}{h}.$$

Here you can either just say 'this is the derivative of the $\cos(x)$ function, which is $-\sin(x)$', or you could proceed to derive the derivative of the $\cos(x)$ function in the same manner, using the series expansion for $\cos(x)$ given above. This gives the desired result.

Here are some possible related questions:

- Give the series expansion for $\sin(x)$ and $\cos(x)$.
- Use this series expansion to prove $e^{i\theta} = \cos(\theta) + i\sin(\theta)$.
- Evaluate the derivative of the following, from first principles:

(a)
$$x^2;$$

(b)
$$\cos(x);$$

(c)
$$\frac{1}{1-x}.$$

$\square$

Solution to Question 6.36. This is a straightforward application of the product rule, and really the value of this question is as a warm-up for Question 6.37. We have

$$\frac{df(x)}{dx} = \frac{d(x)}{dx}\log(x) + x\frac{d\log(x)}{dx}$$
$$= \log(x) + 1.$$

Here is a possible related problem:

- Differentiate $g(x) = e^x \sin(x)$.

$\square$

Solution to Question 6.37. Hopefully solving Question 6.36 gave you an idea as to how to go about this. From this question, we have

$$\frac{d}{dx}(x\log(x)) = \log(x) + 1,$$

or re-arranging

$$\log(x) = \frac{d}{dx}(x\log(x)) - 1.$$

If we then integrate both sides with respect to x, we see

$$\int \log(x)dx = \int \left(\frac{d}{dx}(x\log(x)) - 1 \right) dx$$
$$= x\log(x) - x + C,$$

where C is a constant of integration. How can we solve this if we don't already have a clue as to its form? The trick is to use integration by parts. This is the analogue to the product rule for differentiation, and is given by

$$\int f(x)g'(x)dx = f(x)g(x) - \int f'(x)g(x)dx.$$

To solve $\int \log(x)dx$, we set $f(x) = \log(x)$ and $g'(x) = 1$ in the above expression. This yields

$$\int \log(x)dx = x\log(x) - \int 1 dx$$
$$= x\log(x) - x + C.$$

Here are some possible related questions:

- Use repeated integration by parts to verify
$$\int e^x \cos(x)dx = \frac{e^x}{2}(\sin(x) + \cos(x)) + C.$$

- As an alternative method to evaluate the previous integral, write $\cos(x) = \mathrm{Re}\left(e^{ix}\right)$, where $\mathrm{Re}(z)$ denotes the real part of z, and proceed with the integration. Additionally, without any further work, what does this method tell you about $\int e^x \sin(x)dx$?

$\square$

Solution to Question 6.38. Motivated by Question 6.37 we will attempt to solve this using an integration by parts approach. This suggests, since each integration by parts will reduce the power of the log by one, that the answer will be obtained using induction.

We begin with our base case, that is

$$\int \log x dx = x\log x - x.$$

Again using integration by parts, we can consider the case $n = 2$:

$$\int \log^2 x dx = x \log^2 x - 2 \int \log x dx$$
$$= x \log^2 x - 2x \log x + 2x,$$

so the method seems to work. Now let's look at the more general question:

$$\int \log^n x dx = x \log^n x - n \int x \log^{n-1} x \frac{1}{x} dx$$
$$= x \log^n x - n \int \log^{n-1} x dx$$
$$= x \log^n x - n \left(x \log^{n-1} x - (n-1) \int \log^{n-2} x dx \right)$$
$$= x \log^n x - nx \log^{n-1} x + n(n-1) \int \log^{n-2} x dx.$$

This motivates the assertion of a hypothesis,

$$\int \log^n(x) dx = x \sum_{j=0}^{n} (-1)^j n \cdots (n-j+1) \log^{n-j} x,$$

where we define $n \cdots (n-j+1) = 1$ for $j = 0$. We have seen this holds for the case $n = 1$. To prove that this is the solution we want, we need to use induction to show it holds for general n. Assume it holds for $n = k$, that is

$$\int \log^k(x) dx = x \sum_{j=0}^{k} (-1)^j k \cdots (k-j+1) \log^{k-j} x.$$

Does it hold for $n = k + 1$? We have seen

$$\int \log^{k+1}(x) dx = x \log^{k+1} x - (k+1) \int \log^k x dx,$$

so using the assumption we have

$$\int \log^{k+1}(x)dx$$

$$= x \log^{k+1} x - (k+1)x \sum_{j=0}^{k} (-1)^j k \cdots (k-j+1) \log^{k-j} x$$

$$= x \log^{k+1} x + x \sum_{j=0}^{k} (-1)^{j+1}(k+1)k \cdots (k-j+1) \log^{k-j} x$$

$$= x \sum_{j=0}^{k+1} (-1)^j (k+1) \cdots (k+1-j+1) \log^{k+1-j} x,$$

confirming the hypothesis.

Here are some possible related questions:

- How do you prove that induction works?
- Evaluate

$$\int x^k (\log x)^l dx.$$

□

Solution to Question 6.39. Doing the inner integral (with respect to y) gives

$$\int_{1/2}^{1/2+x} dy = x.$$

This reduces the problem to evaluating

$$2 \int_0^{1/2} x dx = \left[x^2 \right]_{x=0}^{x=1/2}$$

$$= 1/4.$$

Alternatively, one could draw a picture of the domain of integration and the answer is then obvious.

Here are some possible related questions:

- Show
  (a)
$$\int_0^\pi \int_0^{\sin(x)} dy dx = 2,$$

  (b)
$$\int_0^1 dx \int_{x^2}^1 dy f(x, y) = \int_0^1 dy \int_0^{\sqrt{y}} dx f(x, y).$$

- Let D be the region
$$\{0 \le x \le 1, y \ge x^2, y \le 1\};$$

  evaluate
$$\int \int_D (x + y) dx dy.$$

□

Solution to Question 6.40. This is a great integration question that, to solve from scratch, involves a nice trick. First we will consider deducing the solution by a less direct manner. If you have studied any probability theory at all, you will have seen that the density of the $N(0, 1)$ random variable is given by

$$f(x) = \frac{1}{\sqrt{2\pi}} \exp\left\{-\frac{x^2}{2}\right\},$$

for $x \in \mathbb{R}$. You would also be aware that the integral of the density of a proper random variable gives 1, so with a bit of manipulation we can use this to solve our problem:

$$1 = \int_{-\infty}^\infty f(x) dx = \int_{-\infty}^\infty \frac{1}{\sqrt{2\pi}} \exp\left\{-\frac{x^2}{2}\right\} dx$$

$$= \frac{1}{\sqrt{\pi}} \int_{-\infty}^\infty \exp\left\{-y^2\right\} dy,$$

using the substitution $y = x/\sqrt{2}$. Thus

$$\int_{-\infty}^\infty e^{-x^2} dx = \sqrt{\pi}.$$

The alternative method of solution is as follows. Denote by I the integral in question,

$$I = \int_{-\infty}^{\infty} e^{-x^2} dx.$$

Then we have

$$I^2 = \int_{-\infty}^{\infty} e^{-x^2} dx \int_{-\infty}^{\infty} e^{-y^2} dy.$$

$$= \int_{-\infty}^{\infty} \int_{-\infty}^{\infty} e^{-(x+y)^2} dx dy.$$

By considering this as an integral over the entire plane, we change to polar coordinates setting $x = r\cos(\theta)$ and $y = r\sin(\theta)$, $r > 0, 0 \leq \theta \leq 2\pi$. Remembering to include the Jacobian, we then have

$$I^2 = \int_0^\infty \int_0^{2\pi} e^{-r^2(\cos^2(\theta)+\sin^2(\theta))} r\, d\theta dr$$

$$= \int_0^\infty \int_0^{2\pi} e^{-r^2} r\, d\theta dr$$

$$= 2\pi \int_0^\infty e^{-r^2} r\, dr$$

$$= \pi \int_0^\infty e^{-z} dz$$

$$= \pi,$$

which gives $I = \sqrt{\pi}$ and confirms our previous conclusion.

Here are some possible related questions:

- Use the first method to evaluate

$$\int_{-\infty}^{\infty} \frac{1}{1+x^2} dx.$$

- What is the Jacobian in a change of variables?

□

Solution to Question 6.41. We initially treat the more general case of

$$\int_0^\infty \log(x) Q(x) dx,$$

where $Q(x)$ is a rational function. To secure convergence of the integral, we need to assume the denominator of $Q(x)$ is of degree n, at least 2 greater than that of the numerator m, and that the denominator of $Q(x)$ does not vanish for any non-negative real x.

Consider the contour C formed by taking a loop around the branch cut on the negative real axis and a larger circle, as in the Figure 6.1.

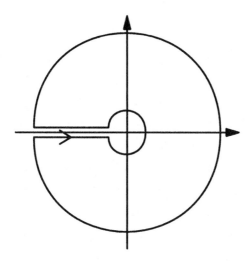

FIGURE 6.1. Contour formed by taking a loop around the branch cut on the negative real axis.

The inner circle has radius ϵ, the outer radius R. We then consider the integral

$$\oint (\log z)^2 Q(-z) dz = \int_{top} + \int_{bottom} + \int_{small\ circle} + \int_{big\ circle},$$

where 'top' and 'bottom' refer to the lines above and below the branch cut. Along the top we let $z = te^{i\pi}$, hence t goes from ϵ to R. Similarly, along the bottom we make the substitution $z = te^{-i\pi}$. For the inner circle, define $z = \epsilon e^{i\theta}$, $-\pi \leq \theta \leq \pi$

and for the outer circle $z = Re^{i\theta}$. This gives

$$\int_{top} = \int_{\epsilon}^{R} (\log(te^{i\pi}))^2 Q(-te^{i\pi}) e^{i\pi} dt = -\int_{\epsilon}^{R} (\log(t) + i\pi)^2 Q(t) dt$$

$$\int_{bottom} = \int_{R}^{\epsilon} (\log(te^{-i\pi}))^2 Q(-te^{-i\pi}) e^{-i\pi} dt = \int_{\epsilon}^{R} (\log(t) - i\pi)^2 Q(t) dt$$

$$\int_{small\ circle} = \int_{\pi}^{-\pi} (\log(\epsilon e^{i\theta}))^2 Q(-\epsilon e^{i\theta}) i\epsilon e^{i\theta} dt = \mathcal{O}(\epsilon \log^2 \epsilon) \text{ as } \epsilon \to 0$$

$$\int_{big\ circle} = \int_{\pi}^{-\pi} (\log(Re^{i\theta}))^2 Q(-Re^{i\theta}) iRe^{i\theta} dt$$

$$= \mathcal{O}(R^{m-n+1} \log^2 R) \text{ as } R \to \infty.$$

Observing that we have used a clockwise orientation for our contour, we have, as $\epsilon \to 0$ and $R \to \infty$ (since $m - n + 1 \le -1$),

$$\int_{0}^{\infty} \big((\log t + i\pi)^2 - (\log t - i\pi)^2\big) Q(t) dt$$

$$= 2\pi i \sum \text{Residues} \left\{ (\log z)^2 Q(-z) \right\},$$

or

$$\int_{0}^{\infty} \log t\, Q(t) dt = \frac{1}{2} \sum \text{Residues} \left\{ (\log z)^2 Q(-z) \right\},$$

where the sum is taken over all singularities of $Q(-z)$.

We're now ready to deal with our particular question. Here we are considering the function

$$Q(-z) = \frac{1}{1 - z + z^2}.$$

This function has singularities at $z = \frac{1}{2}(1 \pm \sqrt{3}i)$. Write

$$a = \frac{1}{2}(1 + \sqrt{3}i) = e^{i\frac{\pi}{3}},$$

$$b = \frac{1}{2}(1 - \sqrt{3}i) = e^{-i\frac{\pi}{3}},$$

then the function

$$(\log(z))^2 Q(-z) = \frac{(\log(z))^2}{(z - a)(z - b)}$$

clearly has a residue at a of

$$\frac{(\log a)^2}{a - b} = \frac{-\frac{\pi^2}{9}}{a - b},$$

and a residue at b of

$$\frac{(\log b)^2}{b - a} = -\frac{-\frac{\pi^2}{9}}{a - b}.$$

Thus

$$\sum \text{Residues} \left\{ (\log z)^2 Q(-z) \right\} = 0,$$

and finally

$$\int_0^\infty \frac{\log(x)}{(1 + x + x^2)} dx = 0.$$

Here are some possible related questions:

- Prove the following, using contour integration (note the contours could vary from that used in the above derivation. Think about the location of the singularities):

  (1)
  $$\int_{-\infty}^\infty \frac{1}{(x^2 + 1)^2} dx = \frac{\pi}{2}.$$

  (2) For $t > 0$,
  $$\int_{-\infty}^\infty \frac{e^{itx}}{x^2 + 1} dx = \pi e^{-t}.$$

  (3) For $0 < Re(s) < 1$,
  $$\int_{-\infty}^\infty \frac{e^{sx}}{e^x + 1} dx = \frac{\pi}{\sin(\pi s)}.$$

  (4)
  $$\int_0^\infty \frac{\sin(x)}{x} dx = \frac{\pi}{2}.$$

  □

Solution to Question 6.42. The normal density is

$$N'(x) = \frac{1}{\sqrt{2\pi}} e^{-x^2/2}.$$

We have to show that

$$I = \int_{-\infty}^{\infty} N'(x)dx = 1.$$

The standard way to do this is to show that the square is one. First, note that the integrand is exponentially decaying and smooth so there is no issue with integrals existing. We can write

$$I^2 = \int_{-\infty}^{\infty} N'(x)dx \int_{-\infty}^{\infty} N'(y)dy,$$

$$= \frac{1}{2\pi} \int \int e^{-\frac{(x^2+y^2)}{2}} dxdy.$$

We now change to polar coordinates:

$$x = r\cos(\theta),$$
$$y = r\sin(\theta).$$

We then have

$$dxdy = rdrd\theta.$$

We deduce

$$I^2 = \frac{1}{2\pi} \int_0^{2\pi} \int_0^{\infty} re^{-r^2/2} drd\theta.$$

Since

$$\frac{d}{dr} e^{-r^2/2} = -re^{-r^2/2},$$

the integral is now straight-forward and we get

$$I^2 = \frac{1}{2\pi} 2\pi \left[-e^{-r^2/2}\right]_0^{\infty} = 1.$$

Here are some possible related questions:

- Why would we expect the integral of the normal density to be 1?
- What is the integral of $x^k N'(x)$?
- How would you approximate $N(x)$?

□

CHAPTER 7

Coding in C++

7.1. Introduction

The language of choice in banks for implementing financial models is C++. It is often interfaced with EXCEL; one easy way to do that is to use the xlw open-source software package. This can be downloaded from `xlw.sourceforge.net`.

Let me stress at this point that I have no opinions on whether C++ *should be* the language for quants; it is merely the language for getting a job. Developing some familiarity for the language is a must before going for interviews. The most important thing, however, is not to overstate your ability. C++ is a big language that takes a long time to master and there are many subtleties. In particular, to use it properly requires a firm understanding of object-oriented programming, generic programming, and memory allocation, as well as straightforward functional programming. It therefore makes much more sense to say that you have "basic C++" or a "working knowledge of C++" unless you truly are expert in it. A thorough understanding of classes and virtual functions is a must before claiming any competence in the language.

There are by now various books on how to use C++ in quantitative finance including one by the first author of this book:

"C++ Design Patterns and Derivatives Pricing" by Mark Joshi.

All these books are not aimed at the truly ignorant. They require the reader to have already learnt the basics of C++ and quantitative analysis elsewhere. We list a few books.

"C++ How to Program" by Harvey M. Deitel, Paul J. Deitel. This is an introductory textbook for American undergraduates. This means it goes slow, is comprehensive, uses lots of colour and is easy to read. This book is good if you have not done much computing in other languages.

"C++ Primer" by Stanley B. Lippman, Josee Lajoie, Barbara Moo. This is an introduction to C++ but it is really suited to someone who is very competent in other programming languages. So if you are au fait with programming and want something that will get you going quickly buy this. It is a classic and has sold over half a million copies.

"Thinking in C++" by Bruce Eckel. This two-volume set is about how to use the C++ language properly and aims to teach you the right way to think about C++. In this it succeeds. It is, however, hard going for those who do not know C, as the author assumes some knowledge of that language. It is long and a lot of hard work but if you work through it, you will really know how to program in C++. There is a free downloadable edition at

```
http://www.mindview.net/Books/TICPP/ThinkingInCPP2e.html
```

Once you've got the basics, there are a number of books that aim to get you from the novice level to the intermediate level. These generally discuss small topics one by one rather than trying to be comprehensive.

"Effective C++," "More Effective C++" and "Effective STL" by Scott Meyers. Effective C++ was one of the first books to really discuss how to use C++ as a language rather than focusing on the syntax. Meyers' style is to give you lots of informal advice about the right way to do things and in my experience, if Scott gives you a guideline you really ought to follow it.

"Exceptional C++," "More Exceptional C++," and "Exceptional C++ style" by Herb Sutter. The author presents problems, invites the reader to solve them, and then generally demonstrates that the reader does not understand C++ nearly as well as he thought. There is a particular focus on writing exception-safe code – hence the title. Whilst the presentation can be irritating at times, and I do not buy some of his advice, Sutter will definitely improve your understanding of C++.

"Large-Scale C++ Software Design" by John Lakos. Ever had a large project that turned into spaghetti, or had a project where you were afraid to change certain files because of the time it would take to rebuild the project. This book is on how to avoid such problems by organising your code correctly from the start. Whilst the book is a little dated, and there is a certain amount of overlap with Sutter's books, it is still a good read.

"The C++ Standard Library: A Tutorial and Reference" by Nicolai M. Josuttis. C++ ships with a lot of classes and algorithms; these are called the Standard Library. Learning to use them properly will make your code quicker to develop, more robust and more efficient. Reading Josuttis is a great way to do the learning.

"C++ Templates: The Complete Guide" by David Vandevoorde, and Nicolai M. Josuttis. Everything you ever wanted to know about templates and quite a few things you did not. Templates in C++ have gone way beyond their designers' original intention of providing a way of doing generic programming to being a method of doing computations at compile time. This is the definitive book on the topic.

There are certain books that you should own and consult but should not try to read from cover to cover.

"The C++ Programming Language" by Bjarne Stroustrup. This is the definitive guide to the language from the guy who invented it. Very useful but pedagogy is not Bjarne's strength. If you find it readable then do read it all.

"The C++ Standard: Incorporating Technical Corrigendum No. 1" by British Standards Institute. This has to be one of the driest books ever written, but sometimes you really want to know what the "legal" rule is for some piece of C++ and this book is then great. It is also really good for getting the definitive answer to silly interview questions.

The most effective way to really learn a language is to use it. So read an introductory book and "C++ Design patterns and Derivatives Pricing," and then work through the computer projects at the end of "The Concepts and Practice of Mathematical Finance." You can then discuss with your interviewer what you have coded and how you did it.

Most of the questions in this chapter would be regarded as basic C++ by a C++ expert. If you have difficulty with the majority of them, you really need to brush up on your C++ skills.

7.2. Questions

QUESTION 7.1. What compilers have you used?

QUESTION 7.2. What C++ design patterns have you used?

QUESTION 7.3. What is the difference between an inline function and a macro in C++?

QUESTION 7.4. Is it permissible to throw an exception in a constructor in C++? Justify your answer.

QUESTION 7.5. Is it permissible to throw an exception in a destructor in C++? Justify your answer.

QUESTION 7.6. How would you copy a polymorphic object of unknown type?

QUESTION 7.7. In C++, if a base class has a user-defined assignment operator, is one needed for an inherited class?

QUESTION 7.8. What is the C++ syntax to declare a function pointer?

QUESTION 7.9. What do you know about C++ programming and finance?

QUESTION 7.10. What is a virtual function?

QUESTION 7.11. Implement strcmp.

QUESTION 7.12. What is a virtual destructor and when is it needed?

QUESTION 7.13. If a class B is derived from class A and contains an object of class C, in what order are the constructors and destructors called for an object of type B.

QUESTION 7.14. What does every class come equipped with?

QUESTION 7.15. In what two ways can an object of type A be automatically converted into an object of type B in C++?

QUESTION 7.16. Why does a class that uses memory allocation need a properly written copy constructor and assignment operator?

QUESTION 7.17. Write the code for a sorting algorithm. Discuss the speed and memory of your program. How can you improve it?

QUESTION 7.18. Computer problem: If x is of type int, keep increasing x and plot. What is the graph like? If x is of type float?

QUESTION 7.19. Where are "static" variables stored?

QUESTION 7.20. How is virtuality implemented in C++ ?

QUESTION 7.21. What is the problem with virtualization from the point of view of optimisation? What can a compiler do when a function is not virtualized?

QUESTION 7.22. What is the difference between delete and delete[]? What happens if you use one where the other was expected?

QUESTION 7.23. A student claims that the ?: construct in C++ is redundant since it can be implemented in terms of other language features. He suggests replacing it with the following function

```
int condif(bool condition, int i, int j)
{
    if (condition)
      return i;
    else
      return j;
}
```

Do you agree with the student that for integers there is no difference?

QUESTION 7.24. We present C++ code that gives draws from a standard Gaussian distribution with mean 0 and standard deviation 1. Estimate the number of uniform draws for each Gaussian draw.

```
#include <cmath>

// this gives one uniform and updates seed
double drawUniform(long& seed);
```

```cpp
// draws a standard Gaussian
double drawGaussian(long& seed)
{
    static bool drawNotDone=true;
    static double otherDraw;
    double factor, rSquared, x, y;
    if (drawNotDone)
    {
     do
       {
           x = 2.0 * drawUniform(seed) - 1.0;
           y = 2.0 * drawUniform(seed) - 1.0;
           rSquared = x * x + y * y;

       }
       while (rSquared >= 1.0 || rSquared == 0.0);

       factor = sqrt(-2.0 * log(rSquared) / rSquared);
       otherDraw = x * factor;
       drawNotDone=false;
       return y * factor;

    }
    else
    {
      drawNotDone=true;
      return otherDraw;
    }
}
```

QUESTION 7.25. Write a C++ function that takes as input a character string and returns a new string that is the reverse of its input. Write another variant that performs the reversal in place without doing any memory allocation.

QUESTION 7.26. What is the difference between passing parameters by value, by reference and by pointer?

QUESTION 7.27. Consider the following code:

```cpp
#include <iostream>
#include <memory>
using namespace std;

class Alpha
{
public:
  Alpha() : ptrAlpha(new int)
  {
  }

  ~Alpha()
  {
    delete ptrAlpha;
  }

  virtual void MyFunction()
  {
    cout << "In Alpha" << endl;
  }

private:
  int* ptrAlpha;
};

class Beta : public Alpha
{
public:
  Beta() : ptrBeta(new int) {}
  ~Beta()
  {
    delete ptrBeta;
  }
```

```cpp
  void MyFunction ()
  {
    cout << "In Beta" << endl;
  }

private:
  int *ptrBeta;
};

class Gamma : public Alpha
{
public:
  Gamma() : ptrGamma(new int)
  {
  }

  ~Gamma()
  {
    delete ptrGamma;
  }

  void MyFunction ()
  {
    cout << "In Gamma" << endl;
  }

private:

  int *ptrGamma;
};

int main()
{
  {
```

```
    auto_ptr<Alpha> alpha1(new Beta());
    Gamma gamma;
    Alpha& alpha2 = gamma;
    alpha1->MyFunction();
    alpha2.MyFunction();
  }

  char d;
  std::cin >> d;
  return 0;
}
```

What will the output of this program be? Do you think this program is correct? If not, how would you fix it?

QUESTION 7.28. Consider the following piece of code.

```
#include <iostream>
using namespace std;

class Alpha
{
public:
  Alpha()
  {
    cout << "Creating Alpha" << endl;
  }
  ~Alpha()
  {
    cout << "Destroying Alpha" << endl;
  }
};

class Beta
```

```cpp
{
public:
  Beta()
  {
    cout << "Creating Beta" << endl;
  }
  ~Beta()
  {
    cout << "Destroying Beta" << endl;
  }
};

class Gamma : public Alpha
{
public:
  Gamma()
  {
    cout << "Creating Gamma" << endl;
  }
  ~Gamma()
  {
    cout << "Destroying Gamma" << endl;

  }
private:
  Beta b;
};

int main()
{
  {
    Gamma c;
  }

  char d;
```

```
    cin >> d;
    return 0;
}
```

What does it output?

QUESTION 7.29. Write a C++ function to compute square roots without using the standard library. Wrap your function in a main program so that it can be called from the command line.

QUESTION 7.30. Implement in C++ a data structure to represent a binary tree which contains one integer at each node. Discuss the empty tree. Write a function that takes a tree and returns the tree depth, with an empty tree having depth zero. Write a function that returns the maximum element in a non-empty tree.

QUESTION 7.31. What do you know about `const`?

QUESTION 7.32. Give all the places where you could use the keyword `static`.

QUESTION 7.33. Define the following terms

- What is polymorphism?
- What is an abstract class?
- What is a pointer?
- What is a reference?

QUESTION 7.34. How would you write code to catch all exceptions thrown in a piece of code?

QUESTION 7.35. What is the syntax for making a C++ function have C linkage?

QUESTION 7.36. Are there ways to change the value of a const variable in C++?

QUESTION 7.37. Write a program to implement quick sort.

QUESTION 7.38. Why would you not use virtual destructors for a class for which many objects are created but which has no other virtual functions?

QUESTION 7.39. How do you ensure nobody inherits from a particular class?

QUESTION 7.40. What default methods does the compiler provide when you define a class?

QUESTION 7.41. What's the difference between y++ and ++y ?

QUESTION 7.42. What's the difference between simple virtual and pure virtual?

QUESTION 7.43. Explain how Boost shared pointers work.

QUESTION 7.44. What is the difference between the two STL containers map and set?

QUESTION 7.45. A vector contains 1000 random numbers, find the median.

QUESTION 7.46. What is the difference between a physical address and a virtual address in a computer?

QUESTION 7.47. What is a segmentation fault?

QUESTION 7.48. What is a page fault?

QUESTION 7.49. What is name mangling in C++ and why is it used?

QUESTION 7.50. What is RTTI?

7.3. Solutions

Solution to Question 7.1. The answer to this one can only be the truth. However, it is worth adopting some defensive behaviour to make sure that your answer is not too feeble.

In particular, it is good to have used one Microsoft compiler and one non-Microsoft one. At the time of writing, Visual Studio 10.0 Express is available as a free download from the Microsoft website. DevCpp is a good open source IDE (integrated development environment) available for free which is a front end for the g++ compiler. However, it has not been updated for quite a while now. Another open source option is Eclipse with the C++ toolbox. This is harder to use than DevCpp but much more sophisticated and with the same compiler. Netbeans is another alternative. The only truly compliant compiler is the Comeau computing one which is cheap but not free.

Running your code under more than one compiler is a good habit to get into. Each compiler has its own peculiarities and the process of eliminating all errors, warnings and bugs under each can teach you a lot.

Once you have mentioned more than one compiler or IDE, you are likely to be asked about the differences between them. Some points to make are:

- Microsoft Visual Studio supports range checking in debug mode for the STL.
- The debugger in Visual Studio is much easier to use than GDB which is the open source alternative.
- The g++ compiler has the "electric fence" option which is useful for finding memory leaks and out of range errors.
- The g++ compiler with the "-Wall" option gives a wider range of warnings such as telling you to make destructors virtual and to reorder class member initialisers to match declarations.
- Visual Studio gives silly warning messages when you use STL algorithms unless you switch them off.

□

Solution to Question 7.2. Here again, the answer can only be what you have used. However, as usual, you want to be in the position of having a good answer. A good starting point is to read [7]. For each pattern have an example in mind to discuss with the interviewer. Work through the projects in [6] using patterns so as to have plenty of good examples. In particular, be able to explain and give an example of when you have used each of the following:

- strategy;
- template;
- bridge;
- virtual construction;
- decoration;
- singleton;
- factory.

Make sure that you can explain why you used that pattern and not a different one. If there are multiple choices, you should be ready to explain the pros and cons of each of them.   □

Solution to Question 7.3. This question is a little strange in that there is an implication that the two are similar, whereas they actually have very little in common.

We first discuss the keyword inline. Placing this in front of a function declaration tells the compiler that you would like it to replace each call to the function with the code inside the function. This then eliminates the overhead of making a call to the function.

There are subtleties, however:

- it is a suggestion to the compiler not a command to the compiler;
- the code may be longer because the definition of the function is repeated many times;
- the code must be included in the header file so as to be available to clients, so changing it will cause a lot to recompile, and any compile-time dependencies it has, will also be dependencies for clients;
- and on the plus side, the fact that the code is available to the compiler in context of use may allow the compiler to use extra optimisations;
- adding or removing inline should never affect anything other than the efficiency of your program.

A macro is not actually anything to do with the compiler. Instead, it is an instruction to C-preprocessor or Cpp. The Cpp reorganises a file before the compiler starts work by including all files specified, and by expanding macros. A macro is therefore a direct text to text substitution which takes places before the compiler does its job. As such it is a much more error prone tool and should generally be avoided.

The main thing the two approaches have in common is that they allow the coding of simple functions in such a way that they can be used without the run-time overhead of a function call, and without duplicating code.

Here are some possible related questions:

- When are macros really needed?
- When would you inline a function or method?
- What are the dangers when using macros?

□

Solution to Question 7.4. This is a tricky one in that the community seems to be split between those who think it is wrong to throw in a constructor, and those who think it is silly not to. The best response is therefore to say that you know that there are varying opinions on this, and list the pros and cons, and then finish up with your opinion.

The crucial fact to know is that if you throw in a constructor then the destructor for the object is not called. And it will never be called since the object will not exist after a throw during its construction. However, the destructor for each fully-constructed data member is called. If you are in the main part of the constructor that is within the curly brackets, then all the data members are fully constructed and therefore destroyed.

The main argument against throwing in a constructor is that the destructor will not be called, and therefore it will not do the clean-up that is usually done when the object is destroyed. For example, any memory allocated in the constructor will not be released.

It is therefore OK to throw in a constructor provided you ensure that everything is properly destroyed and deallocated. The easiest way to do this is to use smart pointers as data members instead of raw pointers. These will be destroyed on exit and will automatically carry out the required deallocations.

If you make the rule of no throws in constructor, the problem is what do you do if some aspect of construction fails? Constructors do not have return values so you cannot return a failure code. You could create an extra method for every class that says whether construction was successful. Every time you construct an object, a test for success would then be required together with necessary remedial action. This would be rather painful.

Here are some possible related questions:

- In what order are the data members and bases of a class constructed?
- What happens if you attempt to allocate an array bigger than there is memory available for?

☐

Solution to Question 7.5. This is less controversial than the analagous question for a constructor, though you do get the odd contrarian. There are good reasons to never do this.

The fundamental problem is that if two unhandled exceptions exist simultaneously then the C++ standard says that the application will terminate. If destructors are allowed to throw then it is very hard to avoid two happening at once: when an exception is thrown all automatic (i.e. ordinary) objects declared in the current scope are destroyed before the catch is executed. If any of their destructors can throw, you get two at once and a crash.

So never ever throw in a destructor.

Here are some possible related questions:

- In what order are the destructors for data members and base classes called? Why is it done this way?
- What does it mean for code to be exception safe?

☐

Solution to Question 7.6. This is a standard problem and it is discussed at great length in [7]. The standard way to do this is by using a virtual constructor. Note that it is not possible to declare a standard constructor virtual but we can achieve the same effects by making a class method virtual.

We therefore define in the base class

```
virtual Base* clone() const =0;
```

and in each inherited class

```
virtual Inherited* clone() const
{
  return new Inherited(*this);
}
```

The crucial point here is that the inherited class knows its own type and so can copy itself without any problems. The return type is a pointer to an object of the class allocated on the heap since the type is unknown to the calling code.

Note also that the return type is a pointer to the inherited class not the base class; this changing of return types is allowed when overriding in an inherited class.

Here are some possible related questions:

- Would you use a smart pointer or a raw pointer as return type?
- How would you manage the new object's life time?
- Why not use the stack for the new object?

□

Solution to Question 7.7. The short answer is no! Unfortunately, the interviewer may be under the delusion that the answer is yes, so we need to be able to justify the answer.

If I have a class X inherited from Y and I code

```
X a;
X b;

a = b;
```

without defining an assignment operator for X then the compiler uses the compiler-generated one. This calls the assignment operator for each base and member of

X so whether Y has a user-defined operator or an implicit one does not matter. It would actually be a big flaw in the language if it did – changing an implementation detail of the base class should not require recoding of inherited classes.

Here are some possible related questions:

- Same question for copy constructor.
- Suppose a data-member has a user-defined assignment operator, does this mean that the class needs one as well?

□

Solution to Question 7.8. To declare a pointer called "MyPointer" to a function returning an object of type A and taking in an object of type B, the syntax is

```
A (*MyPointer)(B);
```

Note the crucial parentheses around the name of the pointer and the "*." If we want to assign the pointer to a function "MyFunction" then we might have

```
A MyFunction(B);

void f()
{
    A (*MyPointer)(B);
    MyPointer = &MyFunction;
}
```

For further discussion, see Stroustrup Section 7.7, [20].

Here are some possible related questions:

- If "MyFunction" takes in a constant reference to a B, can I do the assignment above?
- What is the syntax if the function is a class data member?

- Do you think that function pointers are useful in C++?
- What is the syntax for templatizing on a function pointer?

□

Solution to Question 7.9. Well, clearly there is no single right answer to this question. However, there is a clear wrong answer: "nothing."

The worst mistake to make, however, is to claim that you know a lot on this topic when you don't. For example, one candidate on interview stated that he had implemented BGM in C++ but was unable to write a for loop when asked. An honest "I don't know any C++ but can program in another language and am keen to learn" is much better than pretending you know more than you do. However, you would do better to wait until you can honestly say that you know something.

The best way to reach that point is to read books on C++ and finance (e.g. "C++ Design Patterns and Derivatives Pricing"), and to implement some models yourself. At the end of [6], there is a list of computer projects which you can work through. If you can go into an interview and say that you have done these in C++ and are able to discuss them, this will count for a lot. Be prepared for questions such as:

- What did you find hard?
- What did you find easy?
- What was your class design for project X?
- What were you results for project Y?
- How did doing the projects affect you understanding of C++?

□

Solution to Question 7.10. Virtual functions are an important aspect of C++. They allow us to defer the implementation of a function declared in a base class to an inherited class. For example, suppose we have a vanilla option class, we can make the PayOff method virtual. We then inherit calls and puts from the option class.

The PayOff method will be defined differently for calls and puts. The user of an option object may, however, not know which sort of option it is, and does not need to since the virtual function for the right sort of option is called automatically.

Here are some possible related questions:

- How do compilers implement virtual functions?
- Do you think virtual functions cause much run-time overhead?
- How do templates compare to virtual functions?
- What does the C++ standard say about how virtual functions are implemented? (The answer is a little surprising!)

□

Solution to Question 7.11. The function strcmp compares two C-style strings and returns less than a negative number if the first is less than the second, zero if they agree and a positive number if the second is bigger.

We define "less than" in a lexicographic sense, i.e. which one would be first in a dictionary?

The function signature is therefore

```
int strcmp( const char *str1, const char *str2 );
```

The correct way to do this problem is, of course, to use the implementation from the C standard library in "String.h". However, the interviewer is probably not looking for that solution and one should always give interviewers what they want, no matter how silly.

The crucial fact here is that that C-style strings are zero terminated. Here's a simple implementation:

```
int mystrcmp( const char *str1, const char *str2 )
{
    while (*str1 != '\0' && *str2 != '\0' && *str1 == *str2)
    {
            ++str1;
            ++str2;
    }
```

```
if (*str1 < * str2)
    return -1;
if (*str1 > * str2)
    return 1;

return 0;
```

```
}
```

Note that although the pointers point to const they are not const themselves. We can therefore increment them. We keep doing so until one string end is reached or a letter differs. We use pre-increment rather than post-increment since it is supposed to be faster.

Here are some possible related questions:

- How would you implement a case-insensitive comparison operator?
- How do you convert a C++ string into a C-style string? What are the dangers in doing so?

□

Solution to Question 7.12. If one has an object of some inherited class that has been dynamically allocated (i.e. created using new,) then when it is deleted via a pointer to a base class object, one has the issue that the correct destructor needs to be called. If the destructor of the base class is virtual, then the inherited class one is called directly and there is no problem.

If it is not virtual, then the base class destructor is called and the object may not be properly deleted. This generally causes a memory leak and may cause even worse problems.

As a general rule, always declare destructors virtual if any method is pure abstract, i.e. not defined in the base class. Some compilers, e.g. g++, generate a warning if you do not declare the destructor virtual in this case. Generally declare them virtual if any method is virtual. If no method is virtual, it is most often not necessary.

Here are some possible related questions:

- What are the disadvantages if any of declaring a destructor virtual?
- Do you think that C++ should make all destructors virtual?

□

Solution to Question 7.13. The basic rule is the more fundamental something is, the sooner it is constructed and the later it is destructed. The reason for this is that an inherited class may want to use the base class during either construction or destruction, but the converse will never be true. NB if you attempt to use the inherited class via a virtual function during base class construction you will come to grief. If the function is pure virtual you will get a run-time error saying you called a pure virtual function. If it is not, the base class version will be called.

So in this particular case, A is constructed then C then B. And for destruction, B then C then A. Note that this means the class data members are available in the constructor and destructor of B.

Here are some possible related questions:

- In a class with several data members, in what order are they constructed?
- In a class with several data members, in what order are they destroyed?

□

Solution to Question 7.14. The compiler will always provide a copy constructor, an assignment operator and a destructor. It is important to realize that these are trivial in the sense that they do the simplest thing they can.

The copy constructor therefore calls the copy constructor of each data member to make a copy. This is called making a *shallow copy*. The assignment operator calls the assignment operator of each data member.

It is OK to use the shallow copy if every data member has a copy constructor that does the right thing. This is generally not the case if data members are pointers, since both old and new objects will point to the same data. This can result in crashes when the pointed-to object is deleted twice. The same issues apply when defining assignment operators.

A non-trivial destructor is needed if and only if the class needs to free resources when the object dies. This is typically deleting allocated memory. A trivial destructor should be declared virtual if the object is likely to be deleted via a pointer to a base class.

The best way to get round declaring non-trivial copy constructors, destructors and assignment operators is to use smart pointers that do all the correct things when the default behaviour is used. This has been dubbed (by Mark Joshi) "the rule of almost zero."

Here are some possible related questions:

- What is "the rule of three"?
- What smart pointers have you used?
- What would you do if you wanted it to be impossible to copy objects from a class?

□

Solution to Question 7.15. The first and best-known method relies on the fact that if a class has a single argument constructor then the compiler will treat it as a conversion operator. So the class declaration for B contains the line

```
B( const A& myObject);
```

or

```
B(myObject);
```

either is sufficient for automatic conversion.

Another method is needed if we wish to be able to convert into objects of type B when the class declaration is not accessible, for example, suppose B was the type

double: we cannot write a new constructor for doubles. This is done by defining
an operator in the class A whose name is B so we include the line

```
operator B() const;
```

in the class declaration for A. When we define the operator, we code it as

```
A::operator B() const
{
  // create object of type B and return it

  ...

}
```

In both cases, we do NOT specify the operator's return type at the start of the
line. For further discussion, see Section 11.4 of [20].

Here are some possible related questions:

- What does the explicit keyword do?
- Do you think that constructors should be explicit by default? Why do
  you think the standard does it the way it does?
- Can you give a non-trivial example where the second methodology is
  useful?

□

Solution to Question 7.16. If a class uses memory allocation then it will use the
new command. This returns a pointer to a piece of dynamically allocated memory.
If we make the pointer a class data member, then the operations of copying and
assignment will cause issues if we use the compiler's default operators.

In particular, the copy constructor supplied by the compiler will be a "shallow" copy constructor, that is it will simply make a copy of the pointer. The effect of this is that the original object and the copy will point to the same piece of allocated memory. This will cause many problems. For example, a properly written object should `delete` the pointed-to memory in its destructor if not before. A shallow copy will cause this to happen twice, and a crash will result.

More generally, even if the deletion is handled correctly in some other way, the two objects will be strongly tied together and the behaviour will not be that of a copying an ordinary object. The issues with assignment are similar, plus there is an additional complication that the object being overwritten will lose its pointer to the memory it had previously allocated. This means that that memory will never be deallocated and a memory leak occurs.

Some additional points to note on this problem are that the class will also need a properly written destructor and that many of the problems can be avoided by using smart pointers. It is also worth mentioning at this point "the rule of three": if a class has one of a destructor, copy constructor and assignment operator, it generally needs all three.

Personally, I prefer the "rule of almost zero": a class should have none of the three except an empty virtual destructor when it has abstract methods. The reason for this is that memory allocation and deallocation is much better handled by smart pointers. Write (or find in `Boost`) once a smart pointer class that has the desired behaviours, and then use and reuse that. This is a lot less bug prone and takes a lot less time when writing new classes. For more on the rule of almost zero see the second edition of [**7**].

Here are some possible related questions:

- What smart pointers do you know?
- Why do abstract classes need virtual destructors?

□

Solution to Question 7.17. The optimal solution to sort an array is to use the Standard Library:

```
#include <algorithm>

MyArray // uses STL sort algorithm to sort input
STLSort(const MyArray& input // array to sort
                 )
{
        MyArray tmp(input);
        std::sort(tmp.begin(), tmp.end());
        return tmp;
}
```

This will not do it in place. If you want to do it without copying the array, then don't copy the array, change the input to non-const and the return type to void.

It is unlikely that the interviewer will be satisfied with this response, however, since they are probably trying to test your skill with algorithms. It is also worth knowing that the STL sort algorithm is not guaranteed to be a *stable sort*, that is it can change the order of equivalent elements (i.e. neither $a < b$ not $b > a$.) If they ask you for a stable algorithm use `stable_sort` instead.

Here is a simple implementation of the insert sort algorithm:

```
template<class T>
void InsertSort(T start, T end)
{
    for(T i=start; i<end; ++i)
    {
        T::value_type value = *i;
        T dec = i;

        while(dec > start && *(dec-1)>=value)
        {
```

```
        *dec=*(dec-1);
        --dec;
    }

    *dec=value;
    }
}
```

The type T is an iterator (or pointer). This allows the code to be generic and applied to a vector of any type with comparison operators. Insert sort is simple but not particularly fast. It works as follows:

- Sort first j elements.
- Take element $j + 1$ and sift upwards until you find the place where it fits in.
- Insert element $j + 1$ in the correct position and shuffle the elements downwards to get the first $j + 1$ elements to be sorted.
- Keep on going until j reaches the end.

Important points to know about it are:

- It is stable.
- It is in-place and requires no extra memory.
- It is order n^2 in complexity.
- The speed depends on how sorted the array already is. If the array is sorted then the speed is order n.
- It can be used incrementally. i.e. sort a stream of numbers as they arrive rather than having to see them all before starting.

There exist faster algorithms which are order $n \log n$. One easy such algorithm is merge sort. With merge sort, one sorts the top half and bottom, and then merges the two. To sort each half, we can recursively call merge until the array is of length one. The main downside of this algorithm is that it is really fiddly to implement without extra temporary memory. Note that one could shift to using another algorithm once the array got small, e.g. use insert sort algorithm if the length is less than 20.

Other algorithms that are popular are heap sort and quick sort. There is extensive discussion on Wikipedia of the pros and cons of various choices.

Here are some possible related questions:

- Do you think it is worth hand-coding STL algorithms?
- Implement merge sort.
- How would you sort a list? (Lists are non-contiguous in memory so random access iterators cannot be used.)
- If objects were expensive to copy and assign, how would this affect choice and implementation of a sort routine?
- Why would you want a stable sort?

□

Solution to Question 7.18. In C++ the maximum value of an `int` is typically $2^{31} - 1$. If we add one to that we get the largest negative number: -2^{31}. Repeating therefore gives us a saw-tooth type wave.

If we take a `float` or `double` then eventually adding one has no effect because the value 1 as a fraction of the number is too small to show up in the significant digits which are stored as the value of the number.

Here are some possible related questions:

- What is the largest value that can be represented by a `double` in C++?
- What is the smallest value that can be represented by a `double` in C++?
- What strategies would you use to minimise floating point round off error in C++?
- How do you access the constant for the largest number in C++?

□

Solution to Question 7.19. There are three main storage areas for variables:

- the heap;
- the stack;
- the data segment.

Static variables are stored in the data segment, all the memory and locations for each variable are assigned before the program starts. They are not necessarily initialised, however, until their declaration is reached in the code.

The heap is used for dynamically allocated memory, e.g. anything allocated using new or malloc. The stack is used for ordinary (automatic) variables.

Here are some possible related questions:

- When are static variables destroyed?
- Give an example of when a static variable would be useful.

□

Solution to Question 7.20. This is arguably a trick question in that the C++ Standard says nothing about how virtual functions are implemented. So the correct answer is "However the compiler writer felt like doing it."

Nevertheless there is a standard approach which most if not all compilers use. This is to have table called the "virtual function table" where pointers to all the virtual functions are stored. There will be one copy of the table for each class. Each object from a class with virtual functions will contain a pointer to the table for its class.

Note that every object is slightly larger if virtual methods are declared. There is also an issue with some compilers as to how many copies of the virtual function table there are. One solution adopted by some older compilers was to place the table in the same translation unit as the definition of the destructor. This meant that if you declared

```
virtual ~MyClass(){}
```

in the header file for your class, then a copy of the virtual function table was put in the object file for every source file that directly or indirectly included it. For this reason, it is sometimes recommended to always define the destructor in the source file. Most modern compilers should be smarter than this, however.

Here are some possible related questions:

- Are static virtual functions possible in C++? Should they be?
- It is possible to call a pure virtual function?

☐

Solution to Question 7.21. There are a number of issues with virtual functions and optimisation. The first is that they are typically called using pointer indirection, that is the processor has to jump to a location contained in a pointer rather than a pre-determined location. This results in a few extra instructions.

The second is more serious: if the compiler and linker do not know what is contained in the function call they cannot perform any optimisations based on its contents. In particular, virtual functions cannot be inlined.

In addition, a virtual function table will be created for the class and every object from the class will need to contain a pointer to it. For large numbers of small objects, this can be a real issue.

One should realize that these are not huge issues unless the code contained in the function is very short. Thus it makes sense when a method is complicated for it to be virtual but for accessor functions there can be a real performance hit.

A further possible issue is that the virtual function tables for different classes can be in quite different parts of memory, this can result in the memory cached in the processor having to change which results in further slow-downs.

Here are some possible related questions:

- If we replaced a virtual function with a function pointer would that help optimisation?
- If we used templates instead would that help?
- Do you think that virtual functions are worth the overhead?

☐

Solution to Question to 7.22. The delete command is used to deallocate memory that was allocated using the new command, that is the memory for a single object. The delete[] command performs the corresponding task when memory was allocated using new[], that is an array of objects.

The C++ standard states if you call the wrong operator then you get *undefined behaviour*. In practice, if you are lucky then you get a memory leak and if you are unlucky you get a crash. (Some people would prefer a crash since it is much easier to spot!)

Here are some possible related questions:

- What happens if you delete a null pointer?
- It is possible to redefine the new and delete commands. How would you redefine them so that they work seamlessly when the wrong operator is called? Is this is a good idea?
- Why do you think the language has the two commands rather than just one?

$\square$

Solution to Question 7.23. The C++ standard states that for the ?: operator only one of the two final expressions is evaluated. If one used the function condif, they would both be evaluated. This has two consequences: speed and side-effects.

In particular, if the expressions are expensive to evaluate then computing both of them will slow the code down. It is also important to realize that in C++ there is little difference between an expression and an operation so the expressions can do things other than return a value. The use of condif will result in any changes that these operations cause occurring for both of them rather than just one.

A secondary speed issue is that a function call would take more time than calling an inbuilt operator.

Here are some possible related questions:

- How would you write code that correctly simulates the behaviour of ?: for integers?
- Extend this code to work for a general type.

$\square$

Solution to Question 7.24. The code describes an algorithm for turning pairs of independent uniforms into two pairs of independent Gaussian $N(0,1)$ draws. The crucial point is that an acceptance-rejection method is being used which means that if the pair of uniform draws lies outside a circle of radius 0.5 centred at $(0.5, 0.5)$, then they are discarded and another pair is drawn.

The probability of a pair being used is therefore the area of that circle, since the area of the square from which the uniforms are drawn is 1. The area of the circle is

$$\pi \left(\frac{1}{2} \right)^2 = \frac{\pi}{4}.$$

The average number of draws per Gaussian draw is therefore

$$\frac{4}{\pi} \sim 1.27.$$

Here are some possible related questions:

- How would you draw points in the unit circle using precisely two uniforms? (and so not using an acceptance rejection method.)
- Would this methodology work with low-discrepancy numbers?
- What other methods of generating Gaussian draws do you know?
- Which method would you use?

$\square$

Solution to Question 7.25. We first give a solution using reverse iterators:

```cpp
std::string reverse_string(const std::string& input)
{
    std::string output;
    output.reserve(input.size());

    for (std::string::const_reverse_iterator
            it = input.rbegin();
         it != input.rend(); ++it)
            output.push_back(*it);
```

```
    return output;
}
```

The use of reverse iterators allows us to count back from the end without doing any subtractions. Note also that we reserve the size of the output string to be correct to avoid doing more than one memory allocation.

Reversing in place is slightly trickier in that we have to swap pairs of elements. We give a straightforward simply coded algorithm:

```
void reverse_string_inplace(std::string& input)
{
    char c;

    for (size_t i=0;
            2*i < input.size();
                    ++i)
    {
      c = input[i];
      input[i] = input[input.size()-1-i];
      input[input.size()-1-i]= c;
    }
}
```

Note the crucial -1 as the last element is the size of the string minus one.

Here are some possible related questions:

- How would the code vary if you were working with C-style arrays?
- Which of the two routines do you prefer?
- If we were working with a vector of expensive to copy objects, how might the routine be coded to work efficiently?

□

Solution 7.26. In terms of syntax, if we use an & then we are passing by reference, if we use a * we get passing by pointer, and in other cases, we are passing by value.

Passing by value copies the parameter passed in. This means that time can be spent on the copying and that changes to the parameter inside the function do not have any effect outside the function.

Passing by reference means that the object used inside the function is the same as the one used outside. This is fast in that no copying occurs. However, changes to the object do have an effect outside the function, this makes parameters passed by reference useful for returning information. If one does not wish to pass back information in a parameter passed in by reference it is normal to declare it const; this ensures that the function does not change it, and signals to the caller that this is the case.

Passing by pointer is similar to passing by reference. A pointer to the object is passed by value. The cost of passing in is small as we are only copying a pointer not a complicated object. We have to dereference the pointer each time we access the object. Pointers have two concepts of const: whether the location of the thing pointed to can change, and whether the pointed to thing can change. This can make them more useful than references: for example, we can swap two pointers without changing the objects pointed to.

Here are some possible related questions:

- Why bother with references when pointers are available?
- If a parameter is called as a const reference, it is possible for the function to change it?

□

Solution to Question 7.27. This is a question about virtual functions and virtual destruction. The first part to note is that the method MyFunction is declared virtual in the base class. Once a method is virtual it is always virtual so it will be virtual in the inherited classes too. The pointer alpha1 is a pointer to an object of type Beta so the invocation of the method will yield "In Beta." Similarly with the reference alpha2, the object pointed to is of type Gamma so we get "In Gamma."

The correctness of the program is more subtle. A important rule to follow is that a function containing virtual functions should always have a virtual destructor, and this program does not. We should therefore be suspicious.

In fact, there is a memory leak caused by this omission. When the auto_ptr goes out of scope, the pointed to-object is deleted but the destructor of the base class is called, not that of the inherited class. This can be fixed simply by putting virtual in front of the base class destructor.

Here are some possible related questions:

- Why do you think destructors are not always virtual in C++?
- What are the pros and cons of using auto_ptrs?
- What is your favourite smart pointer?
- Have you tried the smart pointers in Boost?

□

Solution to Question 7.28. This is a question about order of creation and destruction: if we have a class Gamma inherited from Alpha and containing a data member of type Beta in what order are they created and destroyed?

The general rule is most primitive first for construction and last for destruction. A base class is more primitive than a class inherited from it, and data members are more primitive than the class they are members of. The bases of a class are more primitive than its data members. In this case, this means that we get the output

```
Creating Alpha
Creating Beta
Creating Gamma
Destroying Gamma
Destroying Beta
Destroying Alpha
```

Here are some possible related questions:

- What other possible orderings could you use, and would they be as good?
- Why are there curly brackets around the declaration of the object c? How would the output change if they were deleted?
- What happens if a class has multiple data members?

□

Solution to Question 7.29. The first thing we need is an algorithm to compute square roots. We use a simple one, believed to have been used by the Babylonians. This is based on the observation that

$$y < \sqrt{x}$$

if and only if

$$x/y > \sqrt{x}.$$

We therefore progress from a guess y to the average of it and x/y. Thus we have a sequence

$$y_{n+1} = \frac{1}{2}\left(y_n + \frac{x}{y_n}\right).$$

The limit y will satisfy

$$y = \frac{1}{2}\left(y + \frac{x}{y}\right),$$

and hence

$$2y^2 = y^2 + x,$$

so

$$y^2 = x.$$

Strictly speaking we need to show that the sequence converges. Let

$$f(y) = y + \frac{x}{y},$$

and so

$$f'(y) = 1 - \frac{x}{y^2}.$$

For x and y positive, this will be between 0 and 1, and as long as y lies in an interval $(0, \theta)$ this will be bounded by $M < 1$. This means that for $a, b \in (0, \theta)$

$$|f(a) - f(b)| \le M|a - b|.$$

This implies that applying f is a contraction mapping. In particular, if our first two points are in an interval of length l then the second and third points will be in an interval of length lM. Each application of f will multiply the length of the interval by M and so the length will go to zero and the sequence will converge. Alternatively, the result follows from the *Contraction Mapping Theorem* which can be found in just about any book on analysis, e.g. [**17**].

We present C++ code to implement this method:

```cpp
#include <iostream>

double absval(double z)
{
   return z >= 0 ? z : -z;
}

double squareroot(double x, double tol)
{

  double guess = x/2.0;

  while (absval(x-guess*guess) > tol*x)
  {
    guess = 0.5*(x/guess+guess);
  }

  return guess;
}

int main( int argc, char* argv[] )
{
   if (argc != 2)
   {
     std::cout << "Precisely one argument "
```

```
         "must be given for square-rooting";
    return 1;
  }

  double x= atof(argv[1]);
  double tol = 1E-8;
  double y = squareroot(x,tol);

  std::cout << y  << "\n";

  return 0;
}
```

Note we have not used the function fabs, here since we were told to not use the standard library.

The main program takes two arguments, the first is the number of arguments passed at the command line. The second is a vector of char* arrays. The zeroth element of the array is the name of the executable which is not useful. The first element is the argument we want. We want a double and we have a char*; the function atof converts between them.

Here are some possible related questions:

- What is the rate of convergence of your algorithm?
- What is the highest possible accuracy?
- What other methods do you know for computing square roots?
- Implement the Newton–Raphson method for this problem.

□

Solution to Question 7.30. A binary tree is a data structure consisting of a collection of *nodes*. Each node contains a piece of data and has zero, one or two nodes below it. Every node except the *head node* must be below precisely one other node. No loops are allowed, so each node has a well-defined distance from the top of the tree, and its *daughter nodes* are one further from the top.

There are a lot of ways to represent a tree in C++. One standard way to do this is have each be represented by a piece of data and pointers to two daughter nodes. If the daughter node does not exist then the pointer is null. This approach gives a tree that is quite easy to use but adding data, copying, assignment, destruction and creating the tree involve a lot of fiddly memory handling. One can also find that the nodes are scattered through memory.

We therefore present a method that uses a vector to store all the nodes. The relationships between nodes are represented by indices in the vector. We also include an auxiliary iterator class for traversing the tree.

```cpp
#ifndef BINARY_TREE_H
#define BINARY_TREE_H
#include <vector>

class BinaryTree
{
public:

  BinaryTree();

  class Iterator
  {

    public:

      int operator*() const;
      int& operator*();

      Iterator& Up();
      Iterator& Left();
      Iterator& Right();

      bool IsNull() const;
      bool LeftExists() const;
```

```
      bool RightExists() const;

   private:

      int Location;
      BinaryTree& OwningTree;

      Iterator(BinaryTree& tree, int location);

      friend class BinaryTree;

  };

  friend class Iterator;

  Iterator InsertOrOverwriteLeft(Iterator location,
                                 int value);
  Iterator InsertOrOverwriteRight(Iterator location,
                                  int value);

  Iterator GetHead();

  void InsertOrSetTreeTop(int x);

  bool IsEmpty() const;

 private:


 class TreeNode
 {
   public:
     int above;
     int left;
     int right;
```

```
    int value;
};

std::vector<TreeNode> Nodes;

};

int TreeDepth(BinaryTree& tree);
int TreeDepth(BinaryTree::Iterator iter);


int MaxElement(BinaryTree& tree);
int MaxElement(BinaryTree::Iterator iter);


#endif
```

As well as our main tree class, we have auxiliary classes: the iterator class and the node class. Note that since the iterator allows modification of the tree, it can only be invoked for trees that are not constant objects. If we wished to be able to work with const trees, we would need to define a second iterator class, which is typical in the standard library for template container classes.

Note the use of friend to allow the iterator class to access the private data in the tree, and also to allow the tree to create iterator objects. We represent the empty tree by a vector containing one node which contains all zeros. We make iterators and nodes point to this node when pointing to non-existent nodes.

The implementation is straightforward, once the structure has been decided:

```
#include "BinaryTree.h"

int BinaryTree::Iterator::operator*() const
{
```

```cpp
    return OwningTree.Nodes[Location].value;
}

int& BinaryTree::Iterator::operator*()
{
  return OwningTree.Nodes[Location].value;
}


BinaryTree::Iterator& BinaryTree::Iterator::Up()
{
  Location =  OwningTree.Nodes[Location].above;
   return *this;
}

BinaryTree::Iterator& BinaryTree::Iterator::Left()
{
   Location = OwningTree.Nodes[Location].left;
   return *this;
}

BinaryTree::Iterator& BinaryTree::Iterator::Right()
{
   Location = OwningTree.Nodes[Location].right;
   return *this;
}


bool BinaryTree::Iterator::IsNull() const
{
   return Location ==0;
}
bool BinaryTree::Iterator::LeftExists() const
{
   return  OwningTree.Nodes[Location].left !=0;
```

```
}

bool BinaryTree::Iterator::RightExists() const
{
    return  OwningTree.Nodes[Location].right !=0;
}




BinaryTree::Iterator::Iterator(BinaryTree& tree,
                              int location)
: OwningTree(tree), Location(location)
{
}




BinaryTree::Iterator
BinaryTree::InsertOrOverwriteLeft(BinaryTree::Iterator iter,
                              int value)
{
#ifdef _DEBUG
    if (&iter.OwningTree != this)
        throw("bad iterator");

    if (iter.IsNull())
        throw("can't insert at null location");
#endif

    int newLocation = Nodes[iter.Location].left;

    if (newLocation ==0)
    {
        TreeNode NewNode = { iter.Location, 0, 0, value};
```

```
        Nodes[iter.Location].left = Nodes.size();
        Nodes.push_back(NewNode);
    }
    else
        Nodes[ Nodes[iter.Location].left].value = value;

    return Iterator(*this, Nodes[iter.Location].left);
}


BinaryTree::Iterator
BinaryTree::InsertOrOverwriteRight(BinaryTree::Iterator iter,
                                   int value)
{
#ifdef _DEBUG
    if (&iter.OwningTree != this)
        throw("bad iterator");

    if (iter.IsNull())
        throw("can't insert at null location");
#endif
    int newLocation = Nodes[iter.Location].right;

    if (newLocation ==0)
    {
        TreeNode NewNode = { iter.Location, 0, 0, value};
        Nodes[iter.Location].right = Nodes.size();
        Nodes.push_back(NewNode);
    }
    else
        Nodes[ Nodes[iter.Location].right].value = value;

    return Iterator(*this, Nodes[iter.Location].right);
}
```

```
BinaryTree::Iterator BinaryTree::GetHead()
{
#ifdef _DEBUG
    if (Nodes.size() <=1)
        throw("empty tree");
#endif
    return Iterator(*this,1);
}

void BinaryTree::InsertOrSetTreeTop(int x)
{
    if (Nodes.size() >1)
        Nodes[1].value=x;
    else
    {
        TreeNode node = {0,0,0,x};
        Nodes.push_back(node);
    }
}



BinaryTree::BinaryTree()
{
    TreeNode node = {0,0,0,0};
    Nodes.push_back(node);
}



bool BinaryTree::IsEmpty() const
{
    return Nodes.size() <=1;
}
```

The iterator stores a reference to the tree so it is wholly associated with this particular tree. Note that since the iterator class's constructor is private, it can only be created by a tree. We have not made the copy constructor private so iterators can be copied, however.

We uses lists to specify nodes, this can be done for trivial classes that have no user-defined constructors. When we add a node, we use the push_back method of the vector class and so do not have to worry about memory allocation. We also do not need to define copy constructors and destructors for the tree.

For the final two problems, these are naturally done via recursion. For each, we define a function for the tree which calls another function for iterators since the real issue is how to traverse the tree:

```cpp
int TreeDepth(BinaryTree::Iterator iter)
{
  if (iter.IsNull())
    return 0;

  BinaryTree::Iterator tmp(iter);

  iter.Left();
  int leftDepth = TreeDepth(iter);
  tmp.Right();
  int rightDepth = TreeDepth(tmp);

  return 1+std::max(leftDepth,rightDepth);
}

int TreeDepth(BinaryTree& tree)
{
  if (tree.IsEmpty())
    return 0;

  return TreeDepth(tree.GetHead());
}

int MaxElement(BinaryTree::Iterator iter)
```

```
{
#ifdef _DEBUG
  if (iter.IsNull())
    throw("attempt to take max from null iterator");
#endif
  int value = *iter;

  BinaryTree::Iterator tmp(iter);

  if (iter.LeftExists())
    value = std::max(value,MaxElement(iter.Left()));

  if (tmp.RightExists())
    value = std::max(value,MaxElement(tmp.Right()));

  return value;
}

int MaxElement(BinaryTree& tree)
{
#ifdef _DEBUG
   if (tree.IsEmpty())
     throw("attempt to take max of empty tree");
#endif

   return MaxElement(tree.GetHead());
}
```

The only real subtlety here is that at points we copy the iterators. This is a very fast operation since they only contain a reference and an integer; this would be true even if the tree contained a more complicated data type. This is necessary because the Left() and Right() operations modify the iterator, and it is the unmodified iterator that we want.

Here are some possible related questions:

- Add in an iterator class that works with const objects.
- Write a general class that works with data of an arbitrary type.
- Do the tree the conventional way using nodes and pointers.

□

Solution to Question 7.31. The keyword const indicates that something is constant, that is it cannot be changed. However, there are many subtleties to its use. Here are some of the places it can be used:

- on a variable declaration;
- on an argument of a function or method;
- on a method of a class;
- on a class data member;
- in the declaration of a pointer.

When it is used on a variable declaration, the variable's value cannot be changed after the variable is created so its value must be assigned at that time.

Often arguments to function are passed by reference rather than by value to avoid the overhead of making a copy. If an argument is passed by reference then its value can be changed within the routine and the changes propagate outside. Putting a const stops it changing, and makes it clear to the caller that there is no intention to change it.

When we place a const on a method of a class, it indicates that the class will not change the class's internal state. In particular, inside the method the class's data members cannot be changed easily. However, it is possible to do so if the coder really desires. The easiest way is to declare data members mutable. The const keyword then has no effect on them. This technique can be useful as a method of caching data inside const methods to avoid recomputations. It is, however, very poor practice to use mutable to allow const methods to make essential changes to the class's behaviour. Calling a const method before another method should not affect the result of the second (and any subsequent) method. Once again here the use of const clarifies for the caller what behaviour to expect.

Placing `const` on a class data member means that the data member must be initialised in the constructor's initialisation list, and it cannot be changed thereafter. A nasty side effect of this is that the class cannot have an assignment operator, since such an operator would change the data member's value. It is therefore advisable not to do this, unless you are happy to have classes that cannot be assigned.

Pointers can be `const` in two ways: the object pointed to can be `const`, and the location of the pointer can be `const`. This is distinct from references which can only be `const` in one way.

It is also important to be aware of `const_cast` . This can remove constness from pointers. However, if an object was originally declared `const`, an attempt to modify it using `const_cast` will result in undefined behaviour. These casts are really only useful when interacting with legacy code which has not been written with `const` in mind.

Being keen on the use of `const` suggests that you are a responsible programmer, being unkeen suggests that you are not, so best to be keen on it at an interview!

Here are some possible related questions:

- Repeat this question for `volatile`.
- Do you think `const` adds to the C++ language?
- Is it possible to have two versions of the same function which are the same except for return type and constness? Would this be useful?

□

Solution to Question 7.32. The keyword `static` has many uses in C++. The first and most common one is a `static` variable in a function.

Such a variable is initialised the first time it is encountered, but does not go out of scope when the function exits, instead the value persists until the next time the function is called and it is then reused. This had the advantage of mimicking class-like behaviour in C but is less useful in C++. It can be used in C++ to reduce the time spent on creating objects. Note, however, that this use is incompatible with multi-threaded programming since the function could be entered by two different threads both wanting to access the same data. It is used in the singleton pattern to allow one instance of a class to exist which is a `static` variable member inside a `static` member function.

This brings us on to `static` member functions, such a function is a method of a class which is not associated with an object of the class. It is therefore invoked via

```
MyClass::MyMethod();
```

rather than

```
MyObject.MyMethod();
```

The third use of `static` is to specify a function which has no linkage outside the translation unit. In other words, if we declare a function `static`, we cannot call it from another file. This usage is archaic, since it has been replaced by the concept of an anonymous namespace. It is has now been officially *deprecated*.

The fourth use of `static` is to denote class data members for which there is only one copy for the entire class rather than one for each object in the class. Once again there are issues with thread safety.

Here are some possible related questions:

- What does it mean for a feature of C++ to be deprecated?
- Give a non-trivial use of `static` member data.
- How would you make `static` objects thread-safe?

□

Solution to Question 7.33. *Polymorphism* means "many shapes." It used in C++ to describe the process of having a base class with `virtual` functions that are defined in inherited classes. Thus client code treats an object as if it is a base class object but elements of its behaviour will vary according to which inherited class it is from.

A good example of this is a Payoff class for which the main pay-off is only defined in an inherited class. Thus either a call or a put pay-off could be passed into a routine that treats all pay-offs the same. For further discussion of this example, see [7]. Other standard examples are "a car is a vehicle" with a "drive" method and "a circle is a shape" with a "draw" method.

An *abstract class* is a class that contains a *pure* virtual method. A method is pure virtual if it is virtual and has the specifier =0 at the end. A class is also pure virtual if it is inherited from a pure virtual class and does not override the pure virtual with a non-pure one. An abstract class cannot be instantiated. This means that such a class can only be used via an inherited class which is *concrete* that is not pure virtual. Note that a pure virtual method need not be defined anywhere but it can be if so desired.

A *pointer* is a variable that contains the address of another object. A *reference* is also such a variable. The principal difference is that a reference can only refer to one object which is determined when the reference is created, whereas a pointer can be reassigned to refer to another object. Pointers can also point to nothing and are then called NULL pointers and have the value zero.

Here are some possible related questions:

- Do you think that references add anything to the language?
- What is a smart pointer?
- Calling pure virtual methods: is it possible to call a pure virtual method that has not been defined? Discuss.
- Calling pure virtual methods: is it possible to call a pure virtual method that has been defined? Discuss.

$\square$

Solution to Question 7.34. We place the code for which we wish to catch exceptions inside curly brackets with a try at the front. At the end, we put catch(...). This then catches exceptions of all types.

Here are some possible related questions:

- What is exception safety?
- How do you rethrow an object?
- If I catch an object of type X and throw an object of type Y under what circumstances is Y caught by the catch?

□

Solution to Question 7.35. We code as follows

```
extern "C"
{
// the functions to have the linkage

}
```

Here are some possible related questions:

- What else can the extern keyword be used for?
- Why is extern ''C'' needed at all?

□

Solution to Question 7.36. The answer is yes. The const_cast command exists for precisely this purpose. Be aware that most people do not think it is a good idea, however. Essentially, the way it works is that we have a const reference to a variable. We const_cast the reference to a pointer to a non-constant variable. We can then change the value of the pointed to object via the pointer.

```
void badFunction(const int& x)
{
        int* p = const_cast<int*>(&x);
        (*p) = 25;
}
```

changes the value of x to 25. This will not work unless the variable passed was originally non-const however. If the function was given a hard-coded value at compile time via something like

```
const int y = 10;
badFunction(y);
```

the value of y will generally be 10. However, the standard does not guarantee anything in this case, and specifies undefined behaviour which could be a crash.

Here are some possible related questions:

- Why would you want to change a const variable?
- Have you ever used const_cast?
- How many types of cast are there?

□

Solution to 7.37. Quick sort is a well-known algorithm for sorting elements of an array. The algorithm is quite simple.

- Pick an element of the array.
- Make all elements less than it, go before it, and make all elements bigger than it, go after it.
- Repeat on the two subdivided arrays.

We work recursively until the array to be sorted is of size 1. Sometimes a different algorithm is used when the size gets below a pre-determined threshold level.

The main subtlety when coding is to do it in place, that is without creating a second duplicate array. There is some arbitrariness regarding which element is picked. The element picked is generally called the pivot. The choice of pivot affects the speed. Whilst using the first element works, that choice is known to perform particularly slowly for already sorted arrays. We give an implementation that uses the value at the mid-point of the range.

```cpp
#include <vector>
#include <iostream>
#include <cmath>

void swap(std::vector<double>& data, int i, int j)
{
    double x = data[i];
    data[i] = data[j];
    data[j] = x;
}

int partition(std::vector<double>& data, int left, int right)
{
    int middle = (left+right)/2;
    double pivot = data[middle];

    while ( left < right )
    {
        // move in from left until we get to an element
        // at least as big as the pivot
        while ( data[left] < pivot )
            ++left;

        // move in from right until we get to an element
        // at least as small as the pivot
        while ( data[right] > pivot )
            --right;

        // if the new leftmost and rightmost points
        // have the same value
        // then move in from left since we must have
        // that they both equal
        // to the pivot
        if ( data[left] == data[right] )
            ++left;
```

```
    else
    // if they are different then one
    // must be on the wrong side so swap them
    swap(data,left,right);
}

    return right;
}


// The quicksort recursive function
void quicksort(std::vector<double>& data, int left, int right)
{
    if ( left < right )
    {
        int pivotIndex = partition(data, left, right);
        quicksort(data, left, pivotIndex-1);
        quicksort(data, pivotIndex+1, right);
    }
}
```

Quick sort is popular because it is quick! However, its computational complexity is not guaranteed to be low. In the worst cases, it is $O(n^2)$ whereas other algorithms are $O(n \log n)$. Generally, it performs best on average, however. So its appropriateness depends on whether you want good average performance or good worst-case performance.

Here are some possible related questions:

- If you wanted a guaranteed $O(n \log n)$ performance, what algorithm would you use?
- Is it worth hand-coding such algorithms as opposed to using the one in the C++ standard library?
- If the objects were very big, how would you carry out a sort?

□

Solution to 7.38. The main downsides of a virtual destructor are that it adds a pointer to the data footprint of class objects and that two indirections are required to call the destructor. The first of these increase the size of an object by a few bytes. If you are creating a lot of objects from a very small class this may become noticeable. The second makes it take longer to call the destructor. Again this is only likely to be an issue if you have many light-weight objects.

The relevance of the other virtual functions is that no memory is added if they exist since the class already needs a pointer to a virtual function table for every object already. It is also much more likely that the objects are likely to be referenced through pointers to inherited class objects if the class has virtual functions. The virtual destructor is only relevant if an inherited class object is deleted through a delete command called on a pointer to the base class.

Here are some possible related questions:

- Should the C++ language specification be changed to make destructors virtual by default?
- What do other languages such as Java do?

□

Solution to 7.39. In C++ 2011, there is an easy solution. You simply use the new keyword *final*. This disallows inheritance and you are done.

However, many people are still using old versions of C++ which did not contain this keyword. The standard solution is to declare the constructor private. We then have to declare a second method which calls the constructor so that objects of the type can be created.

A more sophisticated solution is as follows

```
class Difficult;

class DifficultBase
{

private:
 friend class Difficult;
 DifficultBase () { }
};

class Difficult : private virtual DifficultBase
{
public:

};
```

The class Difficult can access the base class's constructor since it is a friend of the base class. However, any class inherited from it will not be a friend of the base class so cannot access its constructor and there is a compile-time error. We are using an essential feature of virtual inheritance here which is that because there can only be one copy of each virtual base, any virtual base's constructor is called by the most inherited class.

Here are some possible related questions:

- Why would you want to do this?
- How would you allow inheritance for the class whilst outlawing virtual overriding for a particular method?
- Have you used C++ 2011?

□

Solution to 7.40. There are four important methods here:

- a default constructor,
- a copy constructor,
- an assignment operator,
- a destructor.

The default constructor takes no arguments and initialises no member variables. If the member variables are from user-defined classes then their default constructors are called. It exists only if there are no constructors defined at all. So defining a constructor that takes some argument will cause it to disappear.

The other three are provided unless they are explicitly defined. They are generally useful when the class does memory allocation and deallocation. If it does not, then they are not needed and indeed it is better not to define them since there is less to go wrong. The "rule of three" states that if you have one of them then you probably need all three. The "rule of almost zero" says that you should aim to be in the case of needing none of them most of time. It is "almost" because often you need to define an empty virtual destructor in order to ensure that deletion via pointers to a base class is handled correctly. For more information, see C++ Design Patterns and Derivatives Pricing, second edition.

Here are some possible related questions:

- What is a "shallow copy"?
- What is a "deep copy"?
- Do you think that following the rule of almost zero is sensible? Why doesn't it rule out classes that do memory allocation?

□

Solution to 7.41. These are called the post- and pre-increment operators. Both increase y by one. The difference lies in the value returned by the operator. y++ returns the value of y before the change, but ++y returns the value of y after the change.

It is actually fairly rare to use the returned value in any case, so it makes little difference. These days ++y tends to be preferred on the grounds that it does not

require the compiler to make a copy of y to return. In practice, if you do not use
the returned value and are working with an inbuilt type, the compiler will optimise
away the difference.

Here are some possible related questions:

- If you are working with a user-defined type will the choice make a differ-
  ence?
- What is ++b when b is a boolean?
- Give an example where the returned value matters.

☐

Solution to 7.42. A virtual function has the keyword virtual function before it.
A pure virtual function has =0 after it when it is declared in the class definition. If
a function is virtual but not pure virtual then you have to provide a definition of its
implementation or get a linkage error. Pure virtual functions generally do not have
to have definitions provided but it is possible to provide one if the code wants to.
The main effect of being pure is that the class becomes *abstract* which means that
objects from it cannot be instantiated.

A class inherited from an abstract class can be instantiated provided all the
pure virtual functions have been overridden by virtual functions which are not
pure. So the main effect of being pure is to force an inherited class to override
the function.

Here are some possible related questions:

- Why might you want to both implement a function and declare it pure
  virtual?
- How do you call the base class version of a function if it has been overridden from within the overriding function?
- Should virtual functions in the base class ever be impure?

☐

Solution to 7.43. This one is a little ambiguous in that it is not clear if they are asking from the user's perspective or the implementor's one. We therefore discuss both of them.

The Boost shared pointer has been included in C++ 2011 and so now can be regarded as the Standard Libary shared pointer. It is an example of a *non-intrusive reference-counting shared pointer.* We next define these terms.

Non-intrusive means that no requirements are made of the class that is pointed to. For example, we do not require the existence of a clone method.

Referencing counting means that the smart pointer keeps count of the number of smart pointers pointing to the underlying object. When that number hits zero, the object is destroyed and the memory is deallocated. In other words, the object is deleted. This is the virtue of smart pointers – there is no need to worry about object destruction, the smart pointer handles it for you.

Shared pointer means that if we copy the pointer, we get another pointer to the same underlying object, so the pointers share the object. The reference count is increased by one when this happens.

In order to create a shared pointer to an object, we first have to allocate it using new so it is on the heap and then pass the dumb pointer thus obtained into a shared pointer object. Of course, this could be done simply by declaring

```
// if arguments to constructor are x
shared_ptr<myClass> the_shared_ptr(new myclass(x));
```

Shared pointers are useful for avoiding unnecessary copies of complex objects whilst ensuring that memory deallocation is handled automatically at the right time. The main danger of them is that one can accidentally end up using the same object in two different ways at the same time unwittingly, resulting in bugs. They are used very heavily in QuantLib. Developers tend to think more in terms of which smart pointer to use rather than thinking about whether to use one.

We now briefly discuss the implementation of the shared pointer in Boost. Since the pointer is non-intrusive, a counter for how many pointers there are for a given object has to be stored outside the object and it has to be available to all such pointers. This means that it is allocated on the heap and each shared pointer must have a pointer to the counter as well as a pointer to the object.

One surprising aspect of the Boost shared pointer is that if you have a pointer to a base class object initialised with a pointer to a derived class object, it uses the derived type's destructor rather than the base class one. This means that you do not have to declare the base class's destructor to be virtual to get the correct destruction behaviour. Thus the pointer has to store the location of the object's destructor.

The Boost shared pointer implementation breaks in the prescence of cycles. That is suppose an object A contains a shared pointer to an object B and B has a shared pointer to A, then the pointers always think that another reference exists and the objects are never deleted. This will happen no matter how big the chain is if it ends back at the start.

Here are some possible related questions:

- What is a weak pointer and what is it used for?
- What other smart pointers exists in Boost?
- An intrusive shared pointer would reduce the clunkiness of the shared pointer so why not use one?

□

Solution to 7.44. A set in the C++ STL is a way of storing a collection of elements that have an ordering defined. They are always stored using the ordering as a sorted collection. They are typically stored as binary trees with *red-black trees* often used. The important detail of their structure is that inserting a new element does not destroy the ordering and is guaranteed to be of logarithmic complexity in the number of elements in the set. Since the set is always sorted, it is quick to find a given element. Sets do not allow duplicate elements. If such elements are desired, the multiset has to be used.

Maps are similar to sets in that the elements are stored in a tree-like structure that allows fast look-up. The essential difference is that in a map, each element has two components of different types, the first, called the key, is used to determine the position and the second is the value. One could view a set as a map in which the value is always equal to the key. Maps do not allow duplicate keys but multimaps do.

Here are some possible related questions:

- What would you use a set to store?
- Give a non-trivial example of using a map?
- Why not just store everything in a vector and not waste time on learning these other containers?

□

Solution to 7.45. We suppose we have a vector of doubles with N elements. We have to find the middle element. We take this to be the element in place $N/2$ rounded down. If N is even, sometimes the preceding element is used. There is a number of ways to tackle this problem. The easiest is simply to sort the array and pick out the relevant element. The interviewer is unlikely to be happy with that solution in that sorting is overkill and results in an $O(N \log N)$ algorithm.

In fact, there are standard algorithms for partially sorting an array so that just the element you care about is in the right place. One way to do so is adapt the quick sort algorithm of Question 7.37. We pick a value that we know is in the arrray. We then move all the elements smaller than it to its left, and all those bigger to its right. It is then in the right place. We then know whether it is bigger or less then the median by examining its index. We therefore know which of the two partitions contains the median. We therefore repeat the algorithm just on that partition. We recurse until we hit the median.

The fact that we only operate on one side at each stage greatly speeds up the algorithm and it is generally $O(N)$ in time but can take longer if we are unlucky. Note that there is nothing special about the median, and this approach can be used to find the nth element for any n.

Here is the code for the median function. We use the partition function already defined for quick sort. We use the value of the mid-point of the unsorted set as our pivot. It takes as input the target index of the element we wish to get right.

```
// The median recursive function
void median(std::vector<double>& data, int left,
                                       int right, int target)
{
        if ( left < right )
        {
            int pivotIndex = partition(data, left, right);

            if (pivotIndex == target)
                    return;

            if (pivotIndex > target)
                    median(data, left, pivotIndex-1,target);
            else
                    median(data, pivotIndex+1, right,target);
        }
}
```

A downside of this approach is that it reorders the original data array. This may or may not be an issue. If it is, then a copy would have to be made, which results in an extra N memory usage.

There is a nice alternative algorithm which is $O(N \log N)$ but does not require extra memory or copying:

- Find the maximum and minimum values.
- Take the middle of the two.
- Scan through and see whether the middle is greater or less than the median by counting how many elements are less than it.
- Repeat performing a binary search until the median is found.

This works better with integers since the algorithm must terminate since each scan through will determine another bit of the result.

Here are some possible related questions:

- Is there are an algorithm which is guaranteed $O(N)$ complexity?

- Are these algorithms in the STL?
- Should algorithms be a compulsory subject in a computer science degree?

☐

Solution to 7.46. *Physical memory* usually means the actual memory of the random access memory (RAM) included in the computer. However, modern architectures usually allow a larger address space including for example disk drives. Addresses in this larger space are said to be *virtual*. When your program accesses these, the memory has to be mapped into physical memory and then assigned a physical memory address so that the CPU can access it. Programs are typically written to use virtual memory and the computer's memory management unit handles the translation of one to the other.

Here are some possible related questions:

- Does using virtual memory slow your code?
- What is pinned memory? What is it useful for?
- Under Windows how much virtual address space is there?

☐

Solution to 7.47. When the CPU attempts to access memory that it cannot physically address, it is called a *segmentation fault*. It generally results in an exception and a program's termination. In C++ they most often occur when a pointer is abused. For example, if an array without bounds checking is accessed out of range, an access violation occurs and we get a segmentation fault. It can also result from dereferencing a null pointer, or by attempting to access a pointed-to object after the pointer has been deleted. Dereferencing never initialised pointers is another possible cause. Trying to overwrite a constant string defined at compile time is also likely to generate a segmentation fault.

Another possible cause is a recursive function never termnating and generating a stack overflow.

Here are some possible related questions:

- Should arrays always have bounds checking?

- What is an "electric fence" with the GNU compiler?
- What is a "bus error"?

□

Solution to 7.48. Operating systems divide memory up into 4 kilobyte pages. A page fault is an attempt by the computer's hardware to access a virtual memory location in a page that not currently mapped to a physical page. The operating system then has to decide how to deal with the fault. Typically, it would map the desired virtual page to a physical page. If there are no spare pages, it would have to first write out a physical page to disk to create space. If the operating system believes that the requested location does not exist, it generates an error instead.

It is important to realize that page faults are often not errors. However, too much swapping of physical memory with disk space will greatly slow a program down.

Here are some possible related questions:

- What are "minor" and "major" page faults?
- How can we reduce the number of page faults in a program?
- Is avoiding page faults worthwhile?

□

Solution to 7.49. Name mangling is the process of changing the name of a function or class in a C++ program to reflect the namespace it is in, and its arguments. The compiler does this as part of the process of turning source code into an executable. The crucial point of mangled names is that overloaded functions with different arguments have distinct names post mangling, as do functions with the same name in different namespaces. Thus they allow the compiler to assume that any functions with the same name are actually the same function.

The mangled name is not specified by the standard so different compilers will mangle in different ways, and this makes combining object code produced by different compilers hard.

Here are some possible related questions:

- How can we stop a name being mangled?
- What are the pros and cons of stopping mangling?
- How might you implement mangling if you had to do it yourself?

☐

Solution to 7.50. RTTI stands for run-time type identification in C++. It allows the querying of an object to discover its type. This can be useful in that we may have a pointer to a base class and not know the type of the object pointed to. It is used when the `dynamic_cast` operator is called and also the typeid operator. It is only available for classes that have at least one virtual function and so a virtual function table.

It allows the possibility of implementing differing behaviour using a switch statement on the type of the object. However, this use is generally condemned since a similar effect can be achieved by adding an appropriate virtual function to a base class but if the code for the base class is not changeable, it provides a solution.

Here are some possible related questions:

- Why do some compilers make RTTI optional?
- Is RTTI within the spirit of C++?
- What is a `dynamic_cast` and why does it require RTTI?

☐

CHAPTER 8

Logic/Brainteasers

8.1. Introduction

This chapter covers a range of cunning, tricky and devious questions. There is little (if any) mathematics involved in solving the questions, instead they usually require you to look at the question from the correct perspective. The keys to success are therefore persistence and practice: there are only so many different sorts of brainteasers and classifying the questions helps a lot.

Most of these problems are easily solved once you know the trick, so it is particularly important you attempt them before checking the solution.

Due to the varied nature of the problems, there is no one 'rule' we can suggest for tackling them. Here are some general pointers, however:

(1) Avoid the junk. A lot of these types of questions are presented in a story-telling kind of way. Look through all the fluff that surrounds the important details and focus on the main problem.

(2) Reduce the problem to a simple case and see what happens. If you're asked how to solve the problem for a group of objects, what happens with one object? Two? Three? Can you see a pattern developing?

(3) Work backwards. If you're asked to solve the problem over a number of steps, how would you proceed if you were close to your goal? And a little further...?

(4) Perhaps most importantly, think carefully! A lot of these problems are written to trick you, so it is worth taking the extra thirty seconds to consider them carefully.

8.2. Questions

QUESTION 8.1. At 3.15pm, how many degrees separate the hour and minute hand of a clock?

QUESTION 8.2. What's 15 cubed?

QUESTION 8.3. A $4 \times 4 \times 4$ cube is made up of $1 \times 1 \times 1$ cubes. If I paint the outside of the cube, how many $1 \times 1 \times 1$ cubes have paint on them?

QUESTION 8.4. An ant wants to get from one corner of a cube of volume $1m^3$ to the opposite corner. How far will the ant travel if it takes the shortest distance?

QUESTION 8.5. A lily-pad doubles in area every second. After one minute, it fills the pond. How long would it take to quarter fill the pond?

QUESTION 8.6. One lap of a racetrack is a mile long. A car drives round it with an average speed of 30 mph. How fast would it have to go on a second lap to have an average speed for the two laps of 60 mph?

QUESTION 8.7. We have a glass of white wine and a glass of red wine. Each has 100mls initially. We have 5mls from the red glass and put it in the white glass and make the mixture homogeneous. We then take 5ml from the white glass and put it in the red. Is there more white in the red or red in the white?

QUESTION 8.8. Imagine a chocolate bar consisting of n squares. How many times do you have to break the chocolate bar to get n individual squares? Does the result depend on the shape of the chocolate bar? Prove it.

Additional question: Suppose you can stack the pieces on top of each other so that you can break several at once. How many breaks then?

QUESTION 8.9. Suppose the two of us go into a pub and order a pint of beer. I drink half the pint. You drink half of the remainder. I drink half of what's left after this, and we continue. How much of the pint do I drink, and how much do you?

QUESTION 8.10. A rabbit has N steps to climb. It can either jump one step or two steps at a time. How many distinct ways are there to the top?

QUESTION 8.11. Snow starts falling sometime before midday. A snow clearing car begins work at midday, and the car's speed is in reverse proportion to the time since the snow began falling. The distance covered by the snow car from midday until 1pm is double that from 1pm to 2pm. When does the snow start?

QUESTION 8.12. What is the smallest number of integer weights required to exactly balance every integer between 1 and 40. Prove it.

QUESTION 8.13. Find the smallest subset of integers that you can use to produce $1, 2, \ldots, 40$ by only using "+" or "-" (each number in the subset can be used at most one time) .

QUESTION 8.14. How many ways can you tile dominoes (2 by 1) on a 2 by n grid without gaps?

QUESTION 8.15. You have four cards, displaying 7, 6, A, C. The claim is: if there is a vowel on one side of a card, then there must be an even number on the other. You may now turn some cards over to test this claim. Which cards would you turn over and why?

QUESTION 8.16. Suppose there are nine marbles in a jar, one heavier than the rest. You have a set of scales and can weigh as many as you want a maximum of three times to ascertain which marble is the heaviest. How do you achieve this?

QUESTION 8.17. There are n lions in a cage. A piece of meat is thrown into the cage. A lion can either eat the whole piece of meat or none of it. If it eats the meat, it falls asleep and becomes to the other lions a piece of meat. What happens?

QUESTION 8.18. You are sitting in a boat in a swimming pool, you throw the anchor over the side. What happens to the level of the water in the pool?

QUESTION 8.19. Let's play a game with 100 balls: 50 white and 50 black and two sacks. You can arrange the balls within the two sacks in any way you want. I then come into the room and pick a ball from one of the sacks. If I pick a black, I win; a white, you win. How do you arrange the balls such that you have the highest chance of winning?

QUESTION 8.20. 50 smart, logical people are on an island. The people either have blue or brown eyes. The island has a certain set of rules. If you can work out that you definitely have blue eyes, then you have to commit suicide at 12 midnight. But you have to be 100% certain – i.e. you have to deduce logically that you have blue eyes. There are no mirrors and nobody can tell you what colour your eyes are.

First, what happens? Then, one day a man from outside the village comes along and tells everybody on the island that there is at least one person that has blue eyes on the island. What happens?

QUESTION 8.21. There is a prison of 22 prisoners in 22 cells. The warden says to them he will take them into a room with two light switches, which will each begin in the down position, and the prisoner may use a switch. However he will take them randomly, one a day. The warden says that as soon as anyone can tell him that all the prisoners have been into the room he will let them free, but if they get it wrong they hang. He gives them one hour to discuss their strategy, and after that there will be no communication. How do the prisoners guarantee their freedom?

QUESTION 8.22. Given a small rectangle completely contained in a large rectangle and a straight edge, draw a straight line dividing the area contained in the big rectangle but not the small rectangle in half. (This means that the difference set is divided into two pieces of equal area.)

QUESTION 8.23. You are asked to play NIM, with the last one to pick up a stick losing. What's the optimal strategy?

There are various versions of the game of NIM but let's consider a simple one. There are n matches, for example 10, on the table. Each turn you can take $1, 2$ or 3 matches. The person who takes the last stick loses.

QUESTION 8.24. Coins on a round table game: we take turns placing coins on a round table, no coins can overlap another coin or the edge of the table. If the player who can't place a coin loses and you can choose whether to play first or second, devise a winning strategy.

QUESTION 8.25. How many petrol stations are there in the UK (or whichever country/city you are currently in)?

QUESTION 8.26. How many piano tuners are there in Oxford?

QUESTION 8.27. Suppose three people are lined up in a row. 3 hats are selected randomly from 2 red hats and 3 white hats and placed on each persons head. No one can see the hat on their own head, but the third person can see the hat on the second and first person, while the second person can see the hat on the first person.

They are all asked what colour hat they have on their own head. The third person says he doesn't know, as does the second. The first person correctly identifies the colour of his hat. What colour is he wearing?

QUESTION 8.28. Suppose you have five jars each containing pills. The pills in four of the jars weigh 10 grams while the pills in the other jar weigh 9 grams. You also have a set of absolute scales. How do you determine which jar has the pills that weigh 9 grams with just one weighing?

QUESTION 8.29. A 4 by 4 by 4 cube is painted on the outside then broken up. How many little cubes have each of 0, 1, 2, 3 painted sides?

QUESTION 8.30. What is the weight of the Earth?

QUESTION 8.31. Two skyscrapers are built perpendicular to the ground, the distance at the top is measured to be smaller than the distance the bottom. Why?

QUESTION 8.32. A bug starts at a vertex A of triangle ABC. It then moves to one of its two adjacent vertices. How many paths of length 8 end back at vertex A? For example, one such path is ABABABABA.

8.3. Solutions

Solution to Question 8.1. There are 12 hours on a clock and hence 30 degrees between each hour. Obviously it takes one hour for the hour hand to move from the 3 to the 4. Since it is one quarter past 3 (i.e. the minute hand will be exactly on 3), there will be 30/4 = 7.5 degrees between the two hands.

Here are some possible related questions:

- How many degrees at a quarter to four?
- What is the first time before quarter past three when the two hands lie on top of each other?
- What is the first time after quarter past three when the two hands lie on top of each other?

□

Solution to Question 8.2. Well, clearly we can plug this in our calculator and read the display. However, in an interview that will not be an option. Instead, you will probably be expected to do it in your head. (If you think that's unreasonable, do not tell them so.)

The correct answer is 3375.

To do this sort of problem, you need to brush up on your mental arithmetic. The first thing is to simply do a few sums in your head and see how they go.

You can also practice estimating the magnitude of solutions. 15 is about half-way between 10 and 20. These cube to 1000 and 8000. Cubing is convex so the answer will be less than the average of these. So guessing that it's not too far from, but less than, 4000 is a place to start.

If you feel that your arithmetic skills need brushing up, then you need to get a book on the topic. One nice book is "Speed Mathematics Using the Vedic System" by Vali Nasser, [11].

One way to get better at cubes is to memorise squares. Thus work out the squares of all numbers below, for example 32, and memorise them. You then only have to do the square by the number in your head. In this case, it would be

$$15 * 225 = 10 * 225 + 0.5 * 10 * 225$$

which is not too hard.

Here are some possible related questions:

- What is 16 cubed? (Express as a power of 2.)
- Estimate the cube root of 5000.

□

Solution to Question 8.3. As usual, there are two approaches: one is tedious and error prone, the other easy. The bad approach is to count the number of cubes on each face and then subtract duplicates.

The easy approach is to count the number of cubes with no paint. These simply constitute a $2 \times 2 \times 2$ cube. So there are 8 cubes without paint. We therefore have

$$64 - 8 = 56$$

cubes with paint.

Here are some possible related questions:

- What about with a $5 \times 5 \times 5$ cube?
- How many cubes will have paint on more than one face?
- How many cubes will have paint on more than two faces?
- What will happen to the fraction of cubes with paint as the number of small cubes goes to infinity?

☐

Solution to Question 8.4 The key to this is to unfold the cube. The problem is the same as asking the distance to go from one corner of a rectangle of size 1×2 to the opposite corner.

This is clearly
$$\sqrt{1 + 2^2} = \sqrt{5}.$$

Here are some possible related questions:

- If the ant can only go on edges, what is the distance?
- If the ant goes along one edge and then cuts across the face, what is the distance?
- If the ant can burrow through the cube, what is the distance?

☐

Solution to Question 8.5. The key to this sort of question is to spot the trick and not to attempt to solve equations. If it doubles in size every second, then it takes two seconds to quadruple in size.

So the answer is
$$60 - 2 = 58$$
seconds. Here are some possible related questions:

- Two trains start 60 miles apart. They head toward each other on the same track at 30 miles per hour. A fly starts in front of one train and flies at 45 mph until it meets the other. It then reverses direction. It does this until it gets squashed. How far does the fly fly?

- What is the formula for the sum of N terms in a geometric series?
- What if the lily pad doubles in the first second, triples in the second, quadruples in the fourth and so on?

☐

Solution to Question 8.6. This is a trick question. The obvious answer of averaging the speeds is incorrect.

Instead, we compute the times needed. Two laps means 2 miles. To travel 2 miles at 60 mph takes 2 minutes.

To travel 1 mile at 30 mph also takes 2 minutes. We therefore have no time left to go round the second time. The car would have to travel infinitely fast.

Here are some possible related questions:

- If the car has a top speed of 120 mph, what's the fastest average speed that can be attained?
- Why doesn't averaging the speeds work?

☐

Solution to Question 8.7. This is a very old one but still seems to come up. There are two main approaches:

- Compute the position after the first pouring and then compute again after the second one.
- Use conservation of mass.

We will do the second one, since it is easier and whether you spot this is the test of how smart you are (or how experienced...)

The crucial point is that there is 100 mls of wine in each glass at the end. This can only be the case if the two amounts are the same.

Not convinced? Well here's the proof in equations. Suppose there are x mls of red in the white and y of white in the red.

Then the red glass contains

$$100 - y$$

mls of red since the other y is white. But there are only x mls more so

$$100 - y + x = 100$$

since we started with 100.

Here are some possible related questions:

- Suppose we pour 6mls on the second pour. What then?
- Suppose we pour 6mls on the first pour. What then?
- What colour will the wine in the white wine glass be after the procedure?

□

Solution to Question 8.8. The key to the first part is to notice that if you have k pieces and break one then you have $k + 1$ pieces. This means that to get from 1 piece to n pieces takes $n - 1$ breaks. This clearly does not depend on the shape of the bar.

For the second part, if we break all the pieces we have, then we can double the number of pieces with one break and we can do no better. This means that we need at least k breaks where k is the smallest number such that

$$2^k \geq n.$$

In this case, dependence on shape is trickier: if any of our pieces only ever has one square in it, then clearly we cannot break it again.

For example, a 2×2 square can be done with two breaks. However, if we take 3 squares in a row with an extra square below the centre one, then any initial break will detach precisely one piece, and we will need at least 3 breaks in total.

Here are some possible related questions:

- Does the shape of the small pieces matter?
- Discuss the 3 dimensional analogue of the two problems.
- What is a toblerone?

□

Solution to Question 8.9. To solve this problem we just need to identify the infinite sums that describe how much each person drinks. The sums themselves will not need to be computed, as we shall see.

Initially I drink $1/2$, leaving $1/2$ in the glass. You drink half of this, or $1/4$, leaving $1/4$ in the glass. Thus my next drink is $1/8$ of a pint, then $1/32$ and so on, while you drink the sequence $1/4, 1/16, \ldots$ In other words,

$$\text{Amount I drink } = \sum_{k=0}^{\infty} \frac{1}{2^{2k+1}},$$

$$\text{Amount you drink } = \sum_{k=0}^{\infty} \frac{1}{2^{2k+2}} = \frac{1}{2} \sum_{k=0}^{\infty} \frac{1}{2^{2k+1}}.$$

This shows that if we let the amount I drink be x, then the amount you drink is $x/2$: I drink twice as much as you. For completeness we should check that the entire pint is drunk. Adding the above two series gives

$$\text{Total drunk } = \sum_{k=1}^{\infty} \frac{1}{2^k},$$

and using summation of a geometric series we see the total proportion drunk is 1. Given I drink twice as much as you, I must have drunk $2/3$ of the pint, while you drink $1/3$.

Here are some possible related questions:

- If instead I drink $1/3$, then you drink $1/3$ of the remainder, and so on, how much more do I drink now? Will the entire pint be consumed? Generalise to a fraction $1/n$ of a pint at each step.
- Take the original question and add a third person, so I drink half, you drink half of what's left before they drink half of the remainder after that and so on. What amount do each of us drink?
- Say I'm a bit thirstier than you, and drink $1/2$ of what's left each time while you only drink $1/3$. Now how much more do I drink?

□

Solution to Question 8.10. This question screams to be solved backwards, that is starting from a position one step away from the top and working our way back to N steps. This is because it is immediately apparent that the number of distinct ways to the top from a position k from the top will be the sum of the number of distinct ways from each possible next position.

To state this mathematically, let $p(k)$ be the number of distinct ways to the top from a distance of k. From this position, we can move either one or two steps, so

$$p(k) = p(k - 1) + p(k - 2).$$

We have our recursive case, now we need an initial (base) case. From a distance of 1 step, there is clearly only one way to the top. We can define the number of unique ways when we are at the top to be 1, or by considering the number from a distance of 2 we see $p(2) = 2$. Either way, we have the base cases

$$p(0) = 1, \quad p(1) = 1, \quad p(2) = 2,$$

which we require two of. Along with our recursive case, this gives the Fibonacci sequence. See Question 6.3 for further details on this sequence.

Here are some possible related questions:

- What if it can move 3 steps as well?
- Formulate and solve a two-dimensional analogue to the problem.

$$\square$$

Solution to Question 8.11. This problem is quite simple if we break it into a couple of steps. The second sentence says the speed is in reverse proportion to the time since the snow began falling, or

$$s(t) = \frac{\alpha}{t},$$

where $s(t)$ is the car's speed, α is the constant of proportionality and t is the time elapsed since the snow began. Our goal is to determine how long before midday the snow began falling. If the distance covered from time t_1 to t_2 is denoted $d(t_1, t_2)$, then we have

$$d(t_1, t_2) = \int_{t_1}^{t_2} s(t)dt = \int_{t_1}^{t_2} \frac{\alpha}{t}dt,$$

since speed denotes the rate of change (derivative) of distance. Let x denote the amount of time it's been snowing for at midday. Then the question states

$$d(x, x + 1) = 2d(x + 1, x + 2),$$

or

$$\int_x^{x+1} \frac{\alpha}{t} dt = 2 \int_{x+1}^{x+2} \frac{\alpha}{t} dt.$$

Integrating gives

$$\log\left(\frac{x+1}{x}\right) = 2\log\left(\frac{x+2}{x+1}\right),$$

$$\Rightarrow \frac{x+1}{x} = \left(\frac{x+2}{x+1}\right)^2,$$

and solving for x gives $x = \frac{1}{2}(-1 \pm \sqrt{5})$. Since x is the time since the snow began at midday, we need a positive answer and we conclude the snow began $\frac{1}{2}(-1 + \sqrt{5})$ hours before midday.

Here are some possible related questions:

- Repeat the question if the car's acceleration is proportional to the amount of time since it began snowing.

□

Solution to Question 8.12. Each weight can either be used or not used. Thus this is really a problem about binary arithmetic. We should therefore use

$$1, 2, 4, 8, 16, \text{ and } 32.$$

How do we prove that it is impossible with 5? There are only $2^5 = 32$ possible combinations so you cannot balance 40 different numbers.

Here are some possible related questions:

- What if I want to balance every number between 1 and 64? Show me how to balance 64 with your chosen weights.
- Write an algorithm that finds the weights needed to balance a number in the range.

- Suppose you can put weights on either scale, so that a number can be used positively or negatively. How many then?

□

Solution to Question 8.13. First, we derive a lower bound on how many numbers we need. If we have k numbers, we can use each of them in three different ways. We can therefore create

$$3^k$$

different numbers. However, note that one of the numbers must be zero, and for every positive number we can also create its negative.

To make numbers 1 through N, we must therefore have

$$3^k \geq 2N + 1.$$

For the case we are interested in, we need

$$3^k \geq 81,$$

so $k \geq 4$.

To see that it can be done with 4, we work explicitly. If we start with 1 then we can get $-1, 0, 1$. To be able to get 2, we must add in 3, we can then get

$$-4, -3, -2, -1, 0, 1, 2, 3, 4.$$

To obtain 5 without any overlaps, we can use 9. We can then get

$$-13, -12, -11, -10, \ldots, 10, 11, 12, 13.$$

Clearly, the next choice will be 27, and with it we can get all numbers from 1 to 40.

Here are some possible related questions:

- What if we need to construct 1 through 50?
- What if we can use each number twice?
- Can you think of a physical application?

□

Solution to Question 8.14. Each domino either lies horizontally across, or is vertical and another vertical domino lies next to it. This means that slicing into two $1 \times n$ grids, these will have the same tilings, and the problem is equivalent to how many ways can you tile a $1 \times n$ grid with squares and dominoes?

Let $F(n)$ be the number of tilings. The first tile is either a square or a domino. If it is a square then the number of possible such tilings is $F(n-1)$. If it is a domino then the number of tilings is $F(n-2)$.

So

$$F(n) = F(n-1) + F(n-2).$$

We have

$$F(1) = 1 \text{ and } F(2) = 2.$$

This means that $F(n)$ is the nth Fibonacci number!

Here are some possible related questions:

- Why does $F(0) = 1$?
- How would you compute $F(10000)$ quickly?
- How many ways can you tile a $3 \times n$ rectangle with dominoes?
- A polyomino of size k can be obtained from one of size $k-1$ by sticking a square to its side. When $k = 2$, we have dominoes and there is only 1 configuration. How many are there with $k = 3$ and $k = 4$?

$\square$

Solution to Question 8.15. This is a test of basic deductive logic. We are testing the truth of a statement of the form "P implies Q." This means that if P holds then Q must also hold. This is logically equivalent to "not Q implies not P" so Q not holding means that P does not hold either.

It does not say anything about what is on the back of odd-numbered cards. The question is ambiguous in that it is not clear whether a card must have a letter on one side and a number on the other. We proceed as if this were the case.

The first card "7" is odd so we should check the back. If the back has a vowel, then the claim is false.

The second card "6" is even so the statement does not say anything about this card. The other side may have a vowel, or it may not.

The third card "A" is a vowel, so we must check that the back is even.

The fourth card "C" is not a vowel, so the statement says nothing and we not look at the back.

Here are some possible related questions:

- Same four cards. The claim is: each card has either a vowel or an even number. How many cards to test the claim?
- Same four cards. The claim is: each card has a vowel and an even number. How many cards to test the claim?
- Same four cards. The claim is: each card has precisely one of a vowel and an even number. How many cards to test the claim?
- How would you express the relation "implies" in terms of elementary logical operations?
- What if a card could have two numbers or two letters?

□

Solution to Question 8.16. On each weighing, we can split the marbles in half and eliminate one half as not containing the heaviest. This would indicate that with one weighing we could compare two marbles, with two weighings four marbles and with three weighings eight marbles. So how do we find the heaviest from a group of nine?

The above reasoning only uses two possible outcomes: if all marbles are weighed then either the first group is heavier or the second group is heavier. However, if we leave some marbles out we introduce a third possibility: that the third group is the one containing the heavier marble. This will be obvious if the two groups weighed have an equal weight.

With this in mind, how do we solve our problem? On our first weighing, compare two groups of four marbles, leaving the ninth marble out. If the two groups of four are of equal weight, the ninth must be the heaviest and we are done. If one of the groups is heavier, we are in the situation of having two weighings remaining with four marbles. The problem is easily solved by weighing two groups of two to find the heaviest pair, and then using your last weighing to find which of the pair is the heaviest.

Here are some possible related questions:

- Can you do this in two weighings?
- What is the solution to this problem if there are eleven marbles?
- What is the maximum number of marbles this problem can be solved for with only three weighings? (Hint: Start with the maximum for two weighings.)

□

Solution to Question 8.17. We have to assume the following:

- the lions are very intelligent;
- one lion is closest to the meat;
- the lions prefer to eat;
- the lions prefer to be hungry and alive over being eaten.

It is unwise to argue with the interviewer over how silly this problem is. (It is, of course, very silly!)

This sort of problem should always be done by induction. You start with no lions and work up.

If no lions, nothing happens.

If one lion, he eats the meat.

If two lions, no one eats the meat since if they do we will be back to one lion, and the lion who ate the meat will be eaten by the above rule.

If three lions, the closest lion eats the meat since they know two lions will not eat the meat.

If four lions, don't eat.

If five lions, do eat.

In conclusion, if the number of lions is even no one eats. If the number of lions is odd, one eats it.

Here are some possible related questions:

- 6 pirates discover a treasure chest filled with 1000 gold coins. After rolling dice to decide the overall order, each pirate will have a chance to explain how he thinks the wealth should be divided up. Following each proposal, all the pirates will vote on it. If a majority agrees then the proposal is adopted. (The majority must be strict.) Otherwise, the pirate walks the plank. What happens assuming a pirate will vote down a division if and only if he thinks he will get more by doing so?
- What if a tie results in the proposal passing?

□

Solution to Question 8.18. We have to consider two effects:

- throwing the anchor into the pool will raise the water level, since it will displace water equal to its volume;
- removing the anchor from the boat will lower the water in the pool, since it will displace water according to its weight when inside the boat.

An anchor will be denser than water so its weight is greater than that of the volume of water equal to its volume. It therefore displaces more water when inside the boat than outside.

The level goes down.

Here are some possible related questions:

- An iceberg floating in the ocean melts. What happens to the sea level?
- Why do you think this question is phrased for a swimming pool and not for a lake?

□

Solution to Question 8.19. The first point to note is that it does make a difference how the balls are arranged for which sack is selected. For example, if one of the sacks has only 1 ball in it, then there is a 0.5 chance that it will be drawn.

This suggests the solution. We place a single white ball in one of the sacks. All the other balls are placed in the other sack. Our chance of winning is then

$$\frac{1}{2} + \frac{1}{2}\frac{49}{99}.$$

To show optimality, we really need to show that this is the best strategy. One solution is to compute the probability of that you succeed in the general case and then to differentiate.

Here are some possible related questions:

- What if there are 3 sacks?
- What if you win only if the first two independent draws are white?
- What if you win only if the first two draws from a single sack chosen at random are white?

□

Solution to Question 8.20. We have to work up from the zero case.

If there was no one with blue eyes then the stranger would not have said someone did. So at least one person does.

Suppose precisely one person has blue eyes. That person knows that the 49 other people have brown eyes and they know that someone has blue eyes. That person then knows they are the one with blue eyes. So they commit suicide at twelve midnight.

Suppose precisely two people have blue eyes. Each of the two blue-eyed people analyses the situation and sees that there are two possibilities:

- I have brown eyes in which case the blue-eyed person will kill themselves on the first day after doing the analysis above.
- I have blue eyes in which case they will not.

When the other blue-eyed person does not commit suicide they conclude it is because they both have blue eyes and both commit suicide at midnight on the second day.

Following this to its logical conclusion, if n people have blue eyes they all commit suicide on the nth day.

Here are some possible related questions:

- If there were 9 people with blue eyes initially, then everyone already knew that someone had blue eyes so why does the stranger saying that someone has blue eyes make a difference?
- What if the stranger lied (but was believed)?
- Suppose you have to commit suicide if you are $p\%$ sure that you have blue eyes. What difference would this make to the problem? Suppose that everyone starts with the prior belief that they are equally likely to have blue or brown eyes?

□

Solution to Question 8.21. The prisoners must elect one prisoner to be the 'captain'. This prisoner will keep count of how many other prisoners he knows have visited the room, and can then tell the warden when they all have. To do this, the other 21 prisoners and the captain have two different strategies they employ upon visiting the room.

For the 21 other prisoners, their strategy is as follows:

(i) When they visit the room, if one or more switches are down they move one switch up. However they only ever move a switch once, if they have moved one in the past and one or more are down, they leave them.

(ii) If both switches are up, they leave them alone. This is regardless of if they have moved a switch before in the past or not.

The captain however, must tally the number of unique prisoners who have been to the room. He does this by counting the number of switches in the up position each time they visit, and then moving any switches in the up position to the down position. When their tally reaches 21, they know every prisoner has been to the room and may tell the warden.

Here are some possible related questions:

- What is the expected number of days until the prisoners are free? Calculate this by simulation.
- How can they make better use of the two switches to optimise the above algorithm? (Hint: How can you count to 31 on one hand?)

☐

Solution to Question 8.22. If a single line divides both rectangles in half it will inevitably divide the difference in half as well. Observe that any line through the centre of a rectangle will divide it in half.

We therefore draw a line through the centre of both rectangles, and we are done. Of course, this requires us to be able to find the centre of a rectangle, however, the centre is at the intersection of the diagonals so that is easy.

Here are some possible related questions:

- Do you think that your solution to the problem is unique?
- Given a rectangular cake with a rectangular piece missing, find two ways to split the remaining cake in two with a single cut.

☐

Solution to Question 8.23. Since a player will take the last stick if and only if there is one left, our objective is to leave only one stick on the table. This shows that the game where the last person to take loses is the same as the game where the last person to take wins with one less stick.

Suppose there are 5 matches on the table and it is our opponent's turn to play. After he plays there will be 2, 3 or 4 matches left so we can take 1, 2 or 3 matches, respectively, to make him lose. So if there are 1 or 5 matches on the table he loses.

We can play the same way if he has to play with 9 to get him to 5. More generally, we always play in such a way as to ensure that there are

$$4j + 1$$

matches on the table for some j. If we cannot do this then we must lose if our opponent plays optimally.

If it is "last player to pick up wins," we aim for

$$4j$$

sticks instead.

Here are some possible related questions:

- If the number of matches were random, would you play first or second?
- If there were several piles, and you could only take from one pile, what's the winning strategy in both variants?

☐

Solution to Question 8.24. Play first. Place the coin in the centre of the table. Each subsequent move, place your coin in the reflection of their move in the centre of the table.

Here are some possible related questions:

- What if the table were square and so were the coins?
- What about other shapes?

☐

Solution to Question 8.25. Initially this seems like an impossible question. It is unlikely that the interviewer will know the answer, so why have they asked the question? What they want to test is how the answer is structured and which assumptions are used to get there.

One approach to this question is breaking it down to how many petrol stations there are in a town/suburb. So for example there are 3 petrol stations in a town of 10,000 people. This town has a large amount of tourists, and hence more cars than one would expect for 10,000 people. Taking this into consideration we could say there is 1 petrol station for 5,000 people. The population of the UK is roughly 60 million, so the number of petrol stations would be close to 12,000.

In fact, one can check the number at the National Audit Office and it was around 12,000 a few years ago.

Here are some possible related questions:

- How many pairs of shoes are bought each year in the UK?
- What is the real estate value of Central Park in New York?

☐

Solution to 8.26. This is similar to Question 8.25 since the interviewer is mainly is interested in how the answer is structured.

First, we need to assume a population for Oxford, say 100,000. Since people who live in Oxford like playing the piano, we'll assume there is one piano for every 4 people, so 25,000 pianos. To keep these pianos playing beautiful notes the diligent owners like to tune them twice a year, 50,000 tunings per year. A good piano tuner can take care of 4 pianos per day and assuming he works 200 days per year he can tune 800 pianos. There is therefore approximately 60 piano tuners in Oxford.

The numbers used in this example are very approximate (and probably wrong) and aren't as important as the way in which the problem is broken down.

Here are some possible related questions:

- Do you think the number will increase or decrease over time?
- How would you get a more accurate number?

☐

Solution to Question 8.27. If the third person saw that the first and second person were wearing red hats then it would be clear that the third person was wearing a white hat. Hence if the third person doesn't know what colour hat they are wearing, at least one of the first two people must be wearing a white hat.

Now the second person knows that either they or the first person must be wearing a white hat, otherwise the third person would have known what colour they were wearing. If the second person sees that the first person is wearing a red hat, they could deduce that they (the second person) must be wearing the white hat. Hence if the second person doesn't know what colour hat they are wearing, the first person must be wearing a white hat.

Here are some possible related questions:

- In the 'Prisoners and hats puzzle' there are four people, two red hats and two white hats. Three of the people are lined up in the same fashion to the above question. The fourth is placed behind a screen and can not see any of the other people. Which of the four people know which colour hat they are wearing, and what colour is it?
- Solve the 'Prisoners and hats puzzle' if there are three red hats and two white hats.

□

Solution to Question 8.28. Take 1 pill from jar 1, 2 pills from jar 2 and continue up to jar 5. If each of the pills weighed 10 grams the total weight would be 150 grams.

However, if jar 1 contains the pills weighing 9 grams the total weight will be reduced by 1 gram (since we have 1 pill from jar 1). In the same way the total weight will be reduced by 2 if jar 2 contains the pills weighing 9 grams. Continuing, the difference between 150 and the observed weight of all the pills tells us which jar contains the pills weighing 9 grams.

Here are some possible related questions:

- How many weighings would it take if two of the jars had pills weighing 9 grams?
- What if one jar had pills weighing 9 grams while another had pills weighing 8 grams?

□

Solution to Question 8.29. An interior cube will have 0 painted sides. An interior to a face will have 1. An edge will have 2 and a vertex will have 3. We need to work out how many of each sort exist. The fully interior cubes form a 2 by 2 by 2 cube so there are 8 of them. Each face has 4 interior faces so there are 24 of these. There are 12 edges and each one gives 2 so we get 24 again. There are 8 vertices so we get 8 with 3.

Here are some possible related questions:

- What about a 4 by 5 by 6 cuboid?
- The answers are 8, 24, 24, and 8. Why the symmetry?
- Reformulate this problem for a tesseract and solve it.

□

Solution to Question 8.30. This is one of those questions where the interviewer is trying to shock with an obscure problem and is looking to see how you will break the question down. A good place to start is with the mean radius of the earth, which most people would be able to guess is around 6,000 kms (6,378.1 kms to be exact). We can compute the volume of the earth, assuming it is a sphere

$$\text{volume} = \frac{4}{3}\pi r^3 = \frac{4}{3}\pi 6,378,000^3 = 1.09 \times 10^{21}.$$

(work out how you could do this approximation in your head). We could then make the naive assumption that the earth is as dense as water at room temperature, which is approximately 1,000 kg/m^3. This would give the weight of the earth to be 1.09×10^{24} kg. It turns out the earth is roughly five-and-a-half times as dense as water and its weight is therefore 5.97×10^{24}kg.

Here are some possible related questions:

- Compute the weight of the earth using an alternative method.
- How long would it take to walk the circumference of the earth?

□

Solution to Question 8.31. We would expect that the tops are further apart than at the bottom due to the curvature of the Earth. However, in this case they are closer. Some possible explanations are

- The buildings are wider at the top than at the bottom.
- They are built on different sides of a valley so they learn towards each other.
- One is the leaning tower of Pisa.

Here is a possible related question:

- Do you think this could actually happen?
- If two skyscrapers were rectangular and not leaning and were 100m tall and 50m apart at the base, what would be the distance at the top?

☐

Solution to 8.32. The bug starts at vertex A and so after one move can be on either vertex B or C. For the next move the bug can take either two paths that lead back to A and two that finish on B or C. From this we can start to see that if the bug is at point A, then in two moves time it can be back at A, via A-B-A or A-C-A, and there will naturally be twice as many of these paths than there were two moves before. At the previous step, the bug on vertex B or C can move to A on the next move or an adjacent non-A vertex, so we have twice as many points and half end back at A.

If we let $a(n)$ represent the number of paths that lead to vertex A after n moves, we have the following recursion

$$a(n) = a(n-1) + 2a(n-2).$$

The initial conditions are simply $a(0) = 1$ and $a(1) = 0$, because we start on A and after one move cannot be on A. Using this recursion the number of paths of length 8 that finish on vertex A is 86.

Here are some possible related questions:

- Now consider a square with vertices A,B,C and D. Starting at A, after 8 moves how many paths end back at A?
- Can you generalise the result for a shape with m vertices and n paths?

☐

CHAPTER 9

The soft interview

9.1. Introduction

The good news is that quant teams tend to interview technically and Human Resources are an afterthought. If this does not sound like good news to you, then you would do well to reconsider your career choice. The bad news is that "soft" questions are sometimes asked, and for fresh graduate jobs this sort of thing can be important.

In this chapter, we therefore go through some of the questions that might be asked and discuss how to handle them. Having prepared answers for all of these will greatly help if the soft interview occurs. We then follow up with some general finance questions that test your general awareness of finance.

9.2. Soft questions and answers

QUESTION 9.1. Why do you want to work in banking?

Solution to Question 9.1. Well, the truth is generally "I got frustrated with an academic career and I want more money." However, it is considered bad form to say this, and if this is really the only reason you may not do well in banking. Work out what the real reason is for you and how to present it. Some points to consider mentioning:

- Dynamism: fast moving, I want to see the real results of my work in a short time frame.
- Teamwork: I want to work with other people rather than on my own. This tends to go down well, although a lot of quants do not have the easiest personalities.

- Transparency: I want to do something where my contribution is clear and recognized.
- Ability to leverage existing skill set.

Do not give negative reasons, i.e., don't say that I didn't like what I was doing before. Banks are not strong on

- ethics,
- reasonableness,

so best not to mention these as reasons to work in banking.

Bankers tend to get upset if you describe their role in negative terms. They provide financial products that other people want to buy and no one's forcing those people. The job of a quant is to help to produce those products, and if the products were not worthwhile no one would buy them. □

QUESTION 9.2. Tell me about X where X is a random phrase from your CV.

Solution to Question 9.2. The important point here is that for everything you write on the CV, have a prepared speech. If you do not want to discuss something, consider whether it has to be on your CV.

In your speech, consider how to market this particular point:

- Can you explain what you did?
- Why it is relevant to banking, and in particular, how is it relevant to the job you are applying for?
- What you learnt from it.

□

QUESTION 9.3. Can you cope with the people around you swearing?

Solution to Question 9.3. Once again the answer had better be "yes." A lot of people in banking are rough around the edges and do not like smoothy types.

If swearing truly bothers you, consider another profession or at least stay well away from the traders. □

QUESTION 9.4. Why don't you want to do X anymore?

Solution to Question 9.4. It is better to try and accentuate the positive aspects of the new job rather than the negative aspects of the old. This should therefore be turned into praise for banking as much as possible. I want to work in teams, I want to do something dynamic, I want to work in a more energetic atmosphere, I want to make more impact.   □

QUESTION 9.5. How would you deal with a difficult person?

Solution to Question 9.5. This one is annoying in that the solution would vary so much according to circumstances. However, the important thing is to demonstrate some ability to take a non-straightforward approach rather than getting into confrontations with them, e.g.,

- Make them think something was their idea so they back it.
- Work round them where possible.
- Butter them up.
- Try to understand what personality traits make them difficult and how you can exploit them.
- Use extreme clarity when dealing with them to avoid misunderstanding and arguments about what was said.
- Be extra polite with them.

                                                                                      □

QUESTION 9.6. What are your weaknesses?

Solution to 9.6. This is a tricky one, in that who wants to admit all their bad aspects? The standard response is "I don't suffer fools gladly." However, this is so hackneyed that you might just come across as glib.

It is probably better to do some self-examination and then think about how to present honestly some of your true weaknesses. If you really think you do not have any, your weakness is certainly poor self-knowledge.   □

QUESTION 9.7. Are you comfortable working to deadlines?

Solution to Question 9.7. The answer had better be "yes." That alone is not enough, you need to show that you have successfully met deadlines in the past and are able to talk about them. This could be as simple as talking about always getting your assignments done early, or talk about how deadlines were involved in previous employment.   □

QUESTION 9.8. What was our share price at closing last night?

Solution to Question 9.8. Always check before going to the interview. People really do ask this.   □

QUESTION 9.9. What big deals have we closed lately?

Solution to Question 9.9. Again always check before going to the interview. People really do ask this. The easiest solution is to look them up on google news beforehand. In general, read the financial press avidly for months so you have a good general knowledge of what's happening.   □

QUESTION 9.10. Where do you want to be five years from now?

Solution to Question 9.10. Once again, the answer is up to you. The important things are to have one, and to make sure it is compatible with the role that you are going for. You should be careful to avoid the impression that you will be trying to leave as quickly as possible.   □

QUESTION 9.11. Explain your thesis.

Solution to Question 9.11. This question is about your ability to explain technical material rather than about how bright you are. To answer it well, the best approach to prepare answers for various sorts of people. You also need to try to assess what the interviewer's background is and what he/she will understand. You can always ask what their own degree/doctorate is in.

In particular, you should prepare answers for

- the arts graduate;
- an expert in another technical field;
- an expert in your own field.

☐

QUESTION 9.12. Do you own any shares?

Solution to 9.12. This question is often used to gauge your interest in finance. Someone who does not own shares, and doesn't even know a little about the top 10 stocks, probably isn't all that interested in finance. When answering the question you have to tell the truth, but you can turn it into a discussion of which shares you might buy and why.   ☐

QUESTION 9.13. What qualities do you offer, apart from being smart?

Solution to Question 9.13. Make sure to be able to think of some good qualities and also how to demonstrate that you have them. For example,

- presentation skills,
- ability to get along with others,
- delivering work on time.

☐

QUESTION 9.14. What do your friends think of you?

Solution to Question 9.14. This is a strange question in some ways as your friends presumably think highly of you, and they so would say lots of positive things: that is why they are your friends. Try, however, to think of something they would say that makes you perfectly suited for the job you are applying for. For example, they might say you are easy to get along with and will therefore fit perfectly into the team.   ☐

QUESTION 9.15. Do you like French food?

Solution to Question 9.15. The answer had better be "yes." Once again have
something to say beyond that. Perhaps you could even mention that French food is
much better with French wine, such as a glass of Château Petrus.   □

QUESTION 9.16. What is the first thing you would do when you arrive at work
on your first day?

Solution to Question 9.16. This one is infuriating. It turned out that the answer
that the interviewer wanted was that you would ask to see how all the hedging of
derivative products was carried out in practice. Perhaps, the point was to see how a
candidate reacted to infuriating questions: don't show that you are infuriated. □

QUESTION 9.17. What have you done that shows that you have star quality?

Solution to Question 9.17. Try to think of something impressive that you have
done, and how you can market what you have done as such. Also, how do they
relate to this role?   □

QUESTION 9.18. What do you know about finance? What books have you read
on the topic?

Solution to Question 9.18. Make sure you have something to say. The most
important thing is to be able to discuss anything you say you have read. It is much
worse to say you have read something and then demonstrate that you know nothing
about it, than to not have read it. This goes doubly when the interviewer wrote
the book.   □

QUESTION 9.19. Why do you want to work for Megabank? (or whoever they to
happen to be.)

Solution to Question 9.19. Try to think of something other than because I am
desperate. Try to find out in advance some complimentary aspects of them, and

talk about those. For example, they may have a reputation in certain areas, or they may be known as a kind employer. □

QUESTION 9.20. Do you prefer working with others or solo?

Solution to Question 9.20. Saying "solo" is dangerous since it indicates that you are not a "team player." On the other hand, a given role may require a lot of solo work. A balanced response leading toward the truth is therefore required. □

QUESTION 9.21. Tell me about an occasion on which you demonstrated leadership skills.

Solution to Question 9.21. This sort of question is where having outside interests and work experience comes in useful. If you do have work experience then pick an aspect from there, thinking about what you did and what it achieved. If you do not have any work experience, then you could use an instance where you were a captain of a sporting team or other club. □

QUESTION 9.22. Are you comfortable working with our in-house computer language instead of C++?

Solution to Question 9.22. If you want the job, the answer had better be "yes." But bear in mind that a job where you do C++ gives you a transferable skill and ability to leverage off many existing libraries, so do you really want the job? Goldman Sachs is particularly notorious for having its own in-house programming language. □

9.3. Finance data questions

The following sorts of questions really are asked so look them up in the Financial Times, the Wall Street Journal or the web before turning up to the interview. Clearly, one should be most on top of the local financial indicators. For longer term understanding of the global economic situation, one good solution is to read the *Economist* every week.

QUESTION 9.23. What is the current level of the FTSE?

QUESTION 9.24. What is the current price of oil?

QUESTION 9.25. Sketch the current UK yield curve and discuss its shape.

QUESTION 9.26. What is the current Fed funds rate? (What does that mean anyway?)

QUESTION 9.27. What is the Bank of England base rate? (And what does that mean anyway?)

QUESTION 9.28. What is the Euro base rate?

QUESTION 9.29. Explain the sub-prime crisis.

QUESTION 9.30. What's the dollar-yen exchange rate?

QUESTION 9.31. Which EU countries have the highest unemployment rates? Why do you think this is?

QUESTION 9.32. Who is the chairman of the Fed?

QUESTION 9.33. Who is the governor of the Bank of England?

QUESTION 9.34. What is the FSA and how is it related to the Bank of England? What happened historically?

CHAPTER 10

Top ten questions

10.1. Introduction

Most interviewers are not very original, and they tend to ask questions that they were asked. Certain questions come up again and again, year after year. Some that were popular in 1999 were still being commonly asked in 2012. For many of them, it is because they are good questions in that they test understanding of key concepts indirectly. Some test it directly. Here we list the ten most popular questions from our experience and that of our question gatherers. Do not go to an interview unless you are totally on top of all of these. Most times you will get asked at least one of them.

10.2. Questions

QUESTION 2.1. Derive the Black–Scholes equation. What boundary conditions are satisfied at $S = 0$ and $S = \infty$?

For the solution see page 22.

QUESTION 2.4. Suppose two assets in a Black–Scholes world have the same volatility but different drifts. How will the price of call options on them compare?

See page 28.

QUESTION 2.11. Is it ever optimal to early exercise an American call option? What about a put option?

See page 36.

QUESTION 2.15. What is meant by put-call parity?

See page 39.

QUESTION 2.41. Team A plays team B, in a series of 7 games, whoever wins 4 games first wins. You want to bet 100 that your team wins the series, in which case you receive 200, or 0 if they lose. However the broker only allows bets on individual games. You can bet X on any individual game the day before it occurs to receive $2X$ if it wins and 0 if it loses. How do you achieve the desired pay-out? In particular, what do you bet on the first match?

See page 58.

QUESTION 2.44. Suppose an option pays 1 if the spot is between 100 and 110 at expiry and zero otherwise. Synthesise the option from vanilla call options.

See page 59.

QUESTION 2.60. A stock is worth 100 today. There are zero interest rates. The stock can be worth 90 or 110 tomorrow. It moves to 110 with probability p. Price a call option struck at 100.

See page 72.

QUESTION 3.2. Suppose we play a game. I roll a die up to three times. Each time I roll you can either take the number showing as dollars or roll again. What is your expected winnings?

See page 96.

QUESTION 5.1. Write an algorithm to carry out numerical integration. How might you optimise the algorithm?

See page 184.

QUESTION 7.10. What is a virtual function?

See page 281.

Bibliography

[1] M. Baxter, A. Rennie, *Financial Calculus : An Introduction to Derivative Pricing,* Cambridge University Press 1996.

[2] D. Brigo, F. Mercurio, *Interest Rate Models - Theory and Practice,* Springer 2007.

[3] W. Feller, *An Introduction to Probability Theory and Its Applications, Volume II,* John Wiley & Sons 1966.

[4] P. Glasserman, *Monte Carlo Methods in Financial Engineering,* Springer 2003.

[5] J. Hull, *Options, Futures and other Derivative Securities,* Second Edition, Prentice Hall 1993.

[6] M. Joshi, *The Concepts and Practice of Mathematical Finance,* Second Edition, Cambridge University Press 2008.

[7] M. Joshi, *C++ Design Patterns and Derivatives Pricing,* Cambridge University Press 2008.

[8] M. Joshi, *More Mathematical Finance,* Pilot Whale Press 2011.

[9] A. McNeil, R. Frey, P. Embrechts, *Quantitative Risk Management: Concepts, Techniques, and Tools,* Princeton University Press, 2005.

[10] C. Moler, C. Van Loan, Nineteen dubious ways to compute the exponential of a matrix, twenty-five years later, *SIAM Review,* Vol. 45, No. 1, 3–48.

[11] V. Nasser, *Speed Mathematics Using the Vedic System,* www.lulu.com.

[12] B. Oksendal, *Stochastic Differential Equations: An Introduction with Applications,* Sixth Edition, Springer 2005.

[13] A. Pelsser, *Efficient Methods for Valuing Interest Rate Derivatives,* Springer 2000.

[14] G. Peskir, A. Shiryaev, *Optimal Stopping and Free-Boundary Problems,* Birkhäuser Basel 2006.

[15] M. Pykhtin and S. Zhu, *A guide to modelling counterparty credit risk.* GARP Risk Review July/August 2007.

[16] L.C.G. Rogers, D. Williams, *Diffusions, Markov Processes and Martingales Volume 1,* Cambridge University Press 2000.

[17] W. Rudin, *Principles of Mathematical Analysis,* McGraw-Hill Publishing Co. 1976.

[18] S. E. Shreve, *Stochastic Calculus for Finance II: Continuous Time Models,* Springer 2004.

[19] I. Stewart, D. Tall, *Complex Analysis,* Cambridge University Press 1983.

[20] B. Stroustrup, *The C++ Programming Language,* Special Edition, Addison–Wesley Professional 2003.

[21] D. Williams, *Probability with Martingales,* Cambridge University Press 1991.

[22] P. Wilmott, *Derivatives: The Theory and Practice of Financial Engineering,* John Wiley & Sons 1998.

Index

π, 218, 224, 225
e, 218, 225
?:, 267, 293
Itô's lemma, 34
15 cubed, 330, 334
29th of February, 189

absolutely continuous measure, 127
abstract class, 273, 313, 321
acceptance-rejection, 294
accessor function, 292
accountancy firm, 12
accuracy
   pricing function, 21, 70
affine model, 179
algorithms, 181–216
alternating series test, *see* convergence,
    alternating series test
American option, 19
analytical function, 218
anchor in pool, 331, 345
ant on a cube, 330, 335
Anti-thetic sampling, 213
ants on a triangle, 93
arbitrageur, 57
arithmetic mean, 225
Asian forward contract, 21, 64
Asian option, 64
assignment operator, 266, 284, 320
auto_ptr, 297

automatic conversion, 266
automatic variable, 291
average, 64

Babylonian, 298
balls
   coloured, 93
   two colours in bag, 331, 345–346
barrier option, 21, 65
base class, 266, 280, 281, 297
Basel, 55
Baxter
   Martin, 16
Bayes' theorem, 105, 106, 133
Bayesian approach, 106
Bessel process, 148, 149, 156
betting series, 20, 58–59
binary arithmetic, 340
binary search, 207, 208
binary tree, *see* tree, binary
Binet's formula, 223
binomial coefficients, 248
binomial distribution
   normal approximation, 136
binomial random variable, 121, 135
binomial tree, *see* tree, binomial
Björk
   Tomas, 16
Black formula, 32
Black–Scholes, 15, 31, 363

drift, 363

Black–Scholes equation, 16, 24, 50, 148, 218, 237
  boundary conditions, 239
  drift, 16, 28
  explanation, 16, 27
  time dependent volatility, 16, 30
Black–Scholes model, 17
bond volatility, 172, 175–176
  price volatility, 175
  yield volatility, 175
Boost, 287, 322
boundary condition, 363
boundary crossing, 94, 146
Box-Muller transform, 214
branch cut, 259
bridge, 275
Brownian bridge, 95, 158
  distribution function, 95
Brownian motion, 93–95, 144, 147, 157, 158, 160, 167
  correlation, 95, 170
  covariance, 94
  crossing times, 95
  independent increments, 157
  integral of, 95
  martingales of, 152
  maximum, 95, 166
bucket, 194
bug, 333, 353
bus, 219, 248
bus error, 327
butterfly, 19, 21, 65

C linkage, 273
C++, xi, 263–328
C++ 2011, 318
C++ standard, 293
C-preprocessor, 276
calculator, 6
calibration, 19
call option, *see* option, call

capital quant, 11
cards
  vowels and numbers, 331, 342–343
catch, 313
Cauchy random variable, 118, 119, 155
Cauchy's estimate, 231
Cauchy's integral formula, 232
Cauchy's residue theorem, 232
Cayley-Hamilton theorem, 192
Central Limit theorem, 92, 124, 224
chain rule, 251, 252
chair, 219
change of measure, 92, 126
characteristic function, 125, 232
characteristic polynomial, 192
chicken nugget, 219, 245
chord, 225
Chung
  Kai Lai, 87, 88
clock, 243
clone method, 322
coin toss, 93
collide, 183
Comeau computing, 274
commercial bank, 12
comparing elements, 199
compiler, 266, 276, 292, 327
complex exponential, 232
complex integration, 254
complexity
  log, 207
computational complexity, 197
concavity, 226
concrete, 313
conditional probability, 97, 158
confidence interval, 105
conservation of mass, 336
const, 273, 283, 303, 310, 311
const variable, 273
const_cast, 311, 314
constructor, 266, 277

continued fraction, 218, 226
continuous functions, 225
contraction mapping, 299
convergence, 218, 236, 259
    absolute, 237
    alternating series test, 237
    in distribution, 125
    ratio test, 237
    weak, 124
convergence in distribution, *see* convergence,
    in distribution
convergence rates, 224
convexity, 225
convolution, 123
copy constructor, 266, 280, 284, 320
correctness, 202
correlation, 91, 156, 219, 241
correlation coefficient, 116
countable, 208
covariance, 116
covariance matrix, 92
cross-variation, 160
cube
    painted, 333, 351
cumulative distribution function, *see*
    distribution function
CV, 3, 8, 356
CVA, xi, 19, 55

data segment, 290
data structure, 273
date, 182
decoration, 275
deep copy, 320
default constructor, 320
degrees between clock hands, 330, 333
Deitel
    Harvey, 263
    Paul, 263
delete, 267, 287, 292, 293
delete[], 267, 293
Delta, 18, 22, 39, 43, 44, 67, 68, 78

delta function, 233
density function, 91, 92, 117, 120, 121, 123,
    130, 154, 227
deprecated, 312
design pattern, 266
desk quant, 10
destructor, 266, 277, 278, 283, 284, 320
DevCpp, 274
diagonalisable, 192
die, 88, 364
differentiable functions, 225
differentiation, 220
    chain rule, 221
    first principles, 220, 251
diffusion process, 146
Dirac delta function, *see* delta function
discrete random variable, 181
distribution function, 91, 94, 120, 121, 154,
    185, 218, 227
divergent series, 236
domino, 331, 342
duration, 176
Durstenfeld, 200
dynamic replication, *see* replication,
    dynamic
dynamic_cast, 328

Earth, 352
    weight of, 333, 352
Eckel
    Bruce, 264
Eclipse, 274
electric fence, 275, 327
equivalent measure, 127
even function, 132
exam
    take-home, 6
    written, 6
EXCEL, 211, 263
exception, 273, 313
    unhandled, 278
exception safety, 278, 314

expectation, 88–90, 95, 96, 98, 99, 101–103,
    106, 112, 120, 130, 132
explicit, 286
exponential random variable, 123, 124, 183
    density function, 118
exponentiation of a matrix, 182, 191–192
extern, 314
extern "C", 314
extrapolate, 206
eye colour, 331, 346–347

fabs, 300
factorial, 182
factory, 275
fair coin, 89, 99, 103, 105
fair game, 88, 89, 95–98, 101, 107
feedback, 7
Feller
    William, 87
Fibonacci sequence, 142, 181, 186–188, 217,
    223, 342
final, 318
first step analysis, 138
Fisher, 200
forward, 18
forward rate, 172–173
Fourier inversion, 233
Fourier transform, 218, 232
friend, 303
function pointer, 266, 281
functional programming, 263

g++, 274, 283
game, 364
Gamma, 21, 68
    sketch, 68
Gaussian distribution, 267
Gaussian draw, 294
Gaussian function, 92, 132
Gaussian random variable, 93, 143
GDB, 275
generic programming, 263, 265

geometric Brownian motion, 149
geometric mean, 225
geometric random variable, 99, 101
geometric series, 101
Girsanov's theorem, 127
global financial crisis, xi
GNU, 327
golden ratio, 223
Goldman Sachs, 5
Grandma, 91, 115, 182
great recession, xi
Greeks
    computing methods, 21, 66–67
        finite-difference approximation, 66
        likelihood ratio method, 67
        pathwise method, 67
Grimmett
    Geoffrey, 87

hat, 332, 350
header file, 276
heap, 200, 290
heat equation, 218, 237
hedge fund, 12
hedger, 57
hedging, 15
Hermitian matrix, *see* matrix, Hermitian
histogram, 182, 193
Hull
    John, 16
Hull–White model, 180

IDE, 274, 275
implied vol, 17
implied volatility, *see* volatility, implied
importance sampling, 211, 213
index laws, 250
indicator function, 32
induction, 223, 224, 254
infinite sum, 103, 338
inflection point, 218, 226
inheritance, 273, 318

inherited class, 266, 280, 281, 297
inline function, 266, 276, 277
insert sort, 288
integration, 220
   by parts, 254
   contour, 220, 258
   principal value, 120
interpolation, 182
interview, 1–14
intrusive, 322
inverse transform sampling, 212
investment bank, 12
Israeli defense force, 209
iterator, 303, 307, 309
Itô's formula, 152
Itô's formula, 94, 95, 148, 150, 153, 162
   product rule, 155

Jacobian, 258
joint random variable, 123
Joshi
   Mark, 88, 263
Josuttis
   Nicolai, 265
jump diffusion model, 81–82

Kadane's algorithm, 197
Knuth shuffle, 200

l'Hôpitals rule, 222
Lagrange form, 235
Lajoie
   Josee, 264
Lakos
   John, 264
largest element algorithm, 183, 215
leap year, 189
Leibniz rule, 242
LIBOR market model
   Markovian, 172, 178–179
lighthouse, 217, 221
lily pad in pond, 330, 335

limit, 217, 222, 251
Lindeberg's condition, 125
linear recurrence equation, 223
linker, 292
lion problem, 331, 344–345
Liouville's theorem, 218, 231, 234
Lippman
   Stanley, 264
local volatility model, 84
log, 17, 34
log laws, 250
log-normal, 94, 147
Longstaff–Schwartz algorithm, 78–79
low discrepancy numbers, 213, 294
lower_bound, 208
LTCM, 71
Lucas numbers, 224

Maclaurin series, 236
macro, 266, 276
malloc, 291
map, 274, 323
marbles, 331, 343–344
Margrabe option, see option, Margrabe
market models, 177–178
Markov functional models, 178
martingale, 94, 102, 103, 113, 127, 146,
   151–153
matrix
   conjugate transpose, 227
   covariance, 116, 125
   determinant, 116
   eigenvalues, 230
   eigenvectors, 230
   Hermitian, 228
   positive definite, 92, 116, 227
   positive semi-definite, 228
   rank, 219, 241
   square, 228
   square root, 218, 228
   symmetric, 228
   transpose, 218, 227, 228

mean reversion, 149, 156
  interest rates, 172, 175
median, 274, 324
memory allocation, 263, 266
merge sort, 290
minimal polynomial, 192
mobile phone, 5
model validation quant, 10
modified duration, 176
moment matching, 213
Monte Carlo, 92, 128, 182, 183, 213, 218, 224
  quasi, 214
Monte Carlo vs. tree, 22, 76–77
Moo
  Barbara, 264
Moro algorithm, 215
multimap, 324
multiset, 323
mutable, 310

name mangling, 274, 327
namespace, 327
new, 283, 291–293, 322
new[], 293
Newton–Raphson method, 300
Nicomachus's theorem, 137
NIM, 332, 348–349
node, 210, 273, 300, 303
  daughter, 300
  head, 300
normal density
  integral of, 220, 261
normal random variable, 92, 124, 153, 161, 218, 227
  density function, 118, 130, 227, 257
  distribution function, 227
  moment generating function, 130
null pointer, 313
numeraire, 32
numerical approximation, 224
numerical integration, 181, 184, 364

numerical techniques, 181–216

object-oriented programming, 263
odd function, 132
open book, 6
option
  American call, 363
    early exercise, 17, 36
  American put
    early exercise, 17, 37
  barrier
    down-and-out call, 39
    price sketch, 17, 38
  call, 94, 148, 149, 237, 281
    approximate formula, 17, 38
    boundaries, 19, 49–50
    convexity, 19, 51–52
    downward jumps, 28
    forward price, 19, 51
    infinite volatility, 17, 40
    normal distribution, 18, 44–45
    payoff, 23
    price, 44
    price sketch, 17, 35
    value with time, 18, 41
  digital, 128
    replication, 20, 59–60
  digital call, 18, 43
    price sketch, 18, 46
  double no-touch, 69
  Margrabe, 48
  mean reversion, 19, 49
  put, 281, 363
  uses, 19, 57
optional sampling theorem, 102, 103, 146, 167
order of convergence, 185
order statistic, 91, 121
Ornstein-Uhlenbeck process, 94, 156
OTC, 55

page fault, 274, 327

parachute, 209
parameter by pointer, 268, 296
parameter by reference, 268, 296
parameter by value, 268, 296
partition, 324
Pascal's triangle, 203
patience sorting, 215
permutation, 200, 218
petrol stations, 332, 349–350
phone interview, 5
physical address, 274, 326
physical memory, 327
piano tuners in Oxford, 332, 350
pill, 333, 351
pint of beer, 330, 338
point of inflection, *see* inflection point
pointer, 273, 311, 313, 314, 326
Poisson process, 95, 164
Poisson random variable, 95
Poisson random variable, 100, 131, 164, 212
polar coordinates, 258, 262
polymorphism, 266, 273, 312
polynomial, 234
polyomino, 342
portfolio theory, 11
positive-definite matrix, *see* matrix, positive definite
post-increment, 320
pre-increment, 320
price equation, 94
prior distribution, 105
prison of 22 prisoners, 332, 347–348
prisoners and hats, 351
private, 303
probability generating function, 165
product rule, 250, 251, 253, 254
pure virtual, 274, 284, 292, 313, 321
push_back, 308
put-call parity, 17, 34, 39, 363

quadratic formula, 226
quadratic variation, 145, 160

quantitative developer, 11
Quantlib, 322
quick, 290
quick sort, 273, 315

racetrack, 330, 336
Radon–Nikodym derivative, 126
rain, 93
RAM, 326
rand, 182
random number generator, 186
random variable
    product, 124, 156
    ratio, 124, 154
    sum, 92, 95, 118, 164
random walk, 94, 145
range checking, 275
rank, 219, 241, 249
    of a matrix, 219, 249
ratio distribution, 154
ratio test, *see* convergence, ratio test
rational function, 259
recursion, 113, 203, 210, 211, 308
reference, 273, 313
referencing counting, 322
reflection principle, 166
Rennie
    Andrew, 16
replacement, 90, 111
replication, 15, 20, 21, 61–62, 64
    dynamic, 62
    static, 61
research quant, 10
residue, 261
rethrow, 314
return type, 286
reverse iterator, 294
Riemann integral, 169
risk-neutral dynamics, stock process, 27
risk-neutral measure, 23, 31, 34
robot, 181, 183, 209
Rogers

Chris, 88
roulette, 90, 93
RTTI, 274, 328
rule of 70, 172–173
rule of almost zero, 285, 287, 320
rule of three, 285, 287, 320

segmentation fault, 274, 326
separable, 178
series, 364
series summation, 100
set, 274
shallow copy, 284, 287, 320
shared pointer, 322
    Boost, 274
shift operator, 233
short rate models, 177
Shreve
    Steven, 16, 88
simulation, *see* Monte Carlo
singleton, 275
singularities, 260
skyscraper, 333, 352
smart pointer, 277, 279, 285, 287, 297, 313,
    322
snow, 330, 339–340
Sobol sequences, 214
software company, 12
sort, 182, 200, 202, 205, 266, 288, 324
sort, stable, 290
speculator, 57
square root, 273, 298
stable sort, *see* sort, stable
stack, 279, 290
stack overflow, 326
static, 267, 273, 311, 312
static replication, *see* replication, static
static cast, 197
static variable, 291
static virtual function, 292
statistical arbitrage, 71
statistical arbitrage quant, 11

steps, 330, 339
Stirling's formula, 200, 203
Stirzaker
    David, 87
STL, 274
stochastic calculus, 95
stochastic differential equation, 31, 94, 148,
    150, 152, 153, 156
stochastic volatility model, 82–83
    smile, 22, 84–85
stock measure, 32, 34
stop loss hedging strategy, 20, 57–58
stopping time, 103, 147, 167
strategy pattern, 275
stratified, 212
strcmp, 266, 282
string, 268, 283
Stroustrup
    Bjarne, 265
subarray, 182
submarine, 183
Sutter
    Herb, 264
swap, 172, 174
swapping elements, 199
switch, 328

Taylor series, 163, 218, 219, 222, 234, 243,
    252
    error, 218, 235
    remainder, 235
template, 282
template pattern, 275
tesseract, 352
throw, 273, 277
    in a constructor, 266, 277
    in a destructor, 266
trading strategy, 102
transcendental equation, 225
trapezium, 185
tree, 111, 183, 210
    binary, 273, 300–310, 323

binomial, 21, 22, 72–74, 77–78
    red-black, 211, 323
    trinomial, 22, 74–76
tree vs. Monte Carlo, 22, 76–77
triangle, 91, 93, 116
try, 313
typeid, 328

undefined behaviour, 293
unhandled exception, *see* exception,
    unhandled
uniform random variable, 91, 107, 118, 224
    density function, 117
    distribution function, 91, 117
    maximum, 91, 118
    minimum, 91, 118
user-defined assignment operator, 280

value at risk, 50
Van der Corput, 214
vanilla option, 281
VAR, 19, 50
variance, 91, 101
Variance Gamma model, 83–84
Vasicek model, 172, 179
vector, 308, 324
Vega, 21, 69–70
    convexity, 85
virtual, 266, 267, 297, 312, 364
virtual address, 274
virtual construction, 275
virtual constructor, 278
virtual destructor, 266, 273, 287, 296, 318
virtual function, 263, 273, 291, 292, 296
    table, 328
virtual function table, 291
virtual inheritance, 319
virtual memory, 326, 327
Visual Studio, 274
volatile, 311
volatility
    hedging, 20, 62

implied, 79
    skew, 22, 79–81
    smile, 22, 79–81
    time-dependent, 16, 30

weak convergence, *see* convergence, weak
weak pointer, 323
Williams
    David, 88
    Ruth, 88
Wilmott
    Paul, 16
wine mixing, 330, 336–337

xlw, 185, 198, 263

Yates, 200

CPSIA information can be obtained at www.ICGtesting.com
Printed in the USA
BVOW09s0720081015

421365BV00005B/26/P